IMAGES
of America

PLAINFIELD

ON THE COVER: These boys are relaxing as they sit in the grass and watch an exciting game of baseball at Plainfield's Electric Park baseball field. The teams were often sponsored by local merchants and businesses. The local baseball leagues were very competitive. Merchants often offered the best players a job so that they would play on their baseball team. (Courtesy of authors' collection.)

IMAGES
of America

PLAINFIELD

Tim and Michelle Smith

ARCADIA
PUBLISHING

Copyright © 2012 by Tim and Michelle Smith
ISBN 978-0-7385-9438-5

Published by Arcadia Publishing
Charleston, South Carolina

Printed in the United States of America

Library of Congress Control Number: 2012938239

For all general information, please contact Arcadia Publishing:
Telephone 843-853-2070
Fax 843-853-0044
E-mail sales@arcadiapublishing.com
For customer service and orders:
Toll-Free 1-888-313-2665

Visit us on the Internet at www.arcadiapublishing.com

This book is dedicated to our family, who has always supported our passion for collecting and researching the history of Plainfield, Illinois.

Contents

Acknowledgments		6
Introduction		7
1.	Early Plainfield	9
2.	A Stroll Through Town	41
3.	Leisure Time	77
4.	Schools and Churches	105
5.	The Plainfield Tornado	121
Bibliography		127

ACKNOWLEDGMENTS

As passionate collectors of Plainfield images, postcards, advertising, and memorabilia, our journey has taken us on countless trips to antique stores, local shows, and auctions. Our passion has grown to include collecting almost anything related to Plainfield, including the rare paper items and photographs that we would like to share with you in this book. The real enjoyment of collecting comes from the people we have met and the friendships that have flourished along the way as we continue on our journey through the history of Plainfield, one image at a time. As we write this book, our hope is to not only document the history of Plainfield, but to also tell the story of some of the wonderful people who have called Plainfield home over the years. Many of these people have helped build our little village into the beautiful town it is today. Unless otherwise noted, all images in this book are from the authors' collection. We would like to thank the Plainfield Historical Society for its assistance with our research. Special thanks go to Amanda and Jason Vulgamott for all their work in creating photographs from our glass negatives. We truly appreciate your help.

INTRODUCTION

The village of Plainfield, Illinois, originally known as Walker's Grove, had its beginnings on the banks of the DuPage River. The Potawatomi tribe was scattered, with a portion in northern Michigan and Ohio as well as along the banks of the DuPage River. The Potawatomi were known by the white settlers to be friendly; however, they were often described as tall, fierce, and fond of hunting. They were the most numerous of all the Native Americans in Illinois at the time. The last of the Potawatomi left the Plainfield area by 1837.

An early fur trader known as DuPazhe and trader Vetel Vermette lived in the area prior to 1820. The DuPazhe cabin was just south of the current site of the Plainfield Central High School tennis courts. Vermette was living in the DuPazhe cabin and trading with the Native Americans into 1830. Rev. Jesse Walker, a Methodist minister, came to the Plainfield area to spread the word of God in the late 1820s. James Walker, son-in-law of the Reverend Walker, came to the area and built a log cabin south of present-day Plainfield. A sawmill was constructed shortly afterwards by James and a few early settlers. This was the start of Walker's Grove. James was the first postmaster and would later become one of the first Will County commissioners. This book contains a document signed by James Walker. It may be the only known existing document signed by this early pioneer. Walker had influence—not only in the beginnings of Plainfield, but also in the development of Will County, Illinois.

The Black Hawk War grew from a disagreement concerning an earlier treaty. Several tribes banded together over the loss of their land and hunting grounds. In the early 1830s, the pioneers converted the log cabin of Stephen R. Beggs into a fort in order to protect settlers in the Plainfield area. There were about 125 men, women, and children in the fort at the time. Most of the very early settlers were from the north, including Canada, Michigan Territory, New York, Vermont, and New Hampshire.

The earliest area of town was first platted by Chester Ingersoll in 1834. He originally named the town "Planefield." Ingersoll later revised the plat, changing the name to Plainfield. His original plat had 13 blocks, which were bordered by the DuPage River on the west, Division Street on the east, Lockport Street on the north, and Ottawa Street on the south. Ingersoll paid $1.25 per acre in 1833 when he purchased the land he platted. In 1845, Levi Arnold platted an "Addition to the Town of Plainfield." The town grew well during the 1840s, but growth slowed down during the late 1840s when the Illinois and Michigan Canal was opened, drawing the economic boom toward the towns along the canal.

Plainfield's central location between Chicago and Ottawa was a boost to its growth in the stagecoach days of the 1830s through the 1850s. After 1850, a plank road constructed of logs was built between Oswego and Joliet and ran through Plainfield. What is now known as Route 30, or the Lincoln Highway, was built over this same road. During this time period, Plainfield had numerous residences, stores, churches, a cheese factory, wagon shops, blacksmiths, and tinsmiths.

Plainfield had a part in the Civil War, with many of its young soldiers volunteering. Edward McAllister's artillery battery mustered in at the beginning of the war and was heavily involved in the Fort Donaldson and Shiloh battles. In addition, over 100 men from the Plainfield area joined the 100th Illinois Infantry volunteer regiment, which fought at over a dozen major battles including Chickamauga, Kennesaw Mountain, and Franklin.

The town prospered with the coming of the railroad and trolley lines. In 1904, Electric Park was constructed by one of the trolley lines and became known as one of the nicest resorts in northern Illinois. Electric Park became a very popular place to visit and relax. People from Chicago as well as the entire surrounding area spent time at the park.

World War I and World War II saw many soldiers volunteer from the Plainfield area. Ulysses Blakely was an advisor for the building of the Lincoln Highway, also known as US Route 30. He helped establish the route in the early 1920s, bringing it through Plainfield. In 1940, US Route 66 was officially routed through Plainfield and merged with Route 30 for a few blocks, making it the crossroads of two of the longest highways in America at the time. Though Plainfield was growing at a moderate pace during the 1950s and 1960s, the village was still known as a small farming community. The schools were excellent, the neighborhoods were pleasant for raising a family, and traffic was low. The village continued to grow over the next several years, and Plainfield remained a fairly quiet Midwestern town. The 1990 tornado forever changed the town, and the growth afterward was tremendous. Some people speculate that the publicity from the tornado coverage on television, radio, and newspapers made the small, quaint village of Plainfield very inviting to residents of Chicago and its suburbs.

The majority of the over 180 images chosen for this book came out of the authors' personal collection of over 1,000 items. Shown is a variety of the buildings, businesses, streets, and early photographs that would indicate how Plainfield appeared throughout a good portion of its rich history. Several of the images in this book are business advertising items and photographs, which will hopefully bring back great memories to readers as well as inform others of what the town was like. Our goal is to share these images with you, the reader, in the hope that they will serve as a reminder and pictorial account of how the town appeared over the years.

One

Early Plainfield

During the 1820s, the Potawatomi Indians lived along the DuPage River, south of present-day Plainfield. By 1829, a few log cabins built by very early settlers were located in the same area. James Walker, son-in-law of Rev. Jesse Walker, came to the area during this time and built a sawmill along the river. This mill was just south of the current Renwick Road one-lane bridge. James became one of the first commissioners of Will County, Illinois, when it was formed in 1836. The first image in this chapter is one of the earliest known Will County documents and was signed in 1836 by James Walker. Chester Ingersoll platted a portion of the town in 1834, and the village grew over the next several years. Plainfield provided a number of soldiers to the Civil War effort, with over 100 men from Plainfield serving in the Will County 100th Illinois Regiment. Plainfield veterans established the GAR Burrell Post No. 3 after the Civil War.

Plainfield had several early justices of the peace and constables. This chapter includes images of these very early, rare, and original Plainfield bonds and oaths of office for these men. Plainfield photographers played an important role in documenting the town as well as capturing images of the residents in the early days. In this chapter, several photographs are included from the authors' Plainfield glass negative collection that depict early scenes of the village. These images indicate how the people, buildings, and streets of Plainfield appeared during this time period.

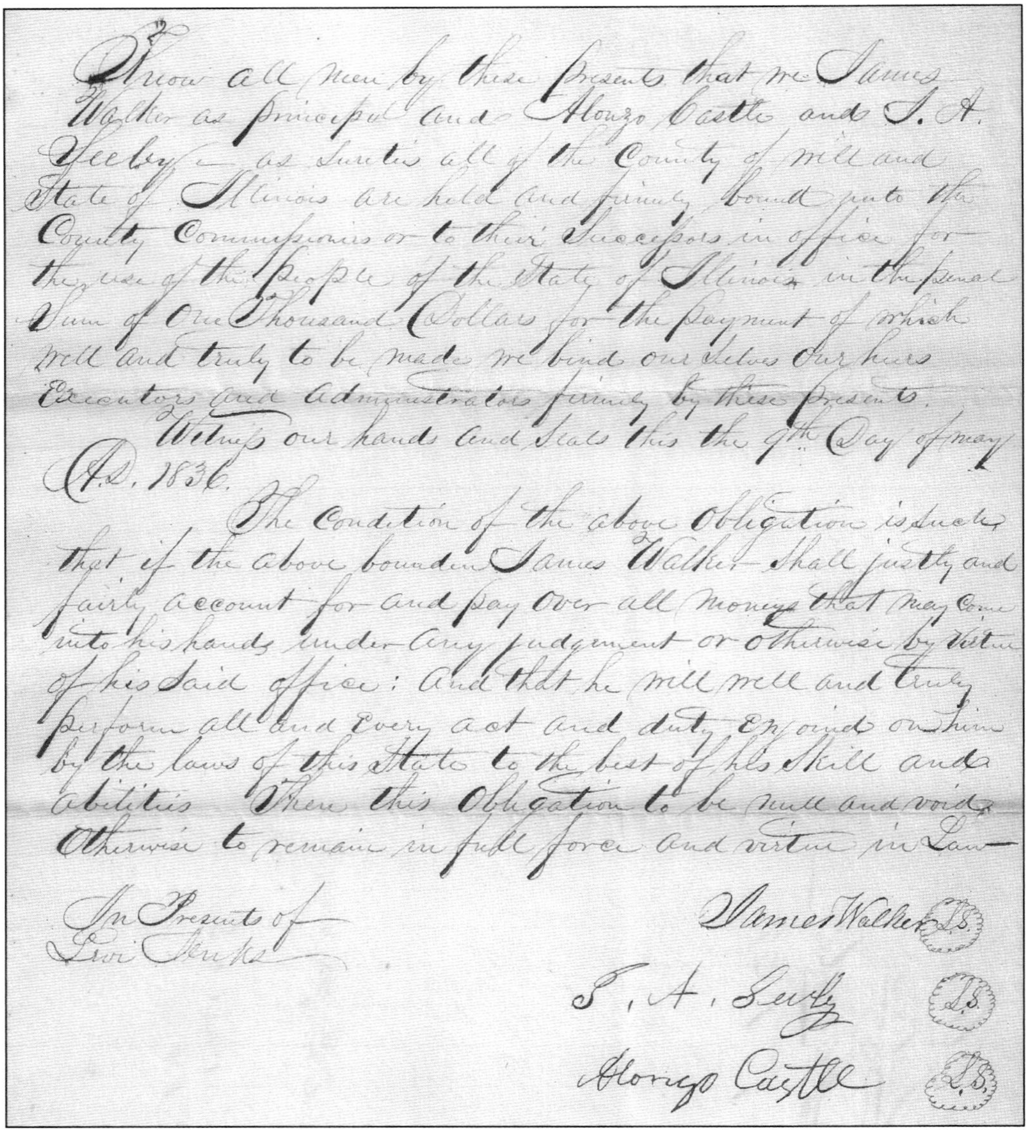

Know all men by these Presents that we James Walker as principal and Alonzo Castle and S. A. Seeley as Sureties all of the County of Will and State of Illinois are held and firmly bound unto the County Commissioners or to their Successors in office for the use of the People of the State of Illinois in the penal Sum of One Thousand Dollars for the payment of which well and truly to be made we bind our Selves our heirs Executors and Administrators firmly by these presents.

Witness our hands and Seals this the 9th Day of May A.D. 1836.

The Condition of the above Obligation is such that if the above bounden James Walker shall justly and fairly account for and pay over all moneys that may come into his hands under any judgment or otherwise by virtue of his said office: And that he will well and truly perform all and every act and duty enjoined on him by the laws of this State to the best of his Skill and abilities Then this Obligation to be null and void Otherwise to remain in full force and virtue in Law—

In Presents of
Levi Jenks

James Walker L.S.
S. A. Seeley L.S.
Alonzo Castle L.S.

James Walker signed this original 1836 Will County $1,000 bond document. Upon the formation of Will County in 1836, Walker was chosen without opposition as one of three county commissioners. This document notes that Walker "shall justly and fairly account for and pay over all moneys that may come into his hands under any judgment or otherwise, by virtue of his said office." It was also signed in the presence of Levi Jenks on May 9, 1836. Jenks was the first Will County clerk. Will County was formed from Cook and Iroquois Counties on January 12, 1836. This is probably the earliest Will County document in existence, and possibly the only remaining document signed by Walker. Below is a close-up of Walker's signature.

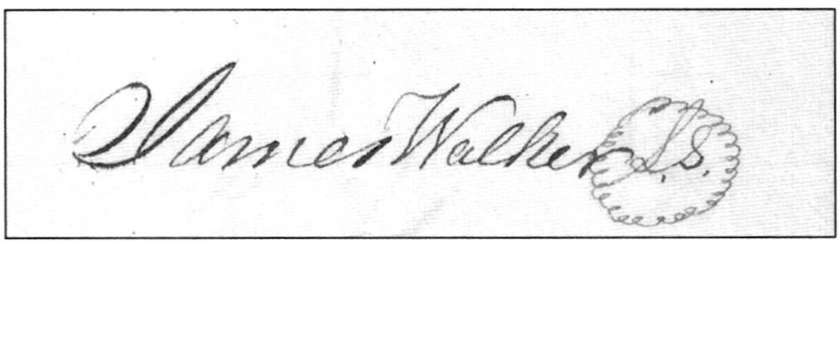

Jonathan Hager is named as the duly elected justice of the peace in the Plainfield election precinct in Will County on this original 1837 Will County justice of the peace bond document. It was signed, approved, and filed at the Will County Courthouse on August 8, 1837. Hager held the position of justice of the peace for 18 years. He and Samuel Sargent opened the first store in Plainfield above a wagon shop. Hager was also the superintendent of one of the first Sunday schools, organized in 1843. His home still stands on Route 126 in Plainfield. James Mathers and Robert Chapman of Plainfield also signed this early Will County document. Below is a sketch of Hager.

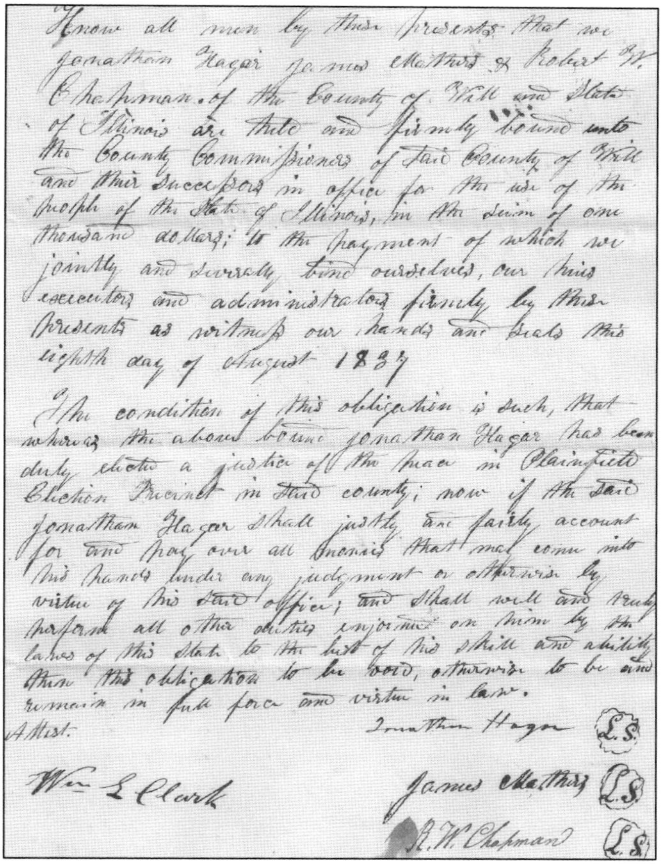

Know all men by these presents that we Jonathan Hager James Mathers & Robert W. Chapman of the County of Will and State of Illinois are held and firmly bound unto the County Commissioners of said County of Will and their successors in office for the use of the people of the State of Illinois, in the sum of one thousand dollars; to the payment of which we jointly and severally bind ourselves, our heirs executors and administrators firmly by these presents as witness our hands and seals this eighth day of August 1837

The condition of this obligation is such, that whereas the above bound Jonathan Hager had been duly elected a justice of the peace in Plainfield Election Precinct in said county; now if the said Jonathan Hager shall justly and fairly account for and pay over all monies that may come into his hands under any judgment or otherwise by virtue of his said office; and shall well and truly perform all other duties enjoined on him by the laws of this State to the best of his skill and ability then this obligation to be void, otherwise to be and remain in full force and virtue in law.

Jonathan Hager (L.S.)

Attest.

Wm L Clark

James Mathers (L.S.)

R.W. Chapman (L.S.)

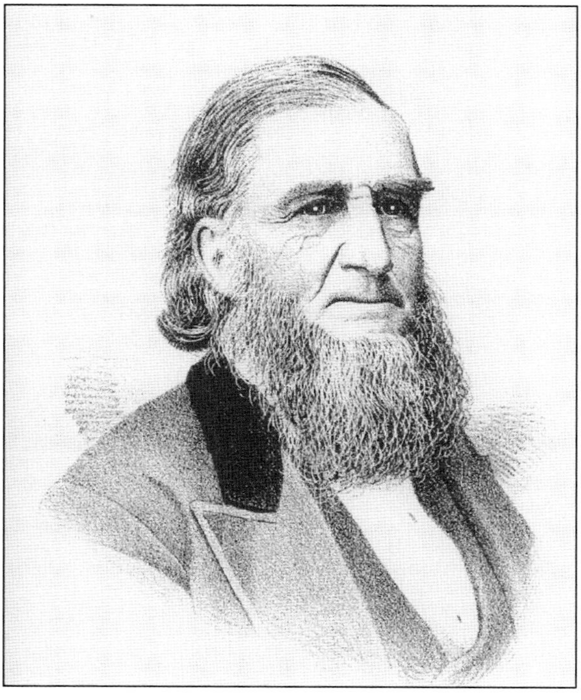

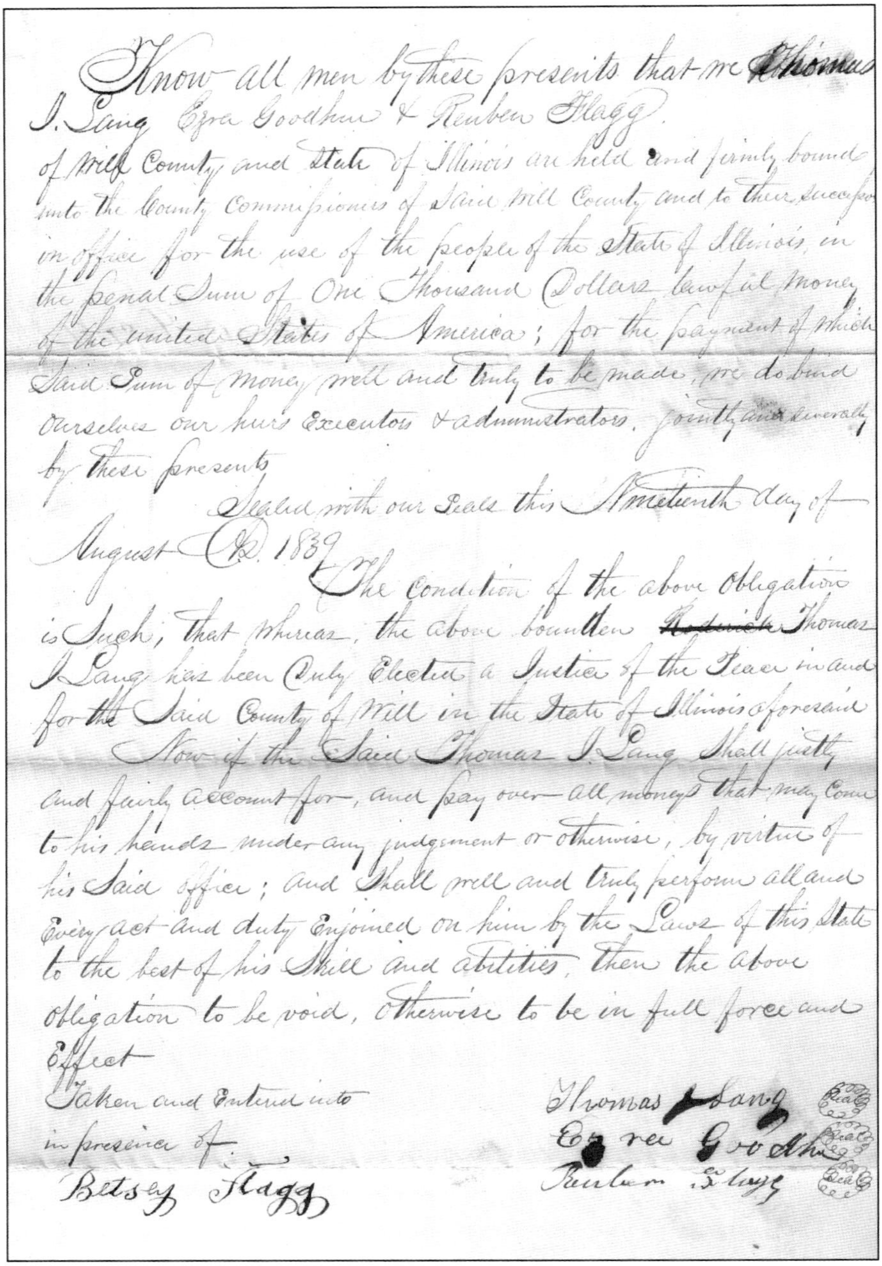

Know all men by these presents that we Thomas J. Lang Ezra Goodhue & Reuben Flagg of Will County and State of Illinois are held and firmly bound unto the County Commissioners of Said Will County and to their successors in office for the use of the people of the State of Illinois, in the penal Sum of One Thousand Dollars lawful money of the united States of America; for the payment of which said Sum of money well and truly to be made, we do bind ourselves our heirs Executors & administrators, jointly and severally by these presents

Sealed with our Seals this Nineteenth day of August AD 1839

The Condition of the above Obligation is Such; that whereas, the above bounden Thomas J Lang has been duly Elected a Justice of the Peace in and for the Said County of Will in the State of Illinois aforesaid

Now if the Said Thomas J. Lang Shall justly and fairly account for, and pay over all moneys that may Come to his hands under any judgement or otherwise, by virtue of his Said office; and Shall well and truly perform all and Every act and duty Enjoined on him by the Laws of this State to the best of his Skill and abilities, then the above obligation to be void, Otherwise to be in full force and Effect

Taken and Entered into in presence of

Betsey Flagg

Thomas J Lang (Seal)
Ezra Goodhue (Seal)
Reuben Flagg (Seal)

Reuben Flagg brought his family to Plainfield in 1830. At that time, Plainfield was part of Cook County. When the Flagg family arrived in Plainfield, they found only a few Caucasian families. In 1833, Reuben hauled lumber from Plainfield to Chicago that would be used in the construction of the first framed house in Chicago. At a land sale in 1836, he purchased 160 acres east of Plainfield, which he cultivated and farmed for many years. Reuben served under General Scott during the Black Hawk War. The Flagg family remained for a time in Plainfield, but they moved to Fort Dearborn during the war, seeking more protection. Upon their return to Plainfield, they found that nothing had been stolen from their home. This 1839 Will County document, swearing in Thomas J. Lang as Plainfield's justice of the peace, is also signed by Reuben and Betsey Flagg along with Ezra Goodhue.

Born on September 9, 1830, Samantha Flagg was the first Caucasian child born in what would become Will County. Her parents were Reuben and Betsey Flag, and her mother's maiden name was Kendall. Samantha died on February 25, 1872, at the age of 41.

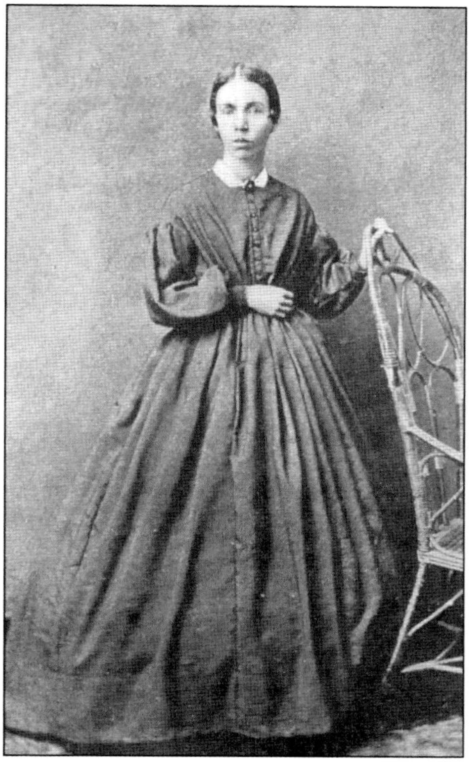

The Halfway House in Plainfield is listed in the National Register of Historic Places. The inn earned its name by being halfway between Chicago and Ottawa, Illinois, on the stagecoach line. The inn's size made it an ideal site to conduct town affairs. The Plainfield Light Artillery used the building as a headquarters from 1856 until the Civil War. The inn closed during the 1880s and was converted into a private residence. (Courtesy of William West Schofield collection.)

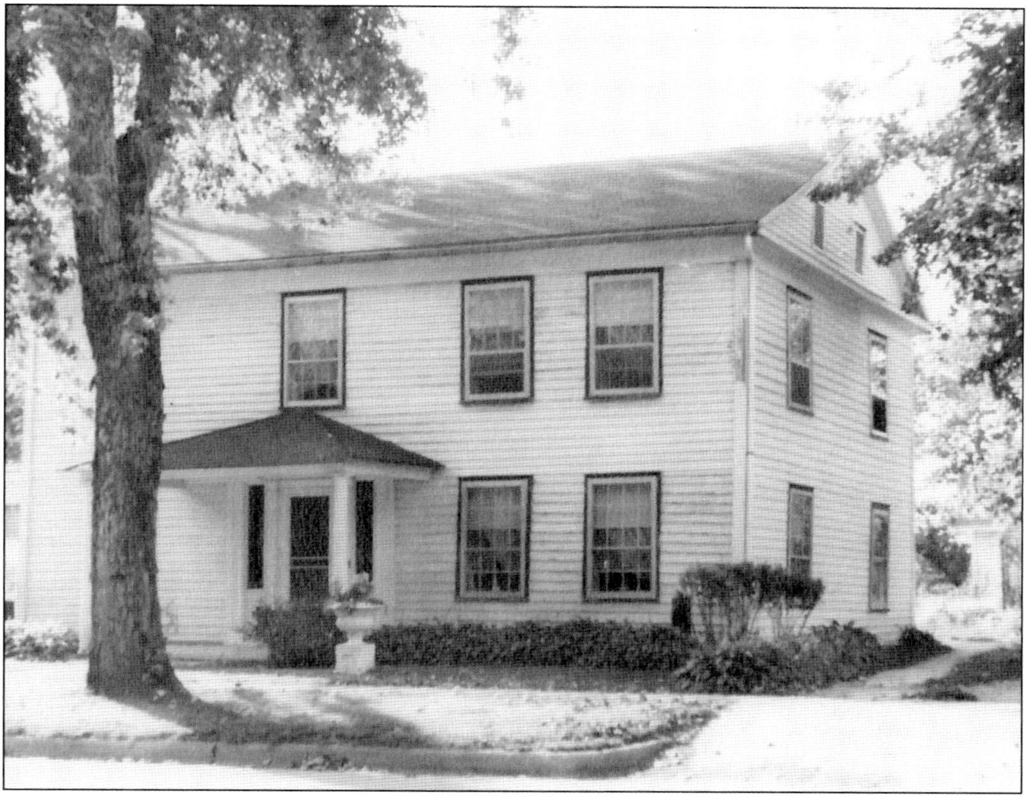

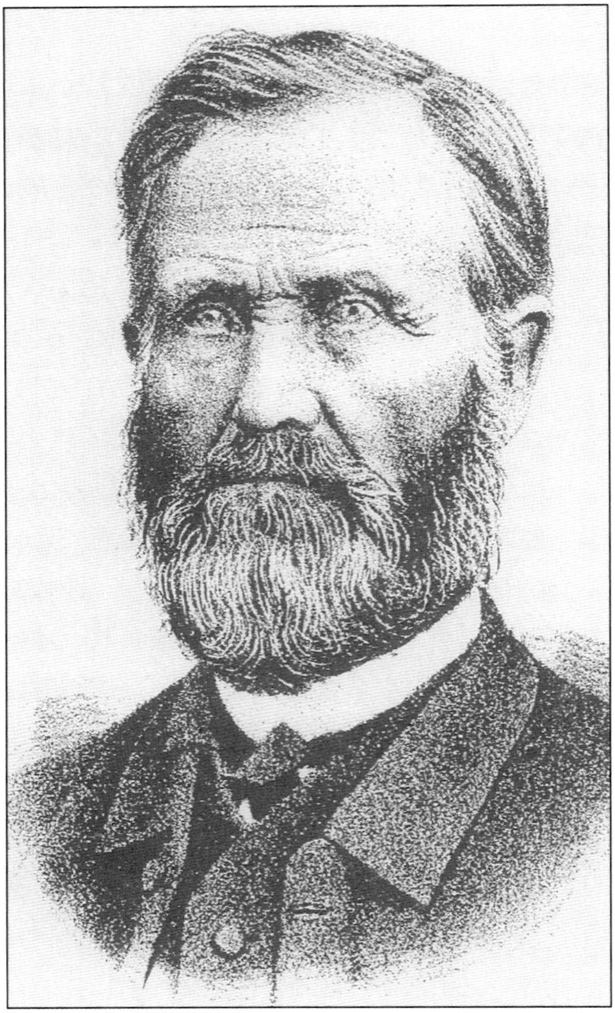

Rev. Stephen R. Beggs was born in 1801. As a young man, he entered the Methodist ministry. In the summer of 1831, Beggs came to Plainfield. Upon the breakout of the Black Hawk War, his Plainfield house was adapted to a fort where several settlers gathered. Beggs was married twice, as his first wife, Elizabeth Heath, passed away in 1866. They had four children by this marriage—Mary E., James W., George W., and Charles W. Beggs. Stephen remarried at age 65 to Sarah (Dibble) Frost.

Alva Culver came to Will County in 1833–1834. This original document is the oath of office for constable, signed by Culver on May 19, 1836, shortly after the formation of Will County that same year. The oath includes the statement, "I do solemnly swear that I will faithfully discharge the duties of my office as constable within the County of Will according to the best of my understanding and abilities, so help me God." Alva was also the supervisor of the Plainfield Township Board in 1852, 1857, and 1859.

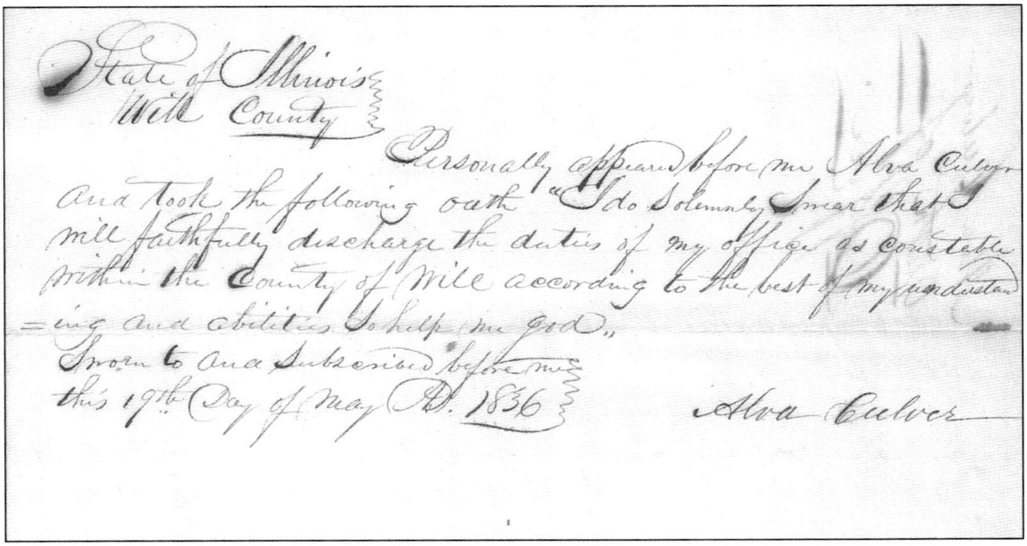

State of Illinois
Will County

Personally appeared before me Alva Culver and took the following oath "I do Solemnly Swear that I will faithfully discharge the duties of my office as constable within the County of Will according to the best of my understan=ing and abilities So help me God."

Sworn to and Subscribed before me this 19th Day of May AD. 1836

Alva Culver

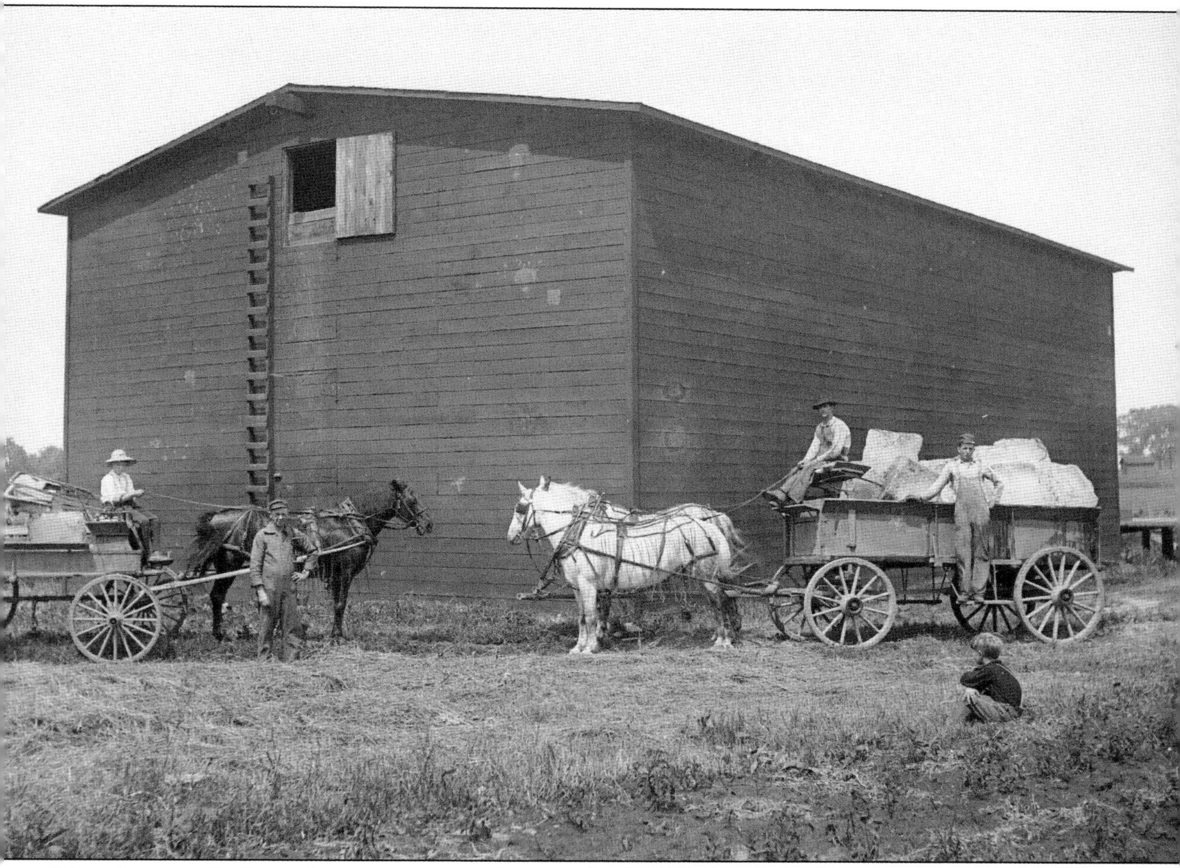

This photograph shows the ice wagons and men in front of the Upton Icehouse in Plainfield. Will Upton, owner of the icehouse, is pictured next to the dark horse. Harvested from the DuPage River, the blocks of ice were taken inside of the icehouse and packed in straw and sawdust to prevent them from melting. These blocks often weighed between 80 and 100 pounds. Icehouses supplied ice to residents before the introduction of the electric refrigerator. William was born in 1862 and married Lillian Foran, born in 1871. They had four children. Lillian passed away in 1919 and William in 1922. Both are buried in St. Mary Immaculate Cemetery in Plainfield.

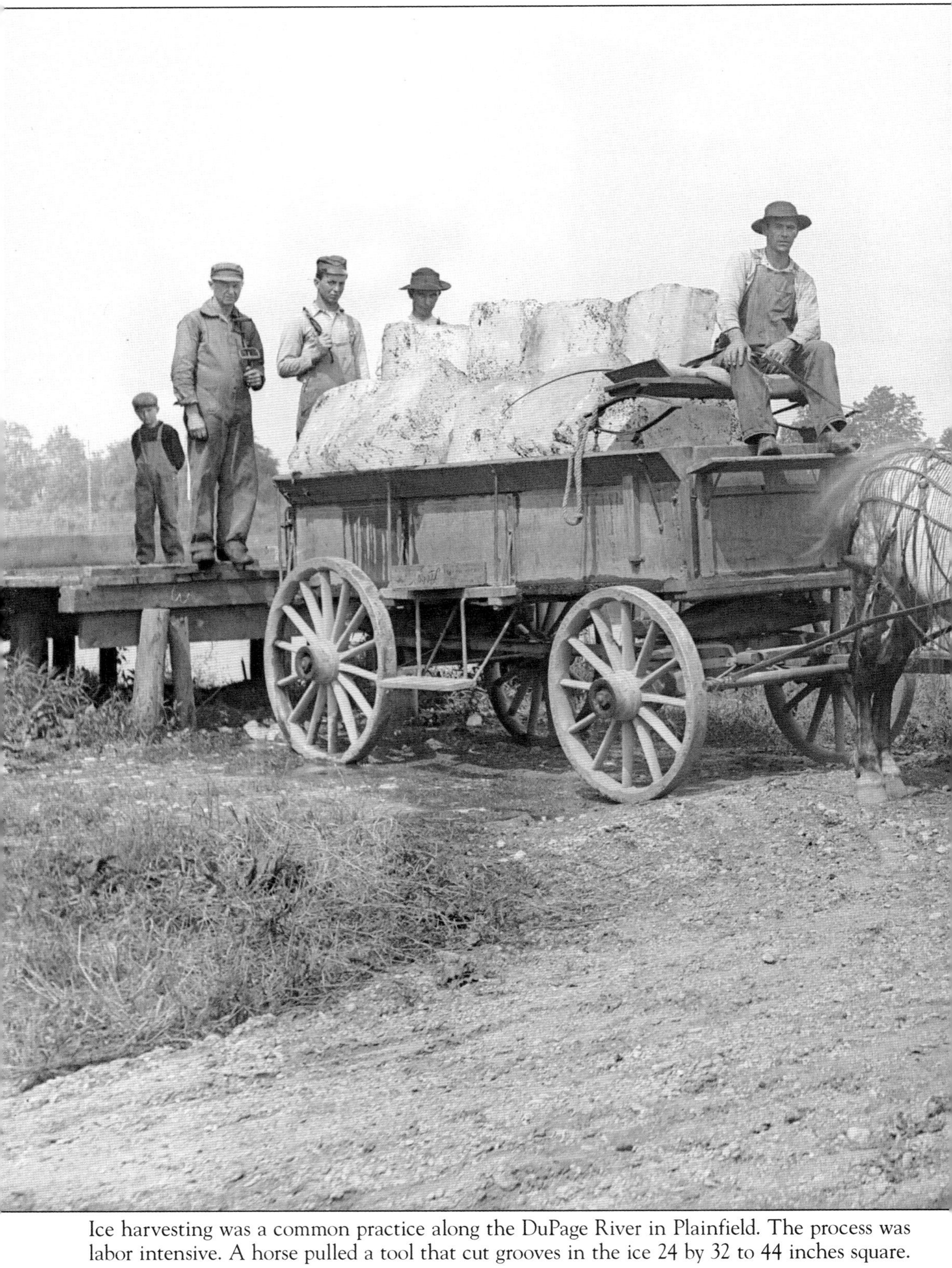

Ice harvesting was a common practice along the DuPage River in Plainfield. The process was labor intensive. A horse pulled a tool that cut grooves in the ice 24 by 32 to 44 inches square.

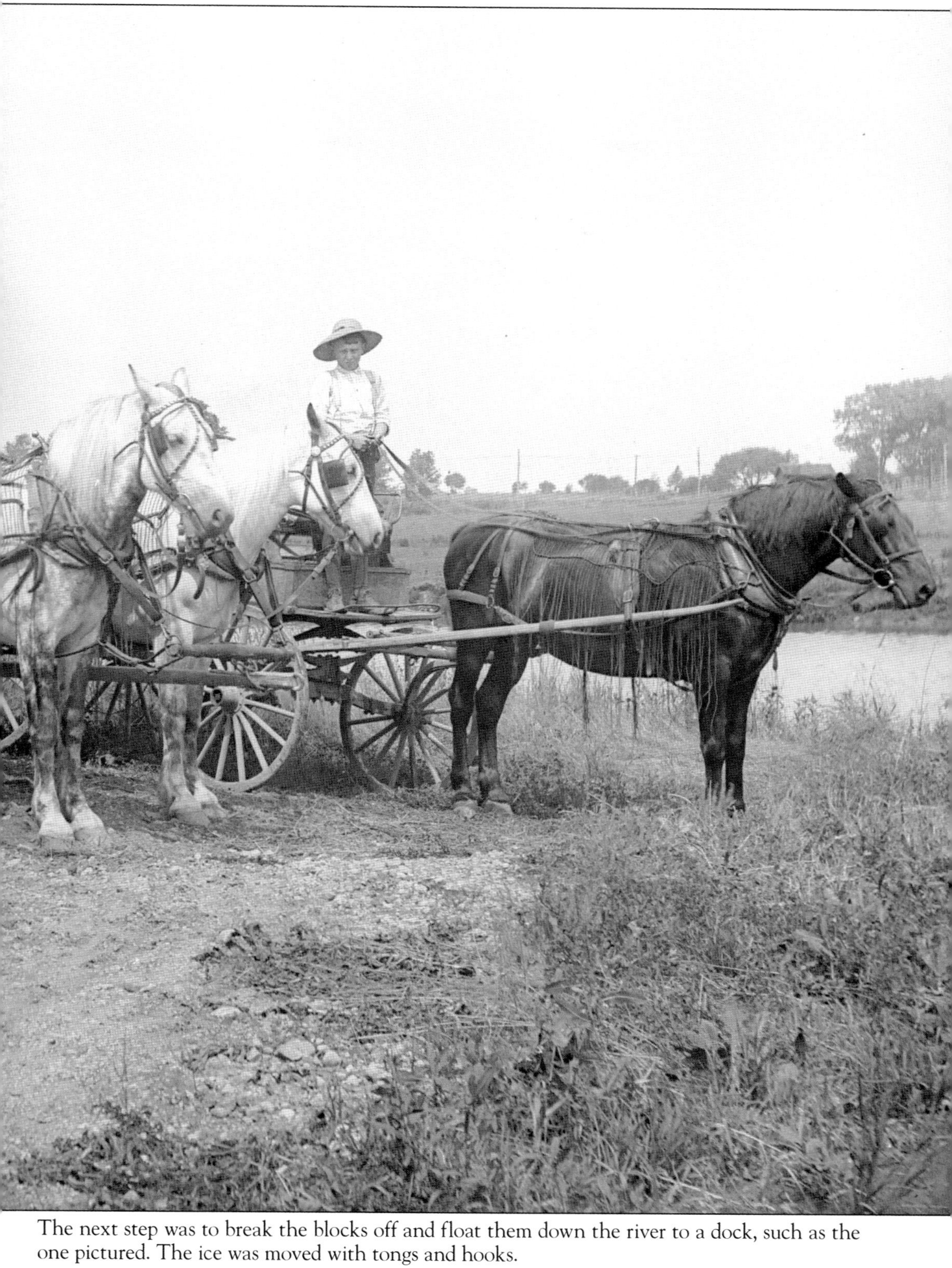

The next step was to break the blocks off and float them down the river to a dock, such as the one pictured. The ice was moved with tongs and hooks.

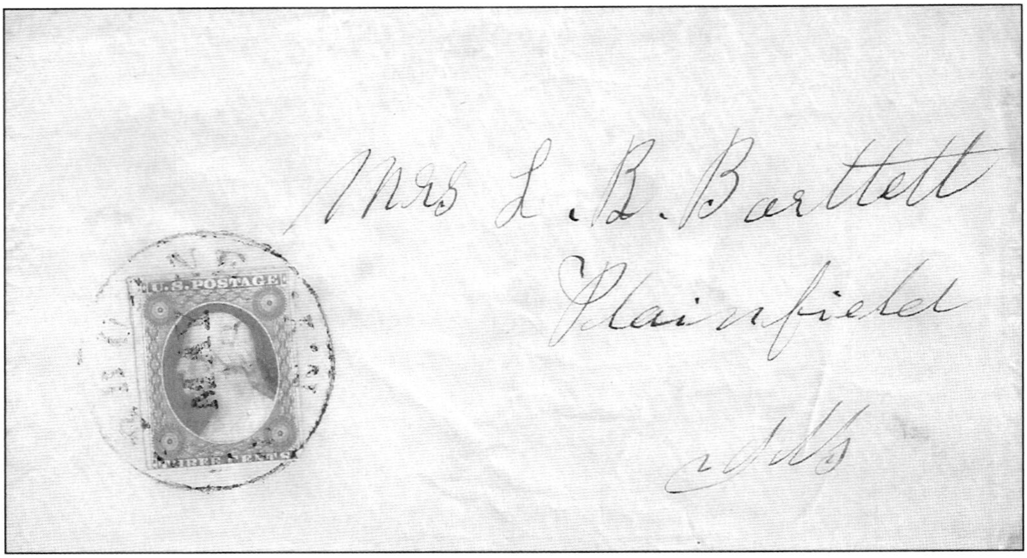

This letter, dated May 17, 1857, is written to Louesa Bartlett of Plainfield and is postmarked from Sherburne, New York. It is from Robert Franklin Bartlett. He writes that he has sold all the old stuff in New York and is lonesome. He also states that the boat he had planned on coming back on has sunk, and he may have to stay longer. Robert writes for her to be "payshant." He signs, "Nothing more from youse husban, R.F. Bartlett." Robert was born in New York in 1818. Robert and Louesa (also spelled Louisa) were married in Will County on December 26, 1843. They had seven children—Adaline, Mary, Casper, Dewayne, Frankie, Kittie, and Harry. The 1873 Will County Plat Book lists Robert as coming to Plainfield from New York in 1836. He is also listed as the Plainfield constable in this plat book. Bartlett Street in Plainfield is named after him.

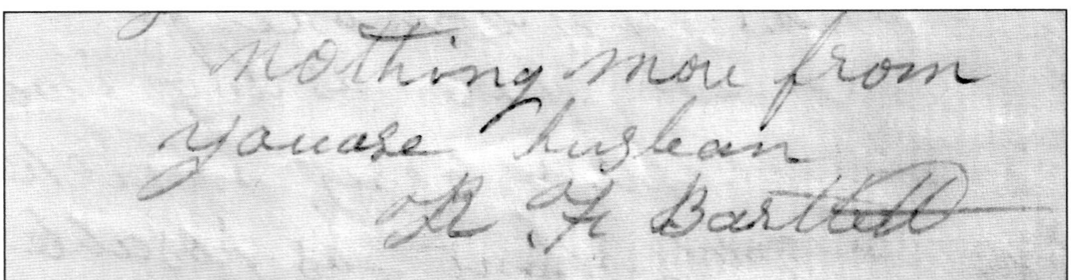

Wilson and Jemima Smith were prominent citizens of Plainfield. Jemima was the daughter of Elias and Christina Hartong, also of Plainfield. The Smiths were both born in the same year—1855. They were breeders of English Shire horses and exhibited them at the Plainfield fairs. At one time, Wilson was the president of the fair association. He also served on the school board as president for eight years, during which time a new high school was built in 1915. He was also one of the founders of the Will County Grange. The Grange is a national association promoting farming and rural public-interest issues.

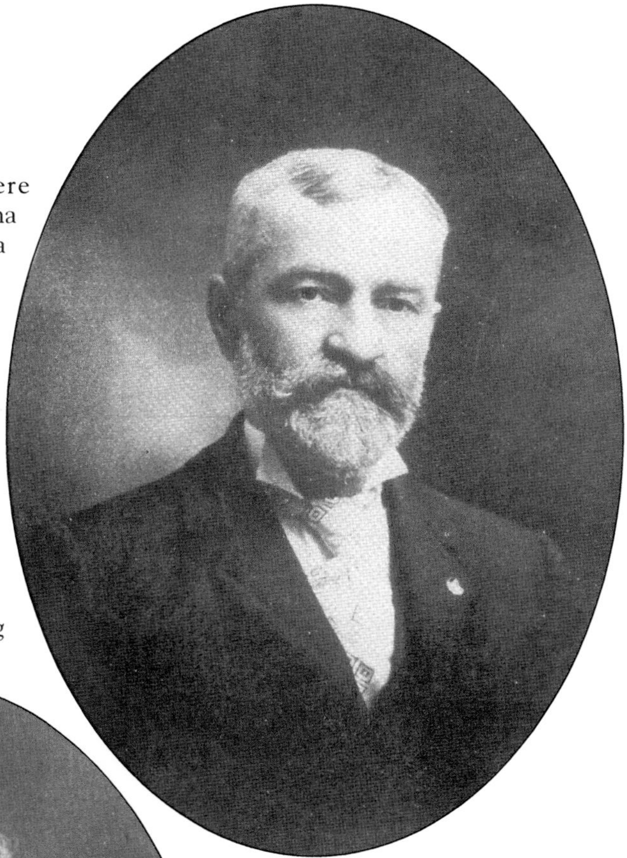

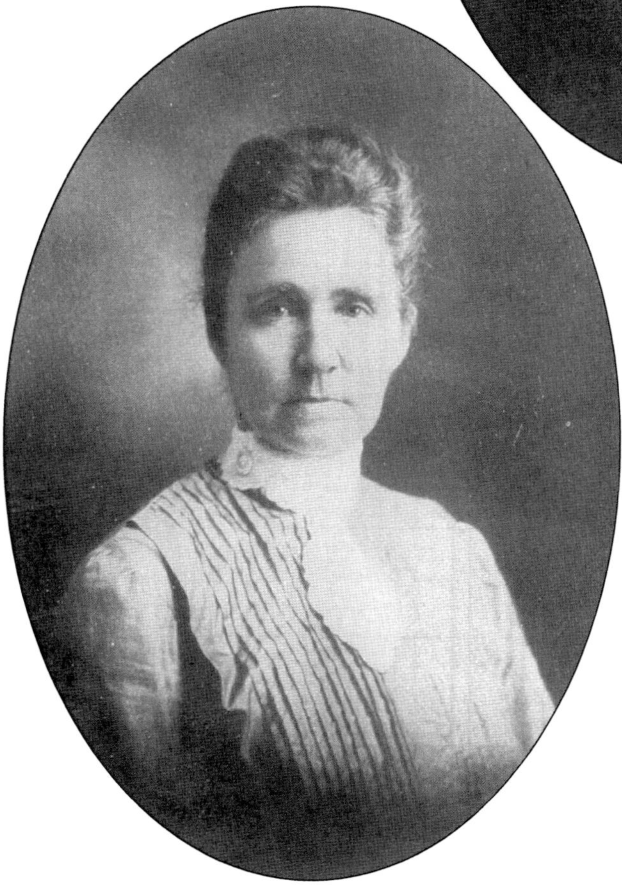

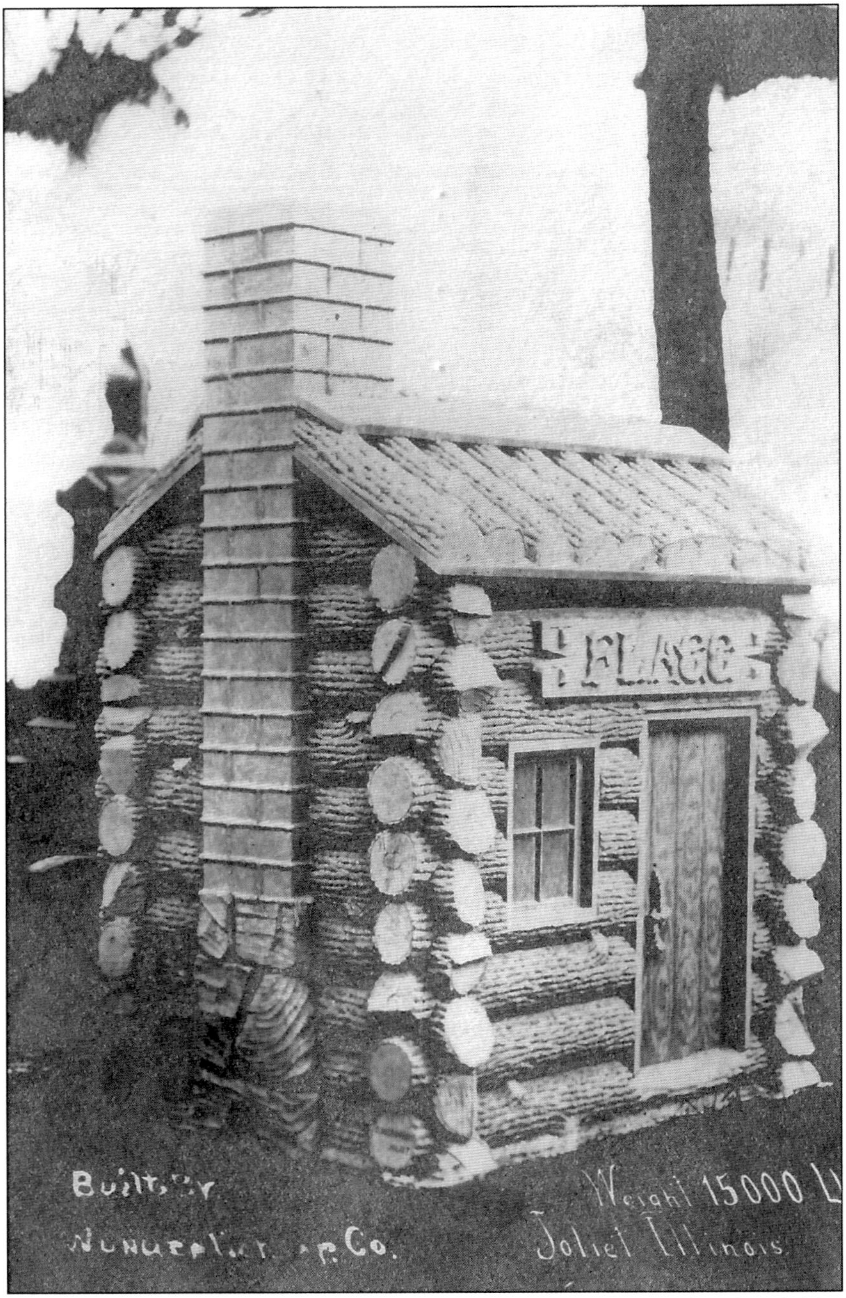

This unusual grave marker, which is in the shape of a log cabin, sits in the Plainfield Township Cemetery. Built by the Wunderlich Company of Joliet, it weighed 15,000 pounds. The log cabin marks the graves of Plainfield pioneer Reuben Flagg, his wife, Betsey, and their children Samantha, Henry, and Mary Jane. Henry was just 15 when he died, and Mary Jane was only nine. There were a total of 11 children in the Flagg family. Betsy (whose maiden name was Kendall) died in 1876. Reuben had learned the stonemason's trade at a young age, but he farmed during his adult life. The Flagg's son George served in the Union army as a first lieutenant in Company K, 8th Illinois Cavalry. George was later a member of the Plainfield Grand Army of the Republic, Burrell Post No. 3.

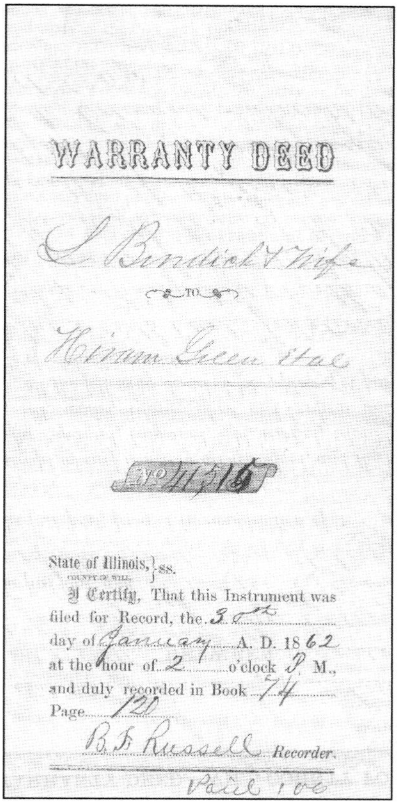

WARRANTY DEED

L Burdick & Wife

TO

Hiram Green et al

No 4151[illegible]

State of Illinois, } ss.
COUNTY OF WILL. }

I Certify, That this Instrument was filed for Record, the 30th day of January A. D. 1862 at the hour of 2 o'clock P. M., and duly recorded in Book 74 Page 120

B. J. Russell Recorder.

Paid 100

This 1862 warranty deed from Lorin Burdick and his wife, Esther, to Hiram Green was for property in Township 36, which is Plainfield Township. Lorin came to Plainfield in 1836 and raised crops on the farm of Reuben Flagg. He later purchased 160 acres in Plainfield Township. Lorin had fought in the war of 1812 and cut lumber for one of the first bridges in Plainfield. In 1878, he died by mistakenly taking Paris green for sulfur. At the time, Paris green was used to kill rodents. Lorin helped lay out the early portion of the Plainfield Cemetery. The recorder on the deed was B.J. Russell. Russell was married to Phoebe Russell, whose first husband, Chester Ingersoll, was an early settler of Plainfield. Below is an original 1866 notary public stamp used by G.N. Chittenden, the Plainfield justice of the peace.

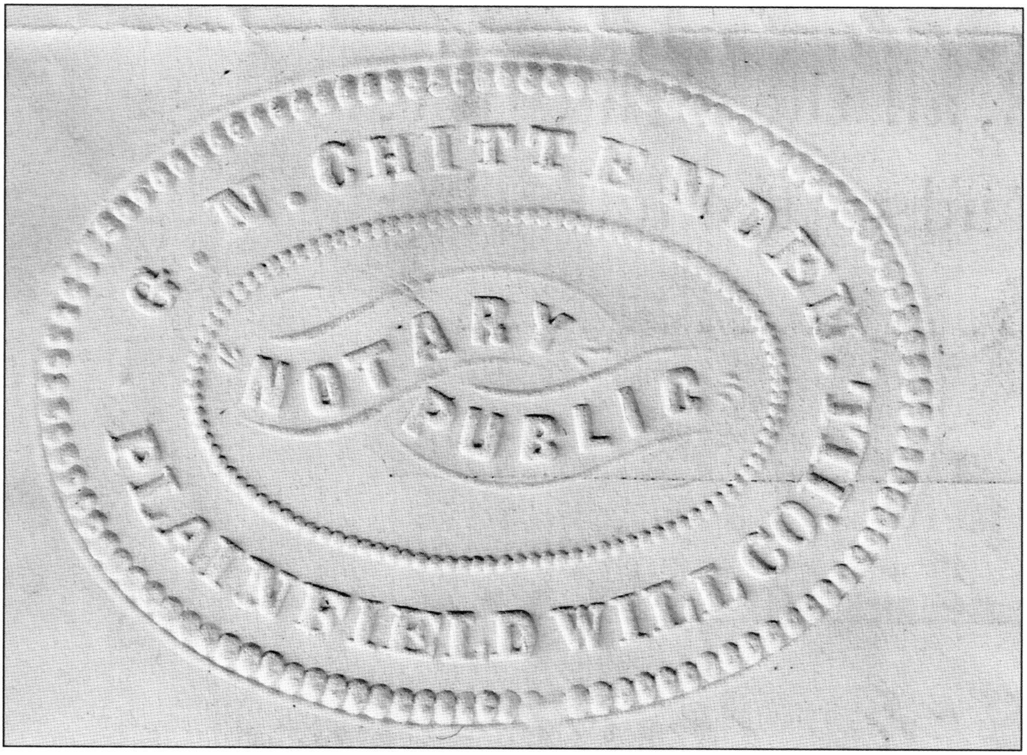

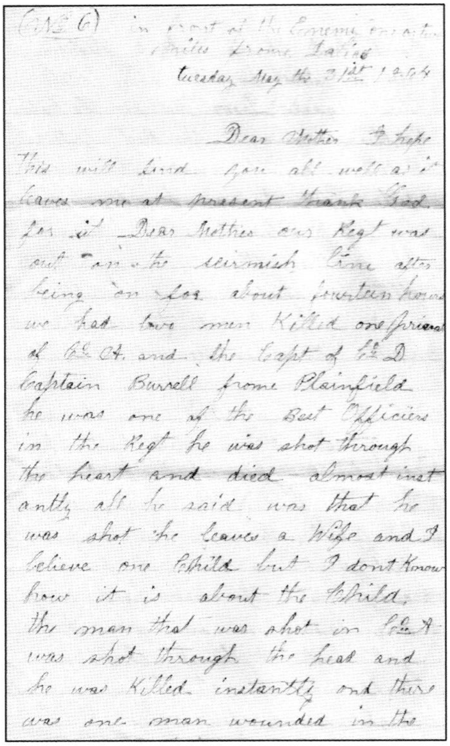

(No 6) in front of the Enemy ... miles frome Dallas
tuesday May the 31st 1864

Dear Mother I hope this will find you all well as it leaves me at present thank God for it Dear Mother our Regt was out on the skirmish line after being on for about fourteen hours we had two men Killed one privat of Co A and the Capt of Co D Captain Burrell frome Plainfield he was one of the Best Officiers in the Regt he was shot through the heart and died almost instantly all he said was that he was shot he leaves a Wife and I believe one Child but I dont Know how it is about the Child the man that was shot in Co A was shot through the head and he was Killed instantly and there was one man wounded in the

In this letter date May 31, 1864, James R. Clark, of the 100th Illinois Volunteer Infantry, writes homes to his mother in Lockport, Illinois, that Captain Burrell, of "Company D" from Plainfield, was killed in battle. The letter reads that Burrell, "one of the best officers in the regiment," was shot through the heart and died almost instantly. James states, "I will finish this at a later time, as bullets are flying around us pretty thick just at this time."

This 1890 "statement of account" letterhead is from P.W. Spangler, who is listed in the 1895 *Will County Directory* as a carriage, buggy, and wagon maker. Peter W. Spangler was born in 1836 and died in 1915. He was married to Mary E. Spangler (née Lee). He served in the 10th Illinois Infantry during the Civil War and was mustered in at age 25 by Edward McAllister of Plainfield. Peter and Mary are buried in the Plainfield Township Cemetery.

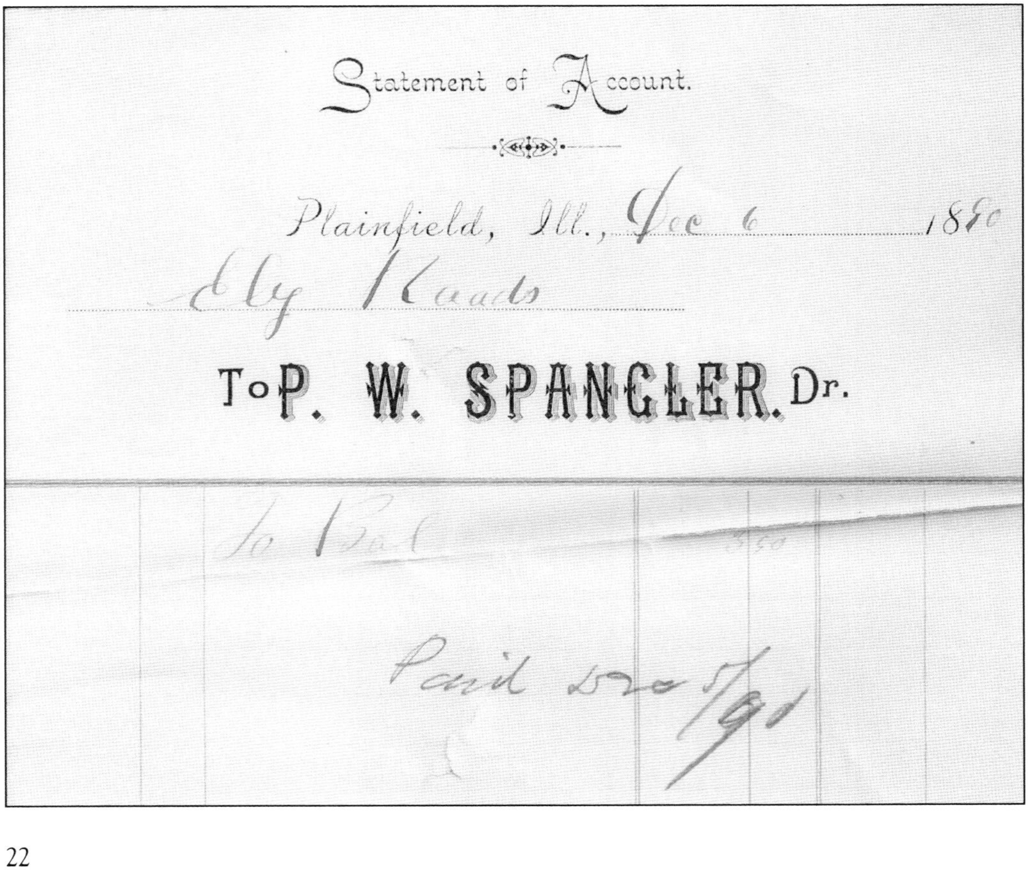

Statement of Account.

Plainfield, Ill., Dec 6 1890

Ely Reads

To P. W. SPANGLER, Dr.

To Bal 3 50

Paid Dec 5/91

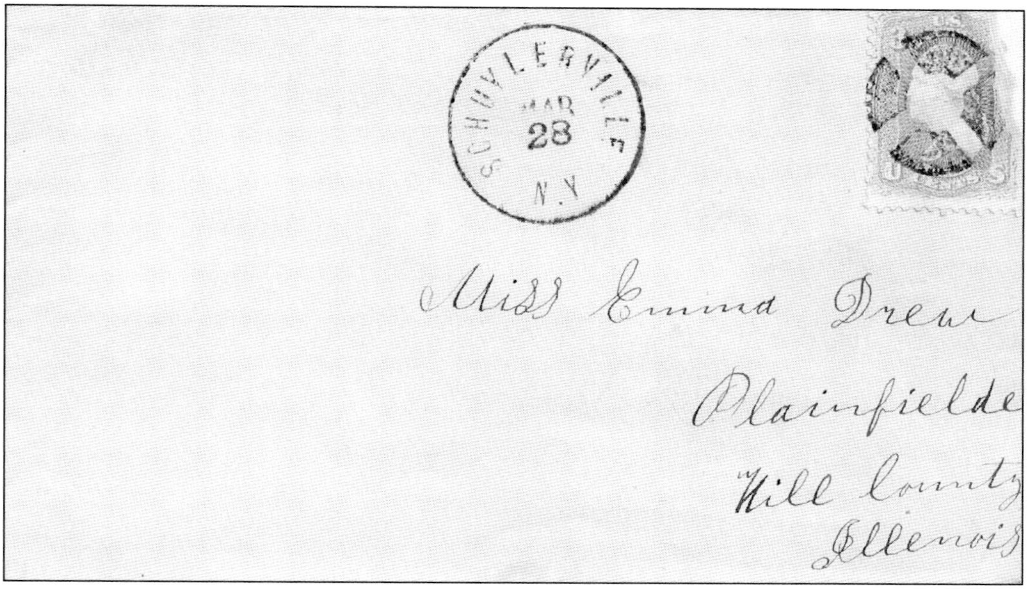

In 1860, Emma Drew is listed as a schoolteacher in Plainfield. Note the spelling of Plainfield with an *e* at the end on this 1860s envelope from Schuylerville, New York. Emma was born in New England in 1839, came to Illinois with her parents in 1845, and married John Sennitt in April 1871. Sennitt started out in 1857 as a farm employee in Plainfield and was later was appointed deputy postmaster of Plainfield in 1860 and postmaster in July 1869. He was responsible for erecting a post office building, which burned in 1898. He built another structure on the same site. John attended Hiram College in Ohio and became well acquainted with James A. Garfield, who would later become president of the United States.

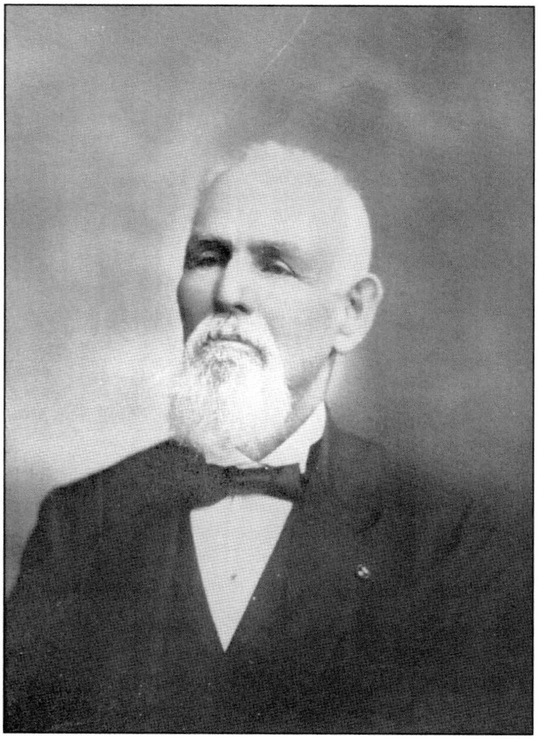

Capt. Edward McAllister was born on December 24, 1828. At the age of 24, he purchased 160 acres in Plainfield Township. At the beginning of the Civil War, Captain McAllister was the first man from Plainfield to enlist and was elected captain of the artillery battery. McAllister's battery fought at Fort Donaldson and Shiloh. At the Battle of Shiloh, it was said that his battery killed and wounded 191 Confederate soldiers in seven minutes. Captain McAllister's battery was at the front, preparing to fire, when a Rebel cannon shot and killed the two horses that were pulling McAllister's cannon. This cannonball traveled through these horses and also killed General Sherman's horse, which was tied to a nearby tree. Captain McAllister was a member of the Bartleson GAR Post No. 6 in Joliet. In honor of Captain McAllister's battery, a monument was erected at the Shiloh battlefield. The monument still stands today.

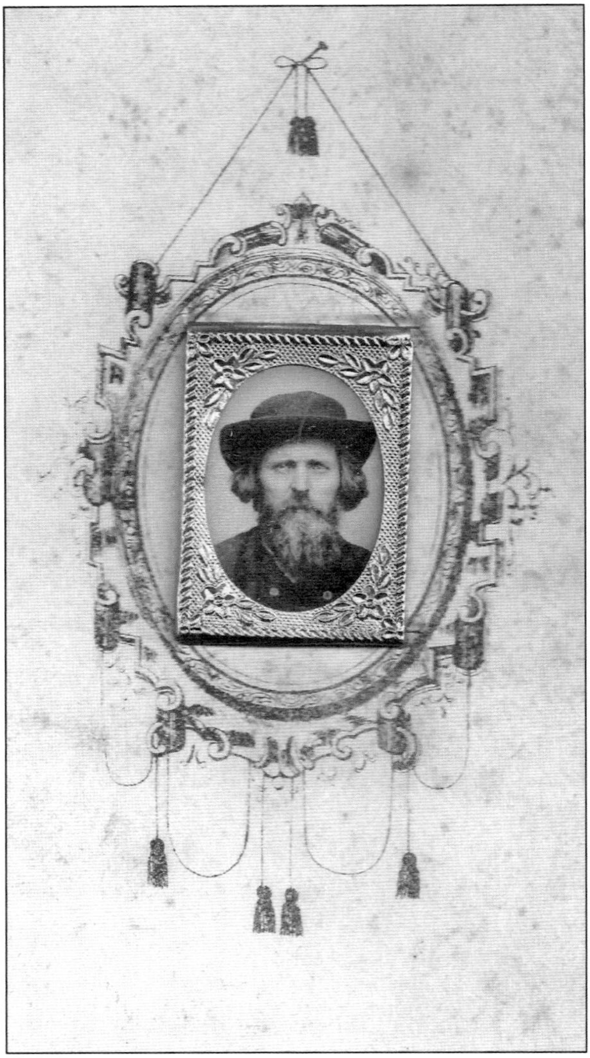

James Platt is listed on the muster rolls for the Civil War 100th Illinois Infantry as being a farmer from Plainfield, Illinois. He joined as a 19-year-old private on August 30, 1862. His brother Joseph mustered with him into Company D of the 100th Illinois on the same day. Joseph died at Nashville on May 1, 1863. In 1864, James was captured at the Battle of Franklin, Tennessee. He was sent to the prison camp in Andersonville, Georgia. Platt returned to the Plainfield area after the war and settled on a farm near Minooka, Illinois. This page from his 1888 farm logbook indicates that he hired one of his Civil War comrades, George McClester, from Plainfield. James paid George $2.50 per day. McClester also served in the 100th Illinois Infantry.

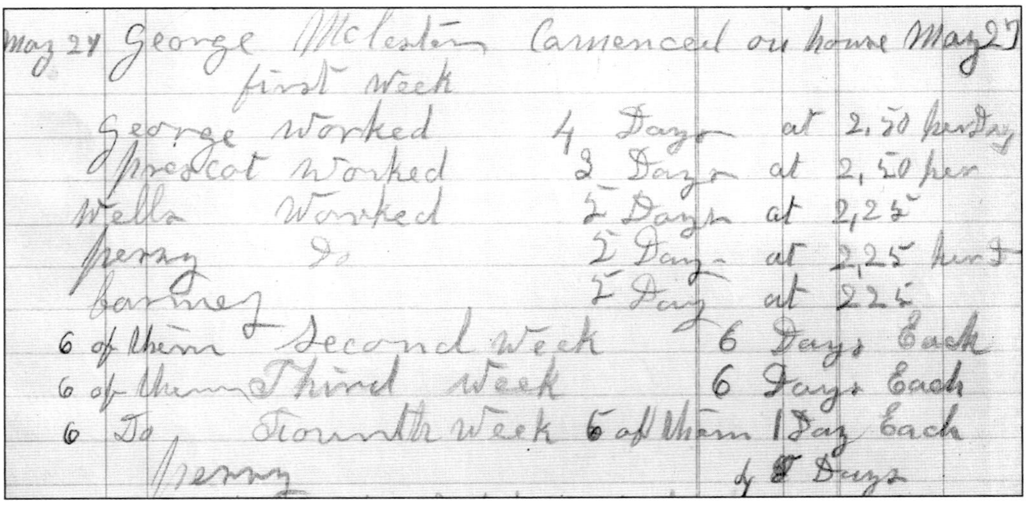

May 27 George McClester Commenced on house May 27
first week
George worked 4 Days at 2,50 per Day
Prescot worked 2 Days at 2,50 per
Wells worked 5 Days at 2,25
Perry Do 5 Days at 2,25 per D
Barney 5 Day at 225
6 of them Second week 6 Days Each
6 of them Third week 6 Days Each
6 Do Fourth week 6 of them 1 Day Each
Perry 4 8 Days

Over 65 of the men living in Plainfield enlisted in the 100th Illinois Infantry during the Civil War. The State of Illinois muster rolls list a total of over 245 men from Plainfield who served as Illinois soldiers in the Union army. The colonel of the 100th was Frederick A. Bartleson, a Will County lawyer. Bartleson was wounded at Shiloh while in the 20th Infantry and lost his left arm. After being promoted to colonel of the 100th, he was captured at Chickamauga and sent to Libby Prison. Bartleson's letters from prison to home were later published in a book titled *Letters from Libby Prison*. The Union army traded prisoners to gain his release; however, after rejoining the 100th, he was shot and killed at the Battle of Kennesaw Mountain in Georgia.

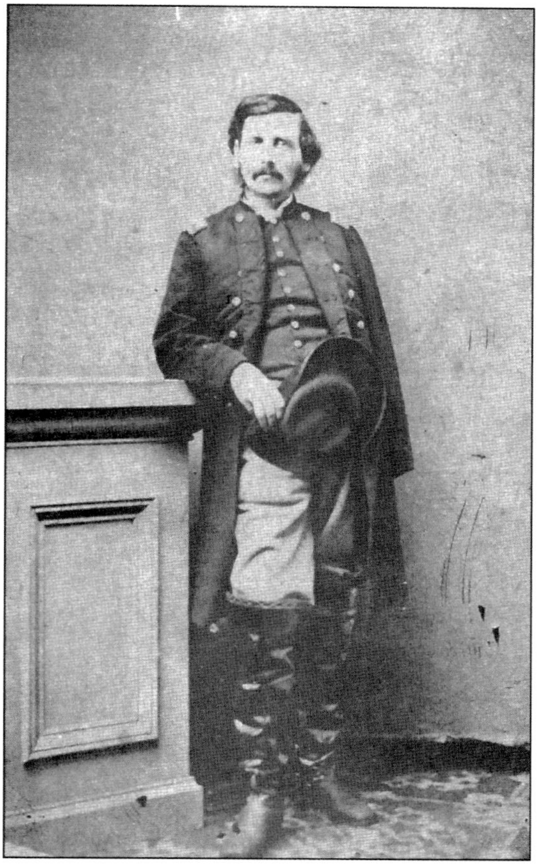

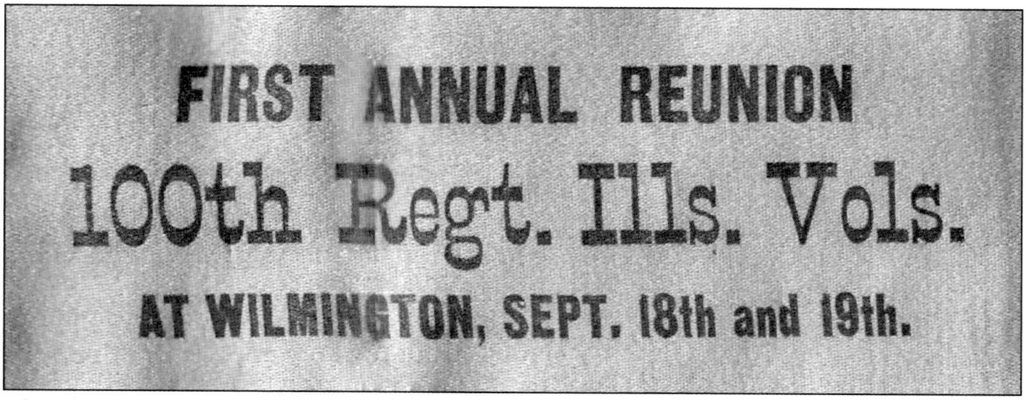

The Plainfield Grand Army of the Republic post was known as the Burrell Post No. 3. The Plainfield Civil War veterans post was named after John A. Burrell, who mustered in to Company D of the 100th Illinois Infantry as a first lieutenant. He was 35 years old and listed as a mason. Burrell was wounded at the Battle of Chickamauga in Georgia. After recovering, he was promoted to captain of Company D of the 100th Illinois. Burrell was later killed instantly while returning to a skirmish line near Dallas, Georgia, on May 30, 1864. It was reported that Colonel Bartleson of the 100th Illinois had tears rolling down his cheeks when he was told that Captain Burrell had been killed. The Plainfield post stayed active until about 1911. This ribbon is from the first annual 100th Illinois Infantry GAR Reunion, held in 1885 at Wilmington, Illinois. The 100th Illinois Infantry would later hold some of its reunions in Plainfield.

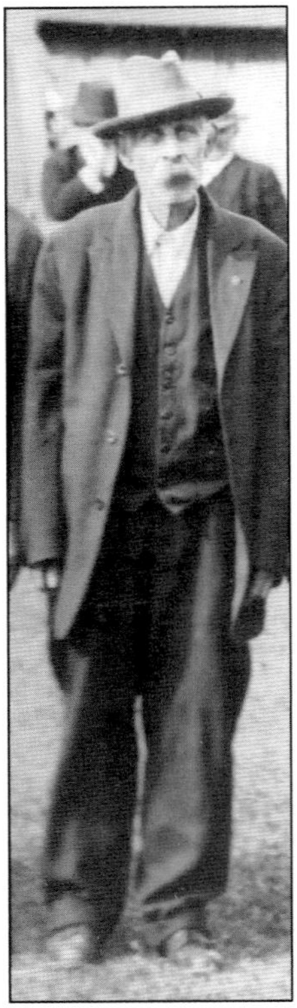

Many early photographs of Plainfield were taken and published by Keene Photography. Later, Keene produced many postcards of Plainfield. The Keene family has long played an important role in the town's history. William Keene opened his blacksmith shop in the early 1840s in Plainfield. His son Anson Keene is listed as "Anson Keen" on the Illinois Civil War database. He joined the 8th Illinois Cavalry in February 1864 at the age of 17. The 8th Illinois Cavalry suffered heavy causalities during the war, with over 250 men lost. Anson is listed as a farmer when he mustered into the 8th Illinois Cavalry. After the war, he was a blacksmith in town for many years. Keene's photograph as a member of the GAR is shown at left. Below is a postcard image taken by Keene Photography of Plainfield that shows city hall being moved.

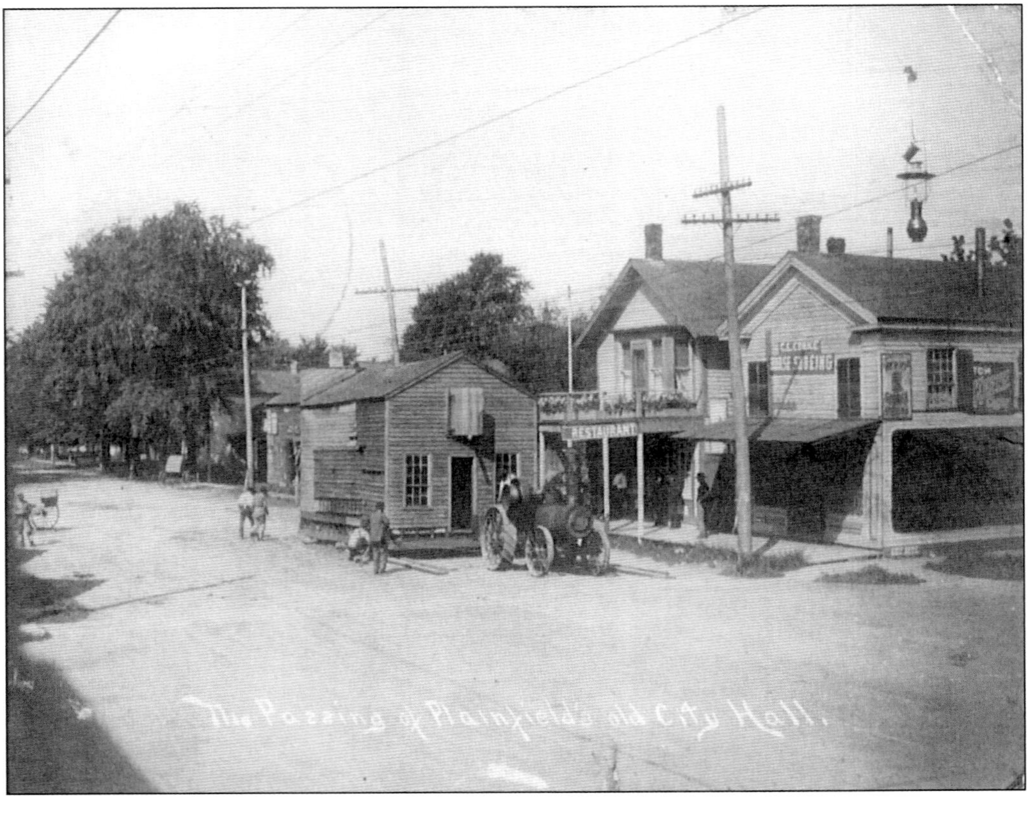

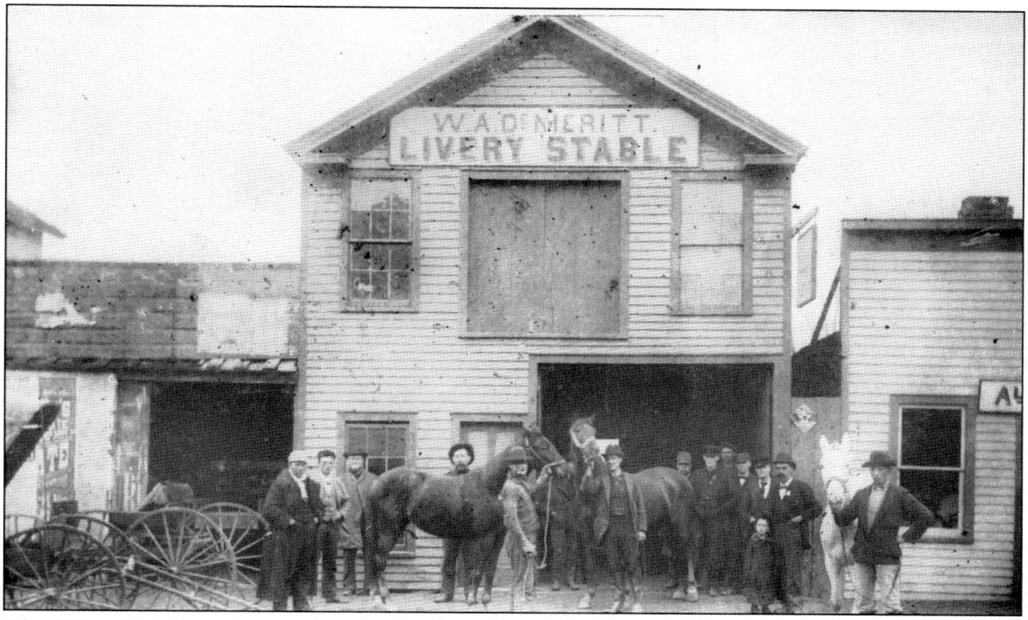

The W.A. DeMeritt Livery Stable, Feed, and Boarding Stable of Plainfield, Illinois, is listed in an early *Will County Directory*. It advertises "Drivers and Carriage Teams, Hacks to meet all Trains, Hacks and Carriages for Weddings, Funerals, Etc." The photograph, taken from a glass negative, shows what appear to be quite a few local men, a young boy, and several horses boarded at the stable. The 1895 *Will County Directory* lists the Plainfield stage drivers, harness makers, blacksmiths, stonemasons, livery, justice of the peace, and wagon makers. Below is an advertisement from the 1895 directory.

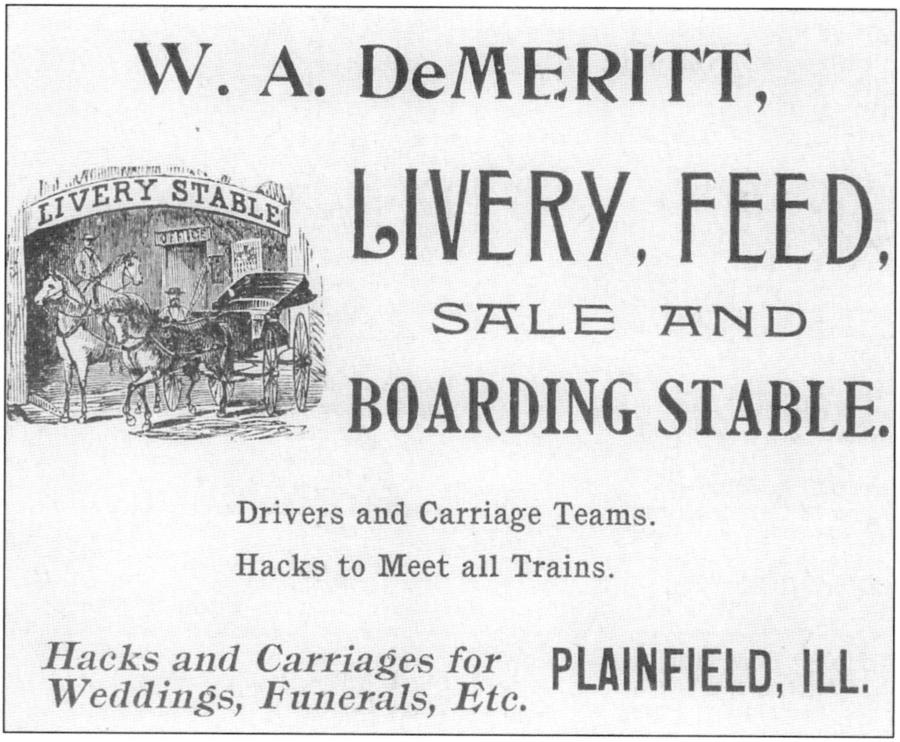

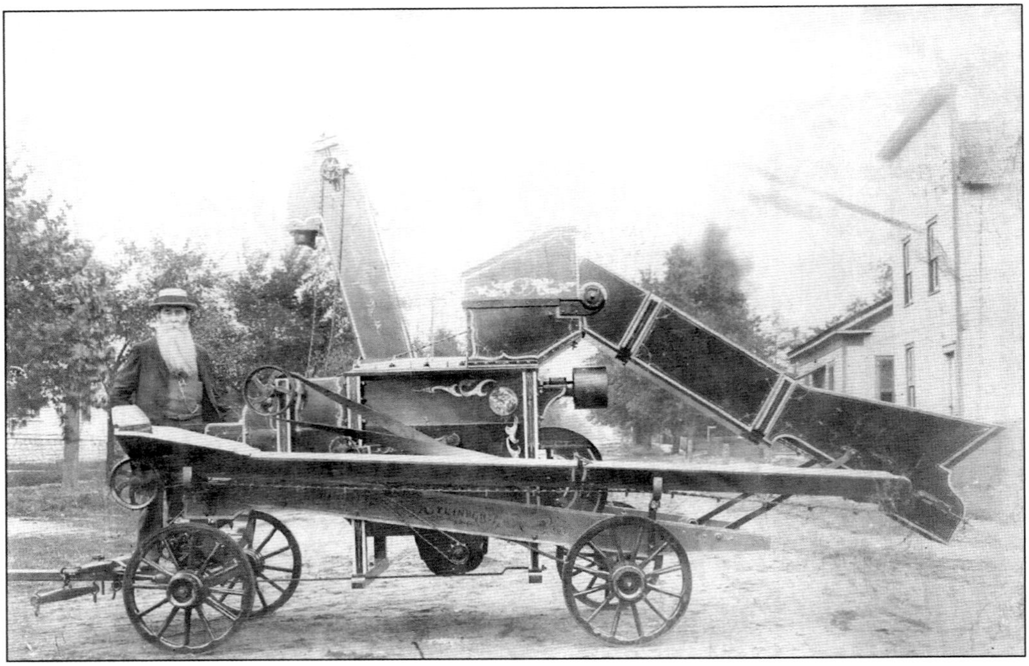

In these 1875 photographs, Andrew H. Shreffler of Plainfield is pictured next to one of his company's corn shellers. The company was started in 1849 as Dillman and Company and was owned by Michael Dillman and his sons. Shreffler was married to Dillman's daughter Elizabeth during that same year. In 1867, the company was incorporated as the Joliet Manufacturing Company, with Shreffler as secretary. In 1873, Shreffler bought out the interest of Michael Dillman, and in 1890, he bought out the interest of L.E. Dillman, becoming the sole owner of the company. These two photographs show Shreffler with and without his hat.

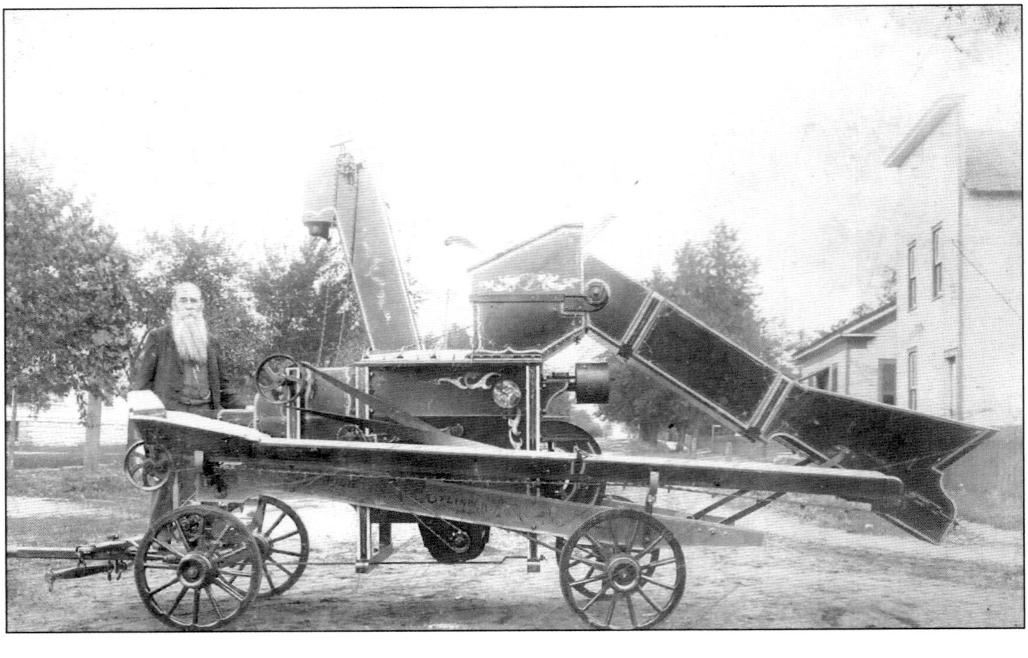

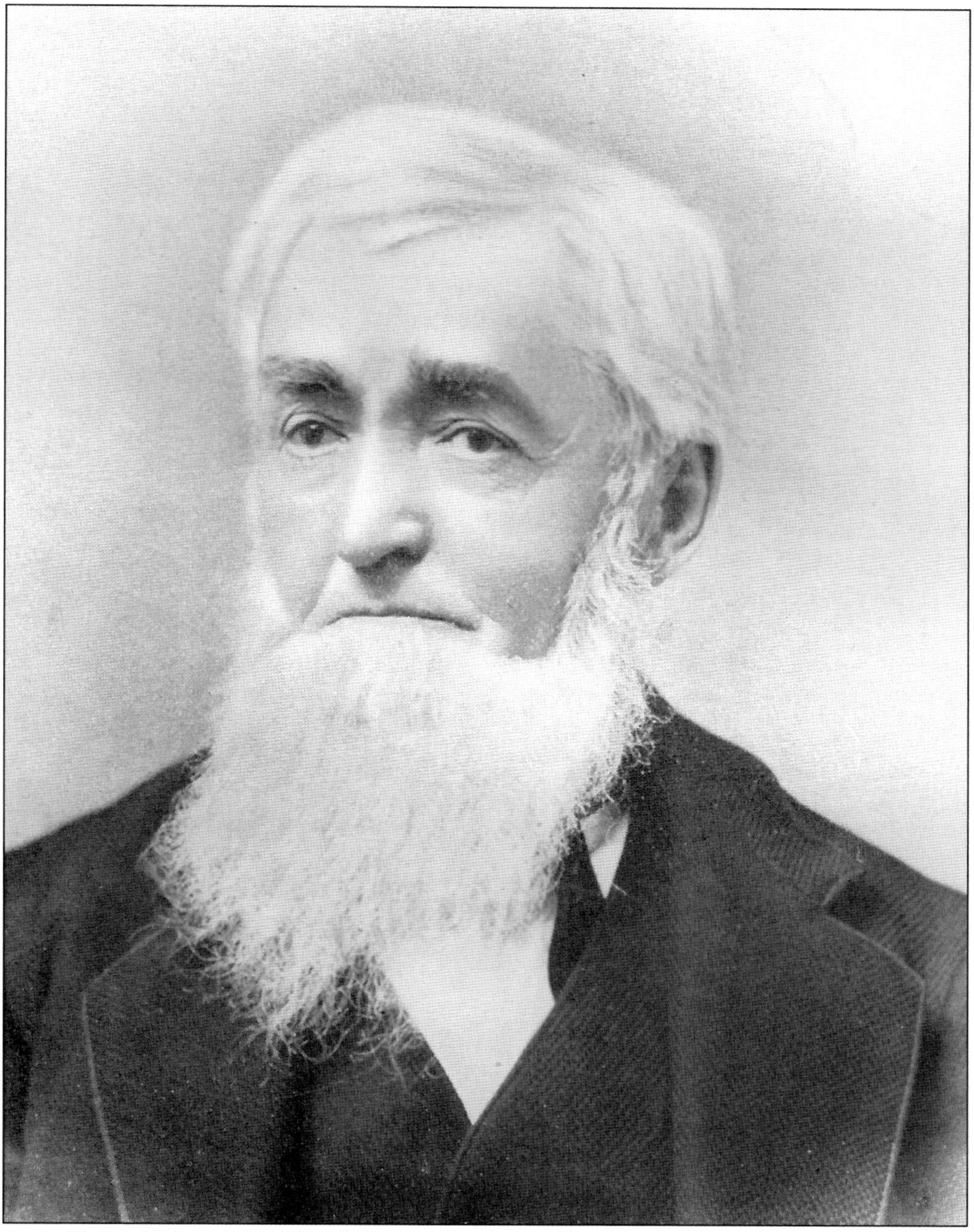

Amos H. Scofield settled in Plainfield in September 1855 at the age of 42. During his first year in Plainfield, he was engaged in merchandising, of which type is unknown. Soon after his arrival, Scofield purchased four and a half acres in Plainfield, selling two lots for residences and keeping the remaining three acres. Scofield also owned some farmland southwest of Plainfield, close to Indian Boundary Road near the Kendall County line. Amos was a strict follower of abolitionist principles during the Civil War. Later in life, he became a Prohibitionist in politics. He was a leading member of the Methodist Episcopal church and served as a Sunday school class leader. He married Elizabeth Rhodes on September 18, 1855. She came to Plainfield with her brother in 1851. Amos passed away on February 23, 1893.

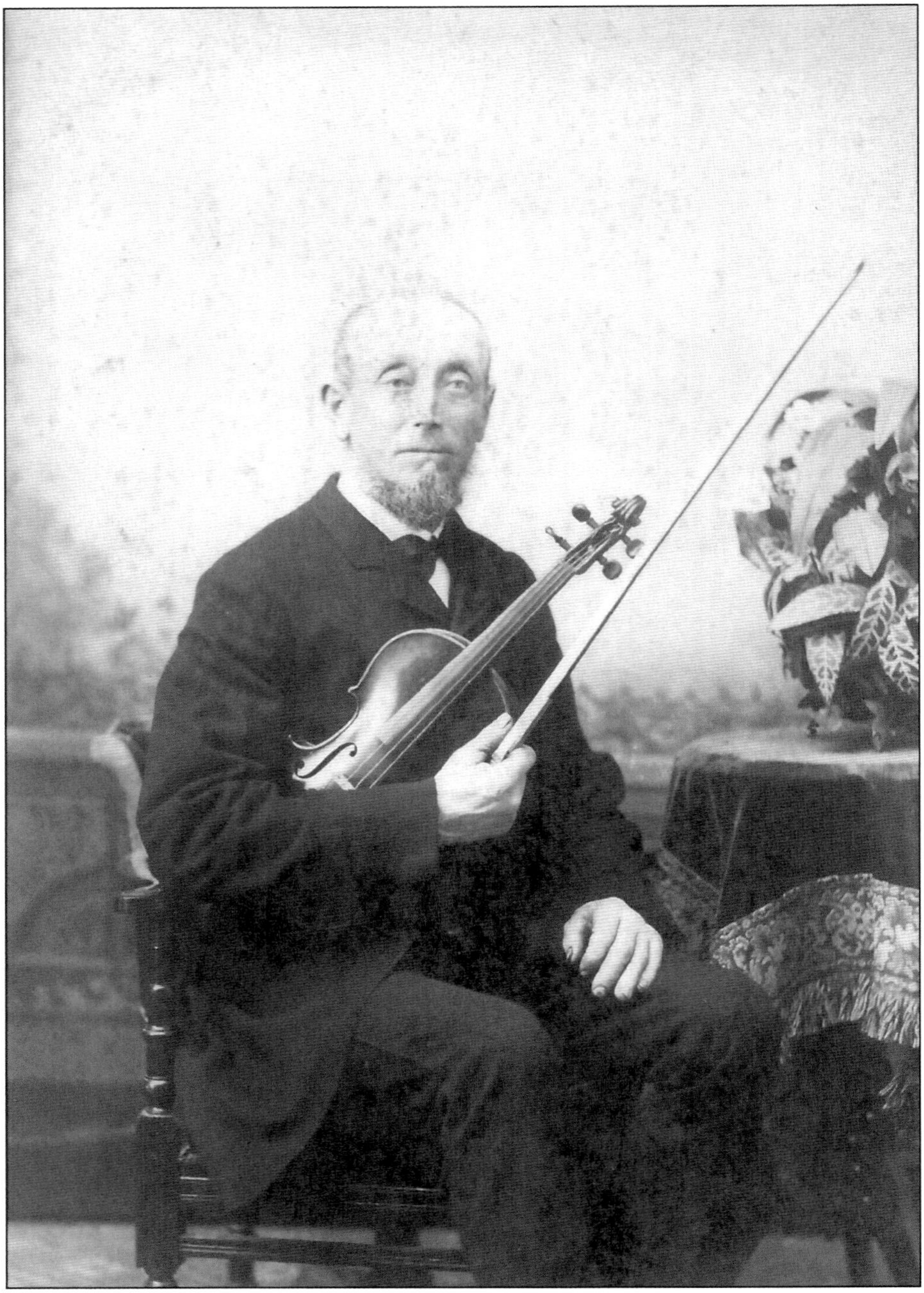

The violinist pictured in this A.H. Mottinger cabinet photograph is Samuel Grundy. A local 1890s newspaper article on the Orpheus Concert Company notes, "When veteran violist Samuel Grundy appeared on the stage, the ball fairly rang with applause, and after rendering a difficult solo, was called back on the stage and he finished with the Scotch air 'The Kerry Dance.' " Grundy and his wife, Janet, were farmers in Plainfield Township in the 1870s. The Grundy farmland was west of Plainfield, on both the north and south side of what is now Route 126, just about a mile west beyond Indian Boundary Road. Samuel was born in 1827 and passed away in 1914, while Janet, born in 1835, only lived until 1897. Both are buried in the Plainfield Township Cemetery.

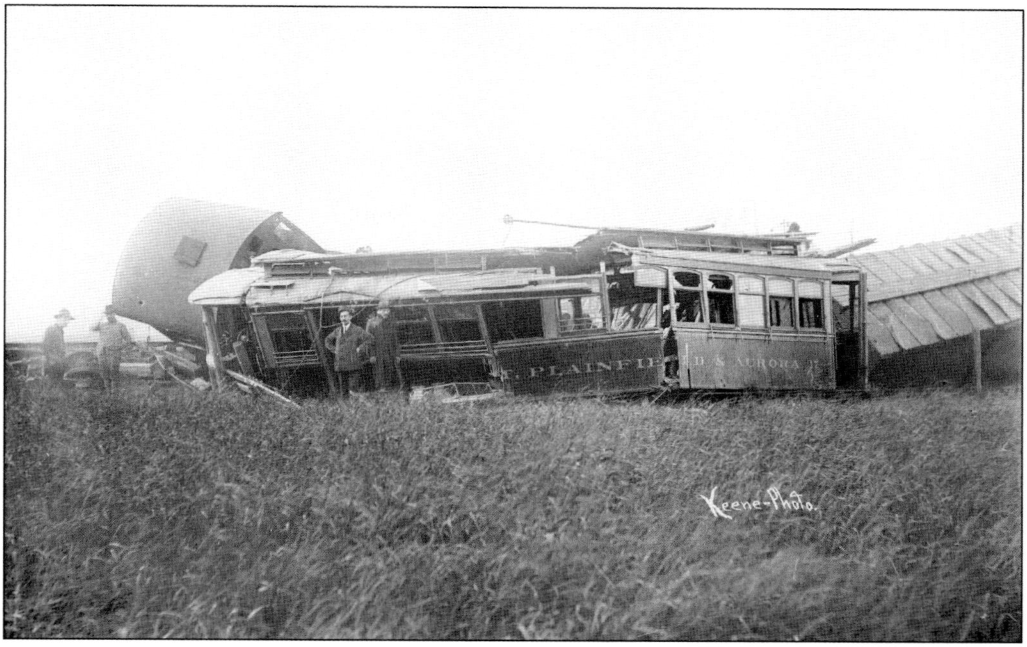

The Joliet, Plainfield & Aurora Railway Company began operation in May 1901 and was later absorbed by the Joliet & Southern Traction Company. Accidents, such as this one near Plainfield, occurred often on the electric trolley lines. Occasionally, the train accident was caused by the railway motorman missing a danger flag signal, and the trolley would run into another train. These tracks were not maintained well, which would also lead to accidents. Note that Keene, a well-known Plainfield photographer, took the photograph. Below is a postcard of a trolley in downtown Plainfield.

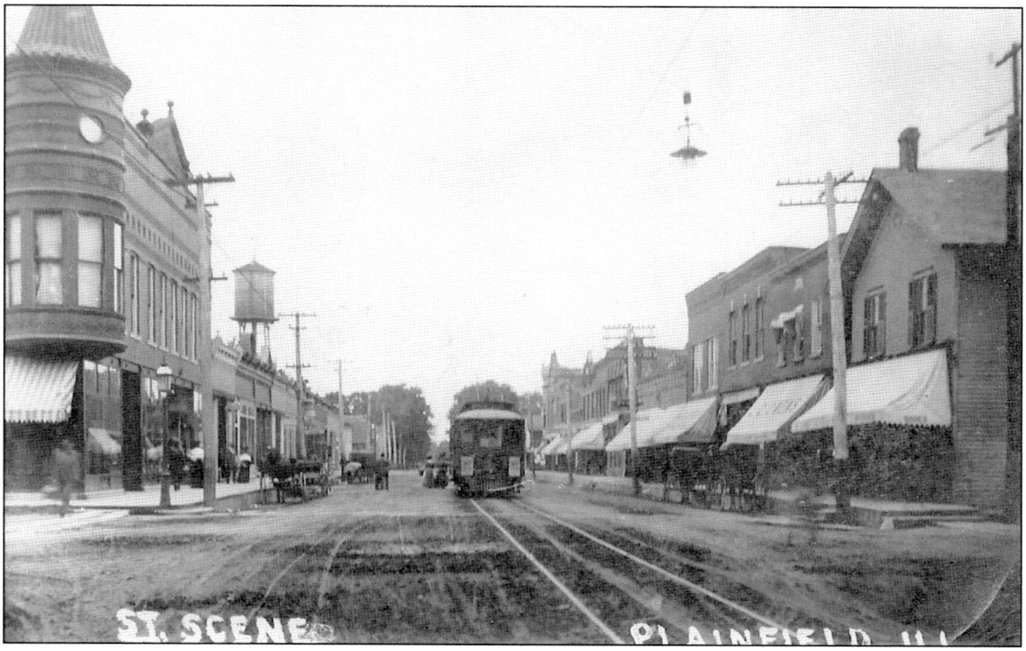

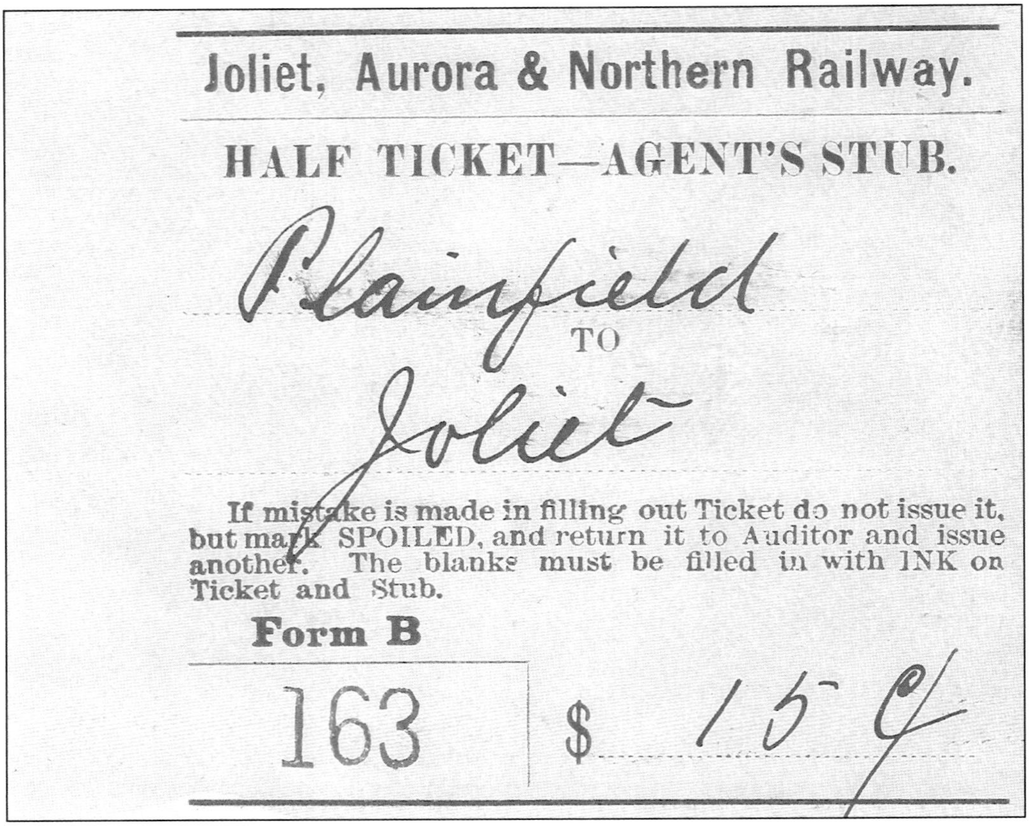

Joliet, Aurora & Northern Railway.

HALF TICKET—AGENT'S STUB.

Plainfield

TO

Joliet

If mistake is made in filling out Ticket do not issue it, but mark SPOILED, and return it to Auditor and issue another. The blanks must be filled in with INK on Ticket and Stub.

Form B

163 $ 15¢

The Joliet, Aurora & Northern Railway was incorporated in 1884. The actual operation of the railway trains began in 1886. This ticket stub is for travel from Plainfield to Joliet. The fare was 15¢, and the ticket is stamped from the Plainfield depot in 1887. The Elgin, Joliet, & Eastern Railway acquired the Joliet, Aurora & Northern Railway in 1888.

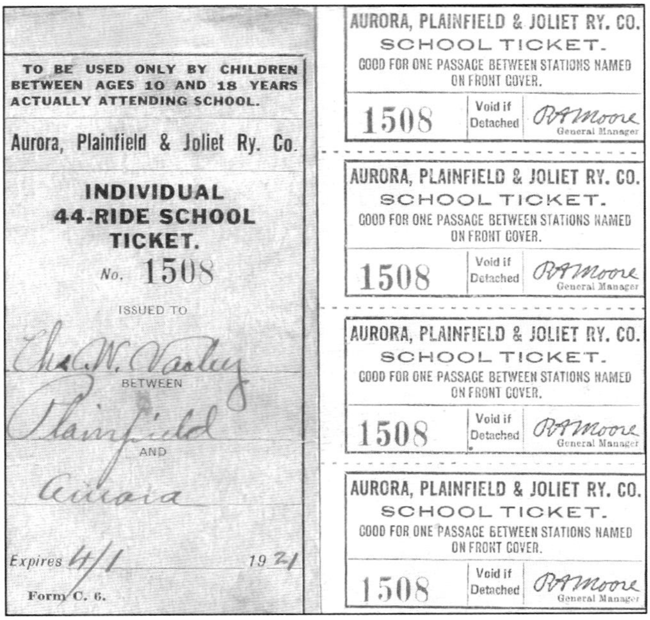

TO BE USED ONLY BY CHILDREN BETWEEN AGES 10 AND 18 YEARS ACTUALLY ATTENDING SCHOOL.

Aurora, Plainfield & Joliet Ry. Co.

INDIVIDUAL 44-RIDE SCHOOL TICKET.

No. 1508

ISSUED TO Chas. W. Vasley

BETWEEN Plainfield

AND Aurora

Expires 4/1 1921

Form C. 6.

AURORA, PLAINFIELD & JOLIET RY. CO.
SCHOOL TICKET.
GOOD FOR ONE PASSAGE BETWEEN STATIONS NAMED ON FRONT COVER.
1508 Void if Detached R.A. Moore General Manager

The tickets in this booklet, issued in 1921 by the Aurora, Plainfield & Joliet Railway Company, were titled "Individual 44-Ride School Tickets." They were good for travel both ways between Six Corners in Joliet, Lily Cache, Plainfield, Normantown, Wolf's, and Aurora. The railway company advertised that the tickets were to be used only by children between the ages of 10 and 18 years who were actually attending school.

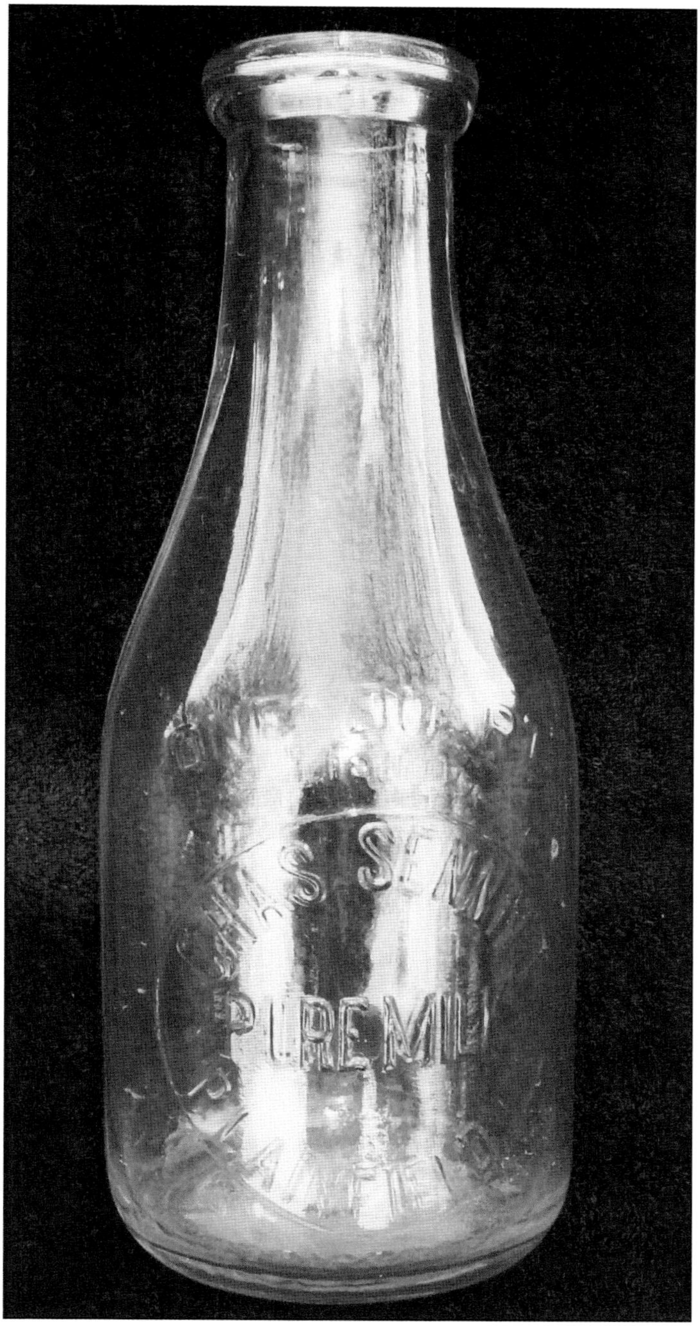

For several years, Charles Sennitt delivered bottles of pure milk to the residents of Plainfield. Today, these embossed milk bottles from the Sennitt farm are extremely rare. This early dairy bottle advertises pure milk, instead of the more common pasteurized milk listed on later dairy bottles. Charles was born in 1882, the son of John and Emma Sennitt. John Sennitt arrived in Plainfield in 1857 and married Emma Drew in April 1871. The Sennitt farm was located on the west side of Plainfield. A portion of Electric Park was built on the Sennitt farm cow pasture. The farm also ran north of the present-day Plainfield depot. Charles died in 1959 and is buried in the Plainfield Township Cemetery.

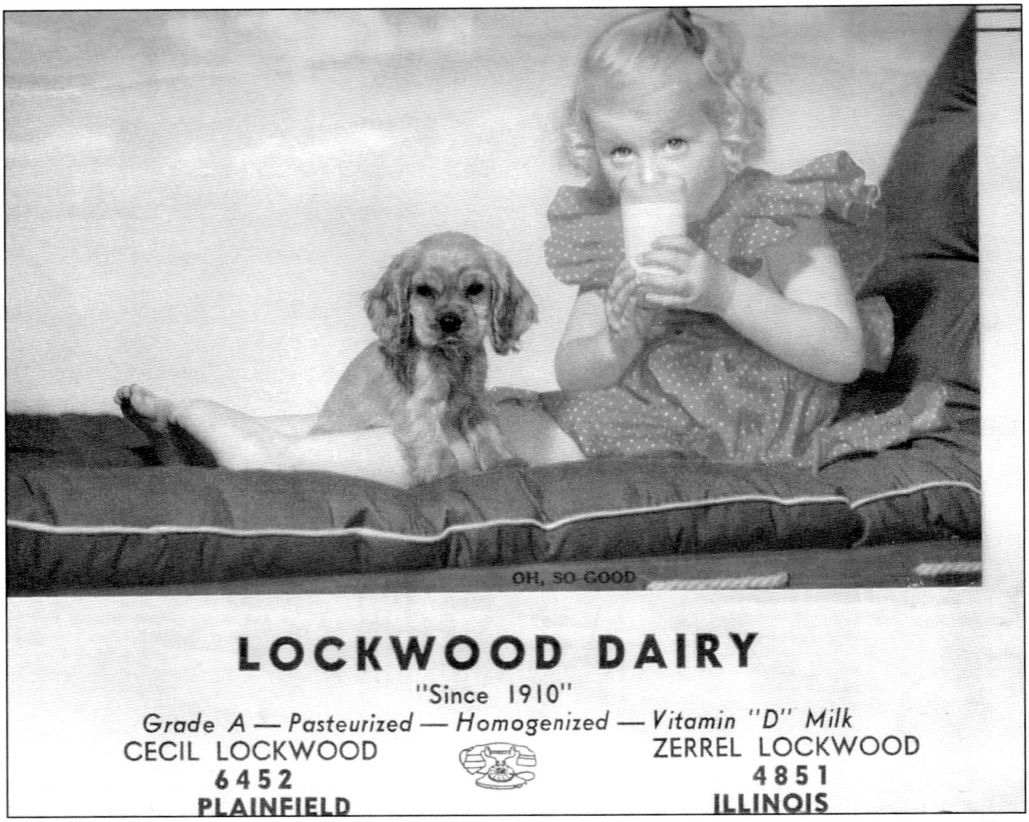

In 1909, Estella (Culver) Lockwood was widowed and left with two sons at home. In an effort to support her family, she decided to turn her small farm on James Street into a dairy, an ad for which is pictured above. She tended and milked the cows, while her sons used their wagon to deliver milk to customers in town. Lockwood Dairy has expanded several times over the years. Lockwood's sons Cecil, Zerrell, and Jerry eventually operated the dairy. The 1945 calendar top below advertises with the slogans "Lockwood Milk—A Surety of Purity" and "Thirty-Five Years of Service to Our Customers."

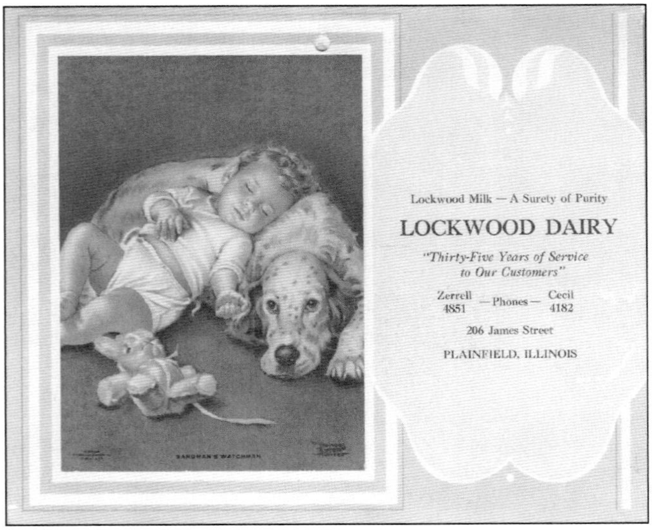

The instructions on this Lockwood Dairy extra-order item (right) suggest placing this signal in the empty bottle with tabs raised to indicate the number of extra items wanted by the customer. The empty milk bottles sat on the customer's porch in an aluminum box, awaiting pickup. Customers could chose from whipping cream, cottage cheese, orange drink, homogenized milk, skim milk, chocolate milk, buttermilk, and eggs. It advertises home delivery since 1910. Below is an early photograph of one of the Lockwood Dairy delivery trucks.

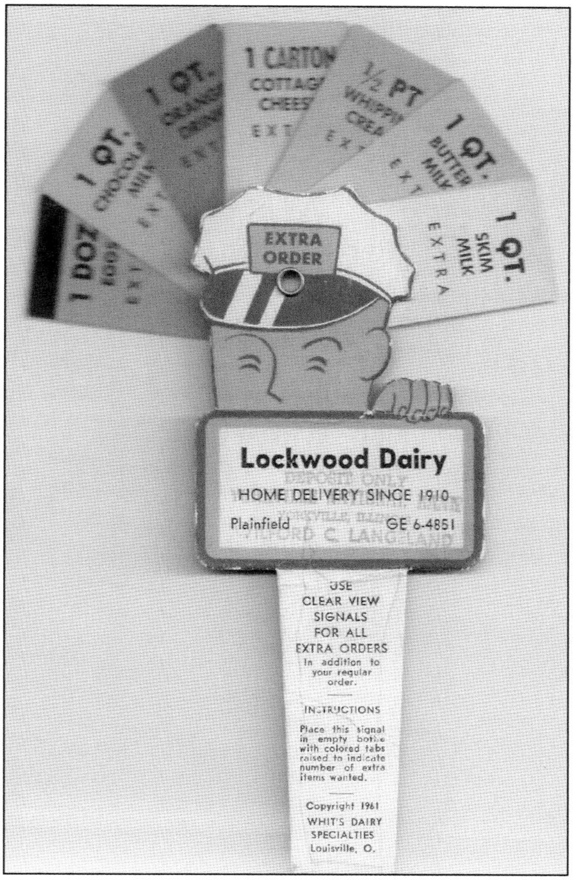

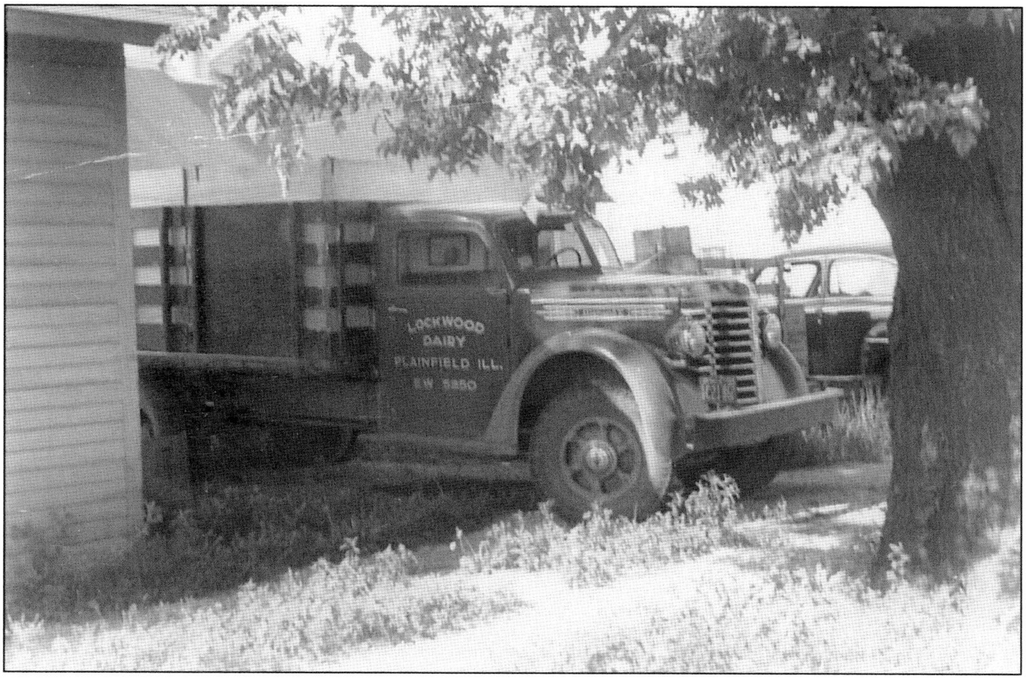

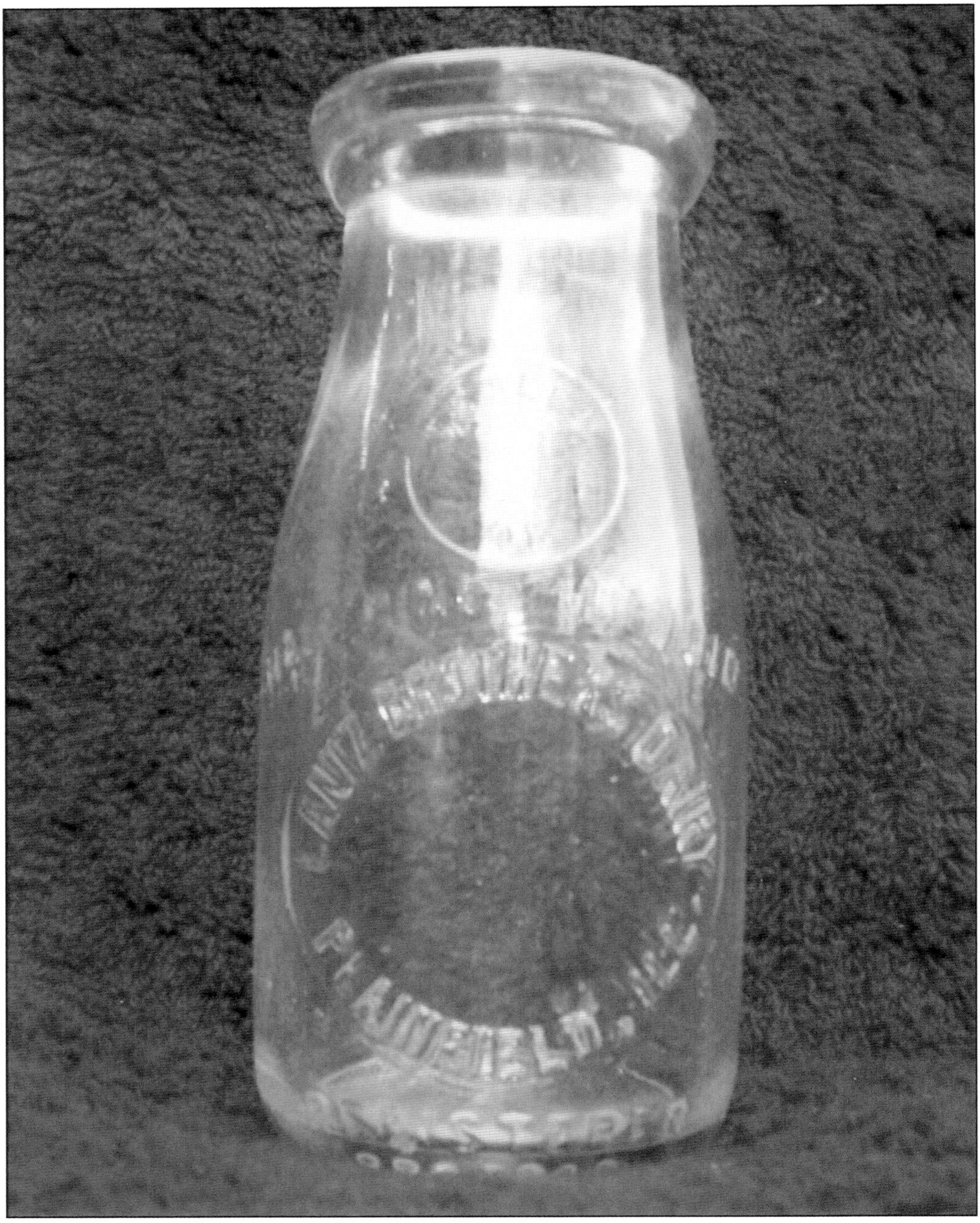

This rare Plainfield half-pint milk bottle is from the Lantz Brothers Dairy. The Lantz Brothers Dairy bottles are very hard to find, with few existing today. This is the only known bottle with "Lantz Brothers" included in the embossing. Catherine Lantz came to the Plainfield-Wheatland area in 1850 from Pennsylvania. She and her children settled in Plainfield after the death of her husband in Pennsylvania that same year. Catherine's sons Daniel and John were farmers in the Wheatland area north of Plainfield. Daniel was an early Plainfield constable. John and his wife, the former Annie M. Schott, had six children and 40 grandchildren.

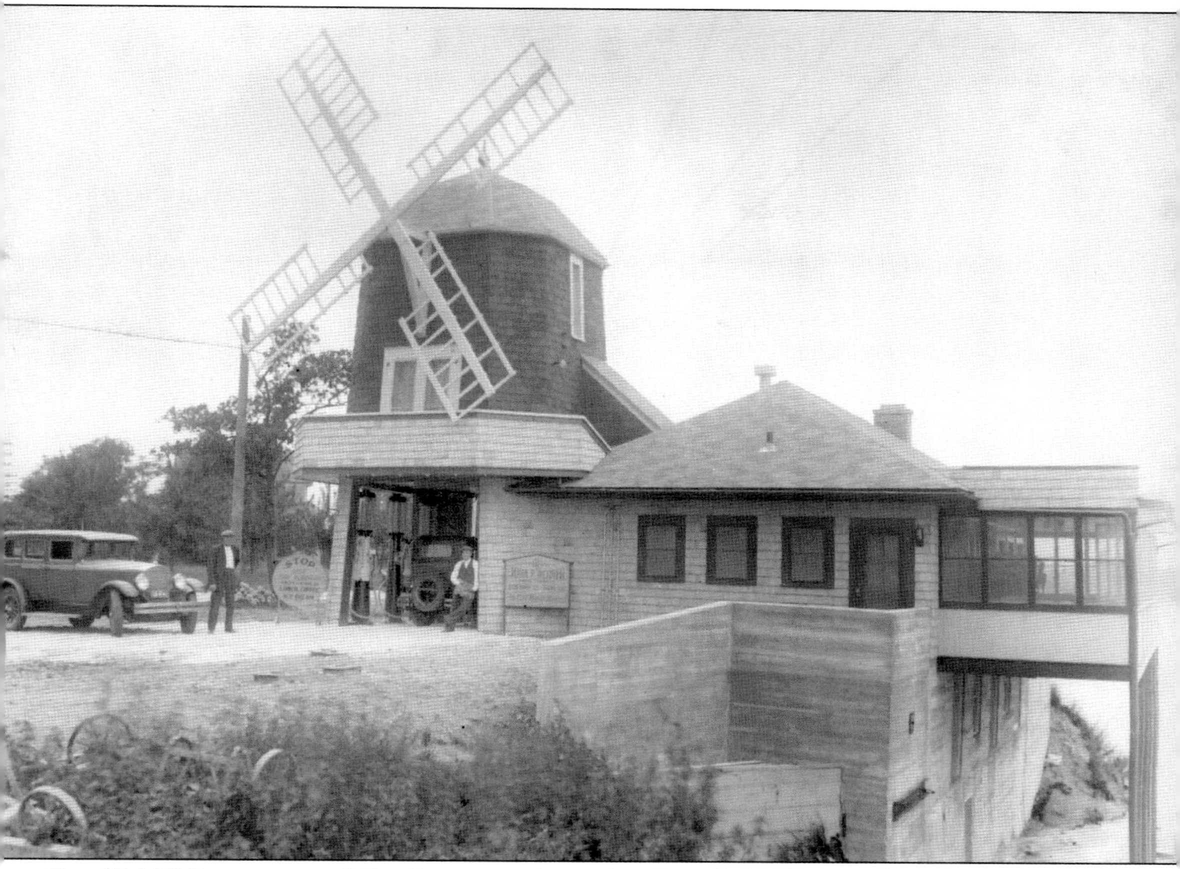

Powell's Mill Restaurant and Gas Station was located on Lincoln Highway at the intersection of US Route 30 and Renwick Road. Decorated with a large Dutch windmill, it was well known for miles around. The sign out front advertises that it is open for business with hot and cold lunches as well as coffee and ice cream. The other sign advertises John P. Werner from 505 Ruby Street in Joliet as the general contractor. This indicates the building was fairly new when this photograph was taken. Werner advertises "Better Built Homes"—however, he must have also built restaurants and service stations. The service station's Standard Oil gasoline pumps are directly under the windmill. This location was a Standard Oil gas station for many years.

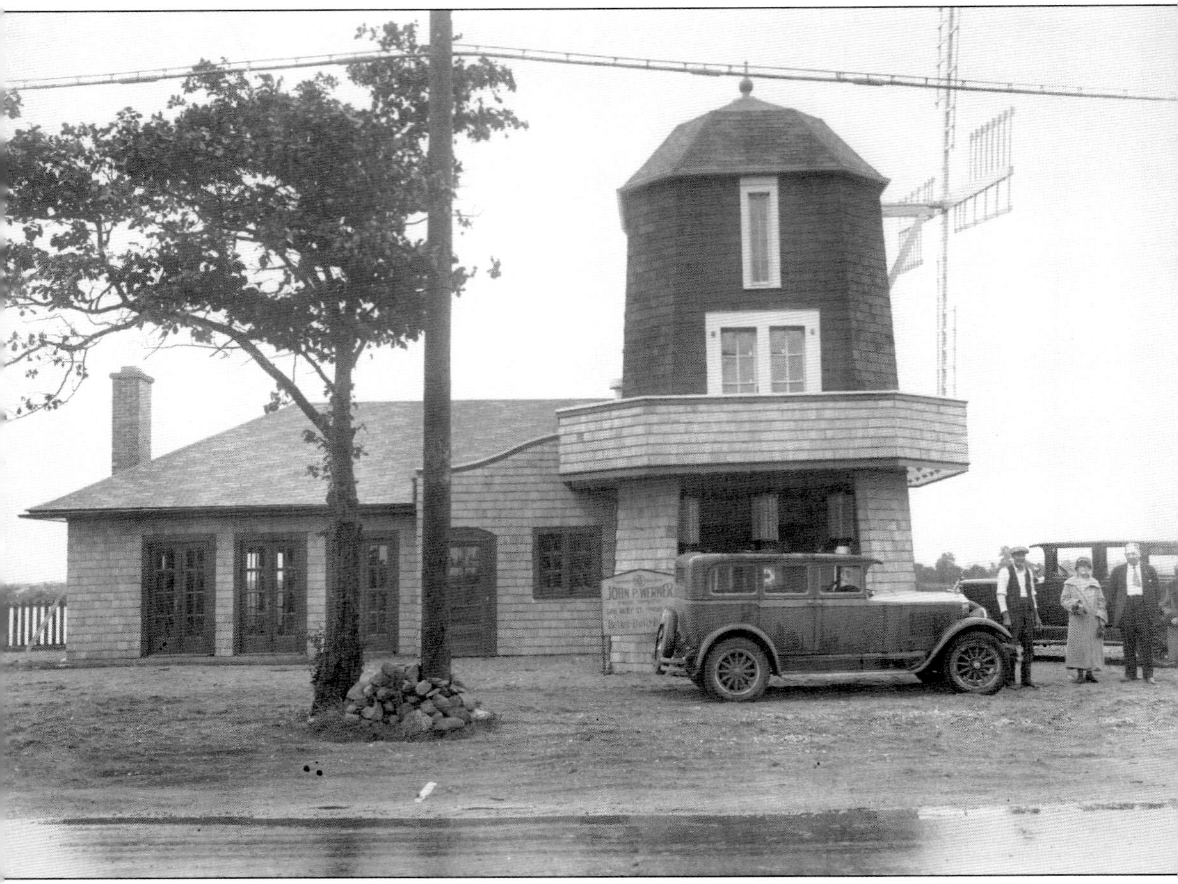

In 1913, the Chicago Gravel Company purchased the property on which the Powell's Mill Restaurant and Gas Station was located. The land was obtained in order to mine gravel, which resulted in the lake being dug after several years. At one point, the gravel company mined 200 train cars of gravel a day from the pit. This spring-fed lake was named Lake Renwick after Frank Renwick, one of the founders of the Chicago Gravel Company. A swimming facility with a bathhouse and a diving board was opened at the lake, all for the price of a $3 season pass. These types of eye-catching restaurants and gas stations were common along US Route 30, much as they were along Route 66. The windmill design was certainly unique and well known in the Will County area.

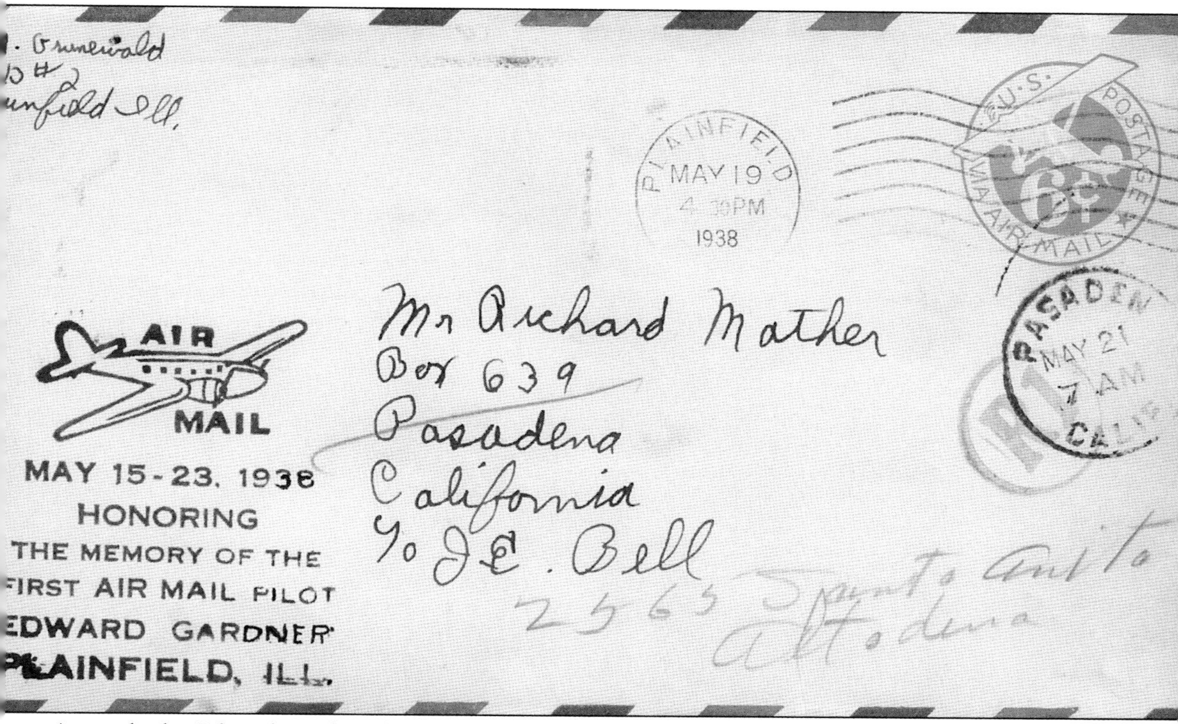

Airmail pilot Edward Gardner from Plainfield, Illinois, was honored by the Plainfield Post Office on May 15–23, 1938. He is credited with making the first airmail delivery between Chicago and New York on September 7, 1918, in nine hours and 18 minutes. While making deliveries to Chicago, Gardner often stopped to visit his mother in Plainfield. After serving the Post Office Department for many years, he worked for the Nebraska Aircraft Corporation. Gardner was killed when his plane crashed in February 1921 while participating in an aviation tournament in Holdredge, Nebraska. He is buried in the Plainfield Township Cemetery. This letter is addressed to Richard Mather in Pasadena, California. Robert Grunewald, a Plainfield High School student, was writing him about the band playing at a ceremony honoring Gardner: "The band plans to play when the air mail plane takes off." He also writes about the upcoming junior prom at the high school in Plainfield.

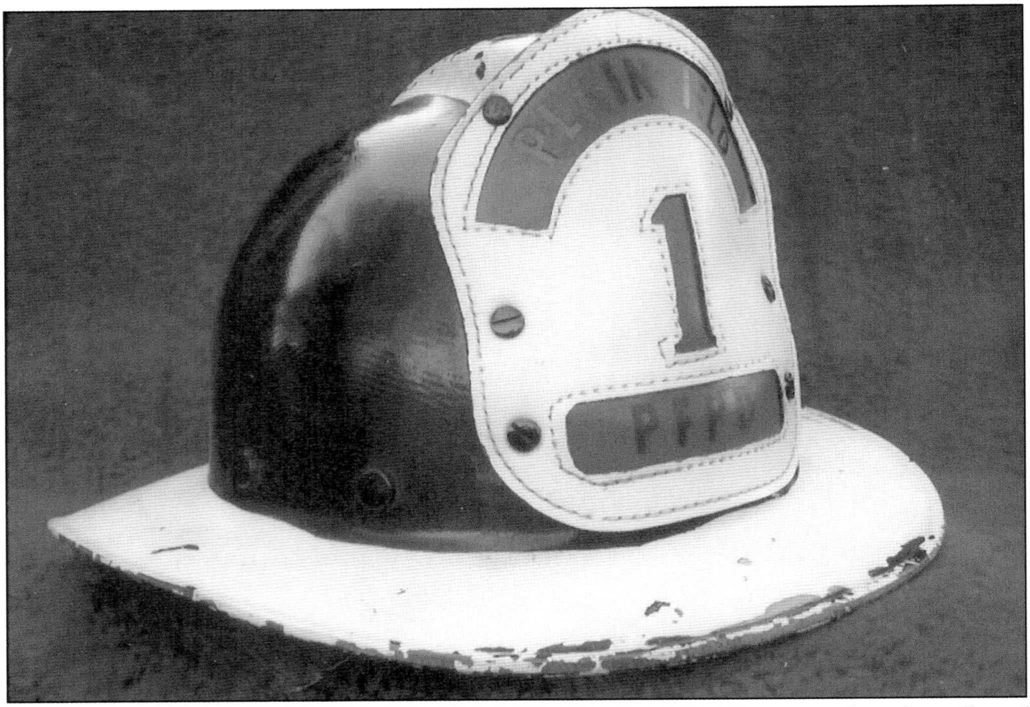

One of the first serious Plainfield fires was reportedly in 1888 and originated in the cellar of Frank Beebe's grocery store. The building was owned by I.A. Clippinger. The insurance company valued the property in the 1888 fire at $4,500, but Clippinger had only $2,500 of coverage on the structure. Other occupants of the building were Gillispie, Evarts, and Davis, who reported $1,300 of loss in the fire. Samuel Gillispie had a blacksmith shop in the area, and J. Evarts was a banker in the building. A sign on the corner later read, "Bank moved on account of intense heat." John Funk sold farm implements in a shed near the building that caught fire. It was also destroyed in the 1888 fire, with a loss of $1,000 in equipment and $80 in office supplies. Funk was not covered by insurance.

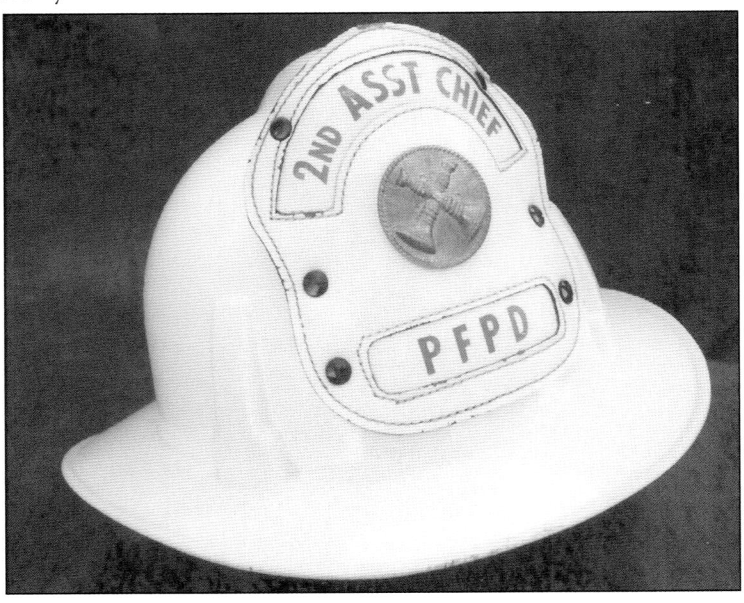

Two

A STROLL THROUGH TOWN

Chester Ingersoll established the village of Plainfield in 1834 after coming to the area in 1831. Ingersoll laid out 13 blocks, which were bordered by Division Street on the east, Lockport Street on the north, Ottawa Street on the south, and the DuPage River on the west. Sometime around 1835, another area northeast of what Ingersoll had platted was laid out near the DuPage River. The area of land between what Ingersoll platted out on the south side and what had been laid out on the northeast side of Plainfield was mostly owned by pioneer Levi Arnold. This land north of Lockport Street was sold off and developed over several years in the 1840s and 1850s. Plainfield's growth in the 1840s was fairly strong, until the Illinois and Michigan Canal opened in 1848. The canal was an economic draw for towns and businesses along it. Plainfield was a central location between Chicago and Ottawa, Illinois. Routes were heavily traveled by stagecoach between the two cities at the time. Despite experiencing large fires in the downtown business district during the late 1800s, Plainfield continued to grow.

The installation of trolley lines along with the completion of the Lincoln Highway were quite a boost to the various businesses in Plainfield at the start of the 1900s and continuing to the late 1920s. After the Depression, Plainfield experienced the typical large growth that many towns saw after World War II. The village held onto its small-town charm through the 1960s and 1970s. The village experienced enormous growth after the 1990 tornado, becoming one of the fastest growing communities in the nation since 1990. This chapter contains images taken from the authors' glass negative collection, which show a look similar to an early western town with dirt streets and wooden sidewalks. It also includes many images of various Plainfield business owners along with business advertisements that will evoke thoughts of days gone by. These doctors, hardware stores, druggists, grocery stores, barbershops, and gas stations all helped develop Plainfield into the special village that it has become over the years.

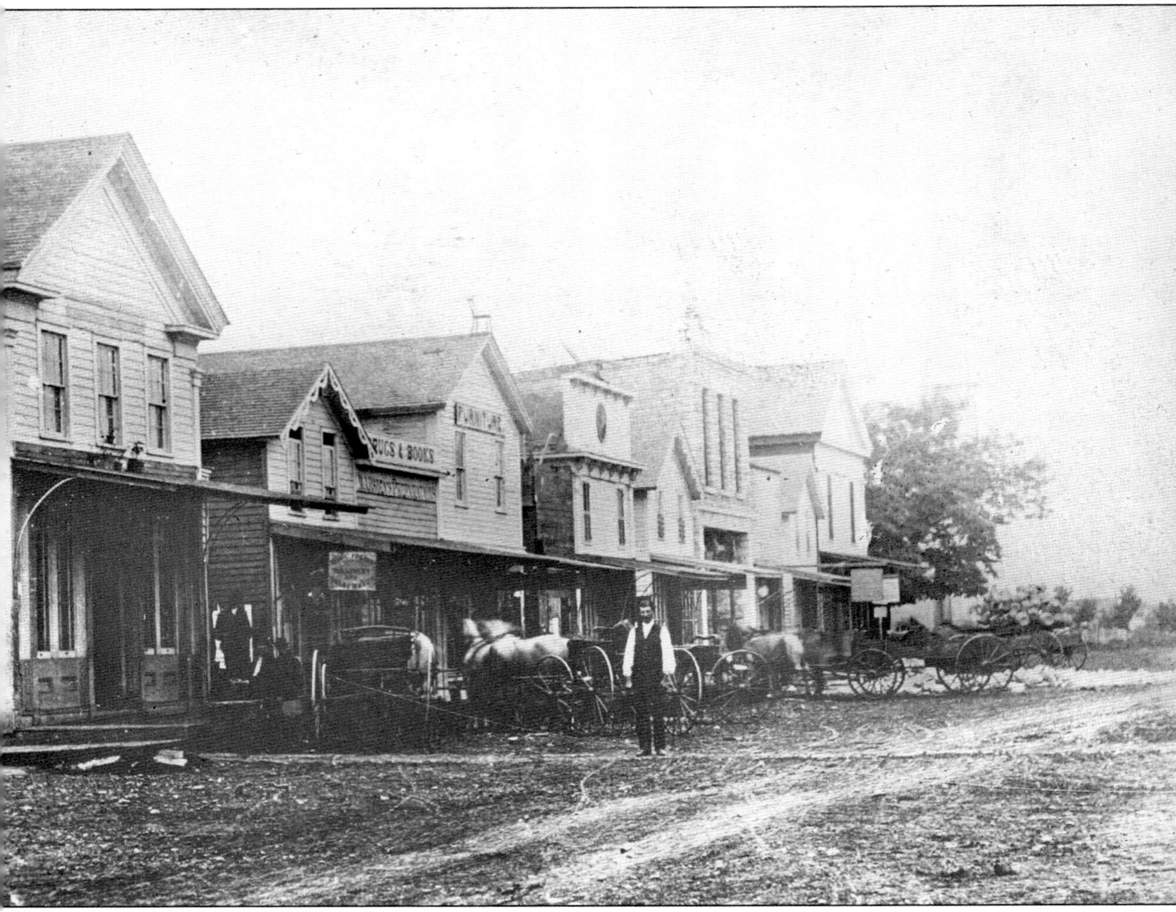

This very early photograph of the north side of Lockport Street looking east has the appearance of an Old West town. The fire of December 31, 1890, and January 1, 1891, destroyed most of the buildings in this image. The last three buildings, however, did survive the fire. The Corbin and Chittenden store at the east end of Lockport Street was one of the structures to survive. Some of the early Plainfield letterhead shown in this book was found on the walls of the store when it was remodeled over 120 years later. The 1895 directory lists the following as some of the business establishments in Plainfield: Austin and Figge Blacksmiths; A.T. Tile Manufacturer; Darr and Cain Hardware Store; W.A. DeMeritt Livery; Sonntag Bros. Harness Shop; the *Enterprise* newspaper; Hays and McCreery Hardware; Jones and Capps Hardware; Marsh and Wood Grain-Coal; Plainfield Bank; L.B. Overman Dry Goods, Groceries, and Hardware; VanDyke and Mottinger Meats; and Weese and Jacobs Restaurant.

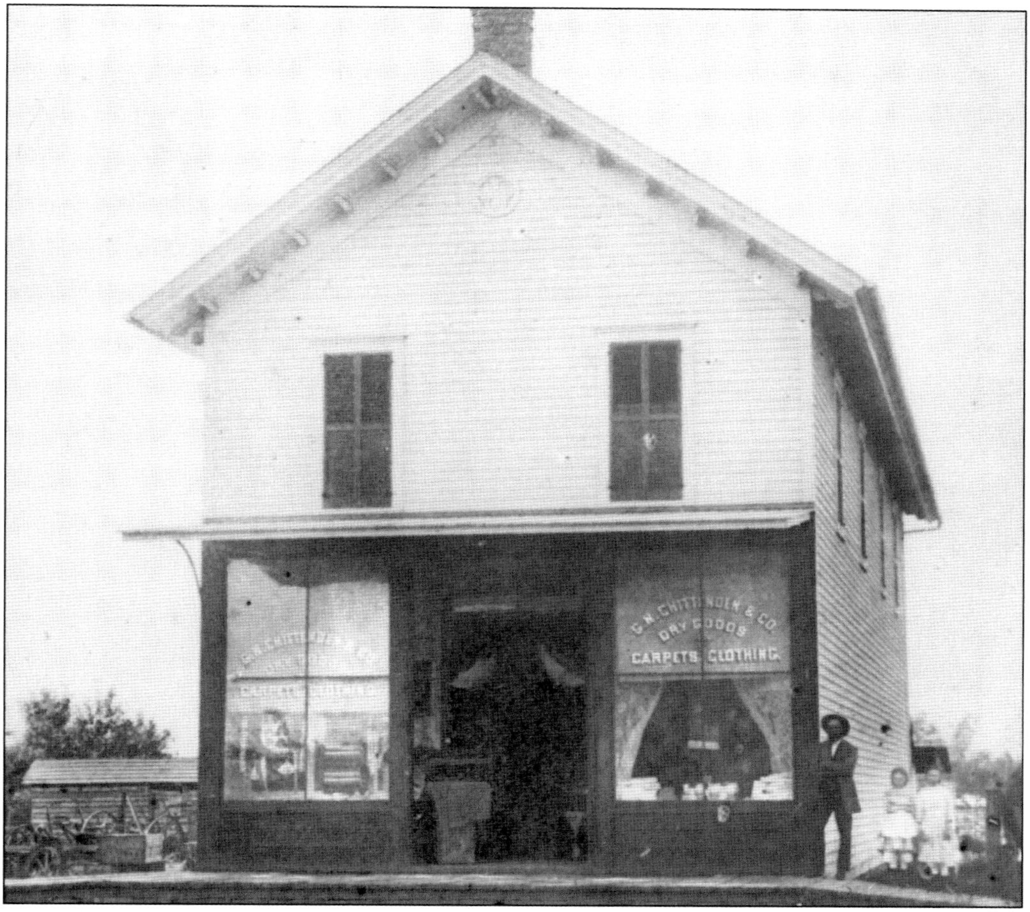

G.N. Chittenden owned one of the first general merchandise stores in Plainfield. In the above photograph, it can be assumed that Chittenden is standing next to his building with his family behind him. He was born in 1818 in Ohio and moved to Plainfield and started his general store in the early 1850s. The store window advertises dry goods, carpets, and clothing. Chittenden held the offices of justice of the peace and township treasurer. He and his wife, Elizabeth, had six children. Their son William was later involved in the store business with Alfred T. Corbin. The store remained standing after the 1891 fire that demolished almost the entire north side of Lockport Street. The building later became the A.C. Steiner Dress Shop.

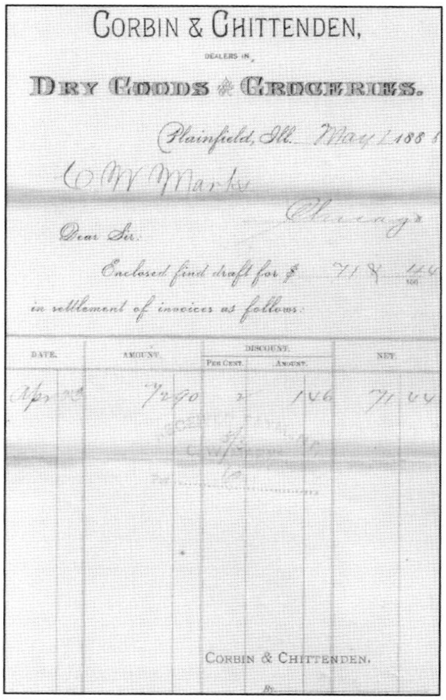

CORBIN & CHITTENDEN,

DEALERS IN

DRY GOODS & GROCERIES.

Plainfield, Ill.

Dear Sir:

Enclosed find draft for $

in settlement of invoices as follows:

DATE.	AMOUNT.	DISCOUNT.		NET.
		PER CENT.	AMOUNT.	

CORBIN & CHITTENDEN.

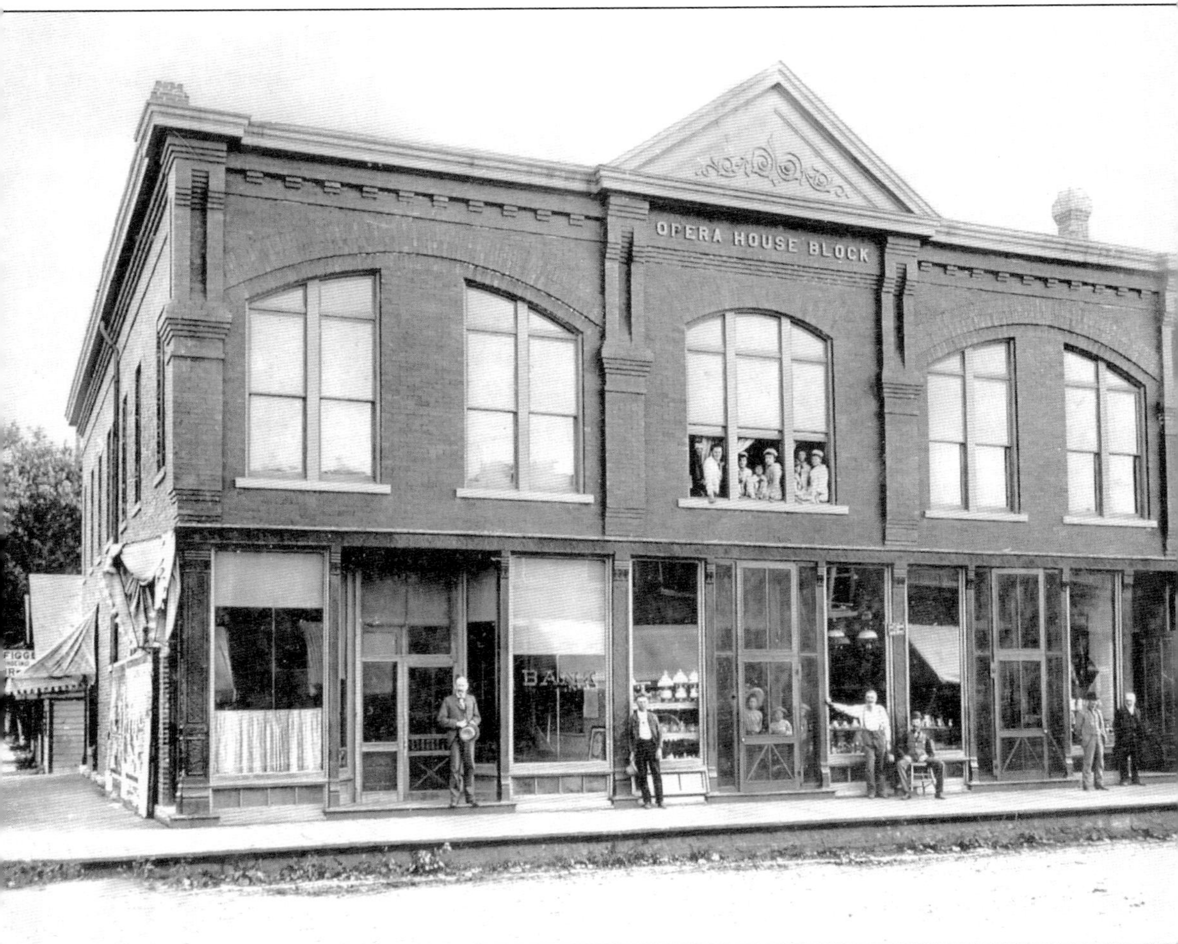

The opera house on the south side of Lockport Street was destroyed in a late-1890s fire. Smoke was found pouring out of the Hays and McCreery store by Harry Hamlin and Lou Mottinger. They had been across the street at the Grand Army of the Republic Hall. It was reported in a local newspaper that even though a dense cloud of smoke poured out, J.W. Prescott, Roy Spangler, and Clint Hartong made their way into the store cellar by crawling on their stomachs on the cellar floor. The fire was found burning in the cellar in front of the furnace. It was reported that "The Plainfield fire engine, considering its size, did splendid work in saving adjoining buildings and those on the opposite side of the street. A.S. Speicher was prostrated by over exertion in leading a frightened horse from the fire, and was taken home in a sleigh."

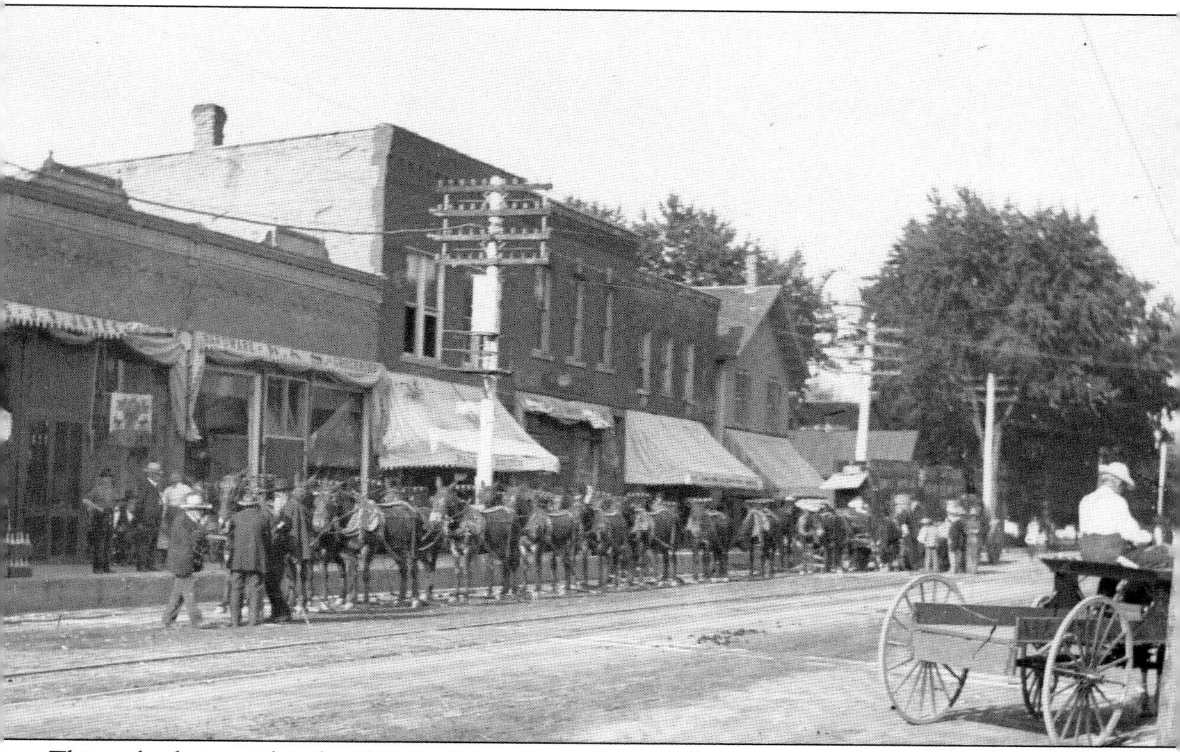

This early photograph, taken from a glass negative, depicts what appears to be a circus wagon on what is now Lockport Street. This was a unique time period, when there were horse and buggies parked on one side of the street, trolley tracks running down the middle, and mules pulling a wagon down the north side. Note the manure in the middle of the street. Also pictured is the J.R. Jones Hardware store to the north, along with the W&S Groceries store. In 1878, Plainfield had two general dry goods stores, two grocery stores that carried hardware, two drugstores, one bookstore, one hotel, one furniture store, five blacksmith shops, two livery stables, one restaurant, three wagon shops, two cider mills, four physicians, and no lawyers.

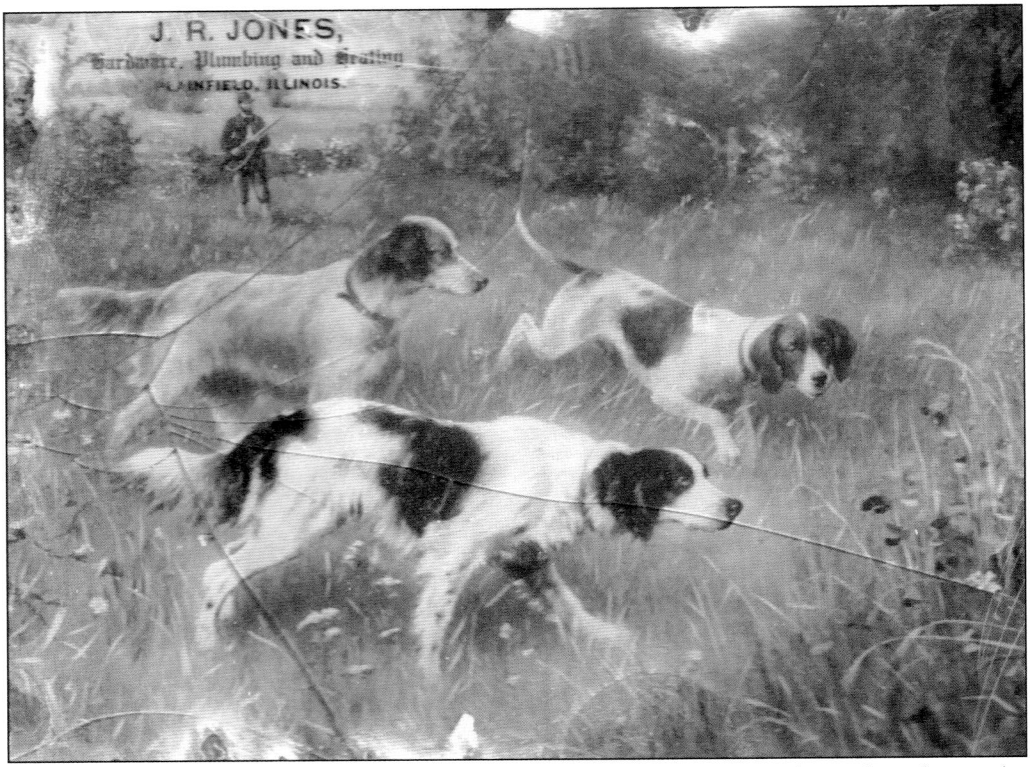

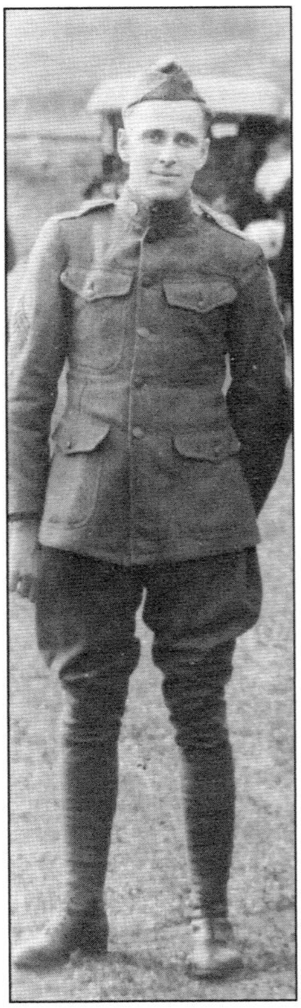

J.R. Jones Hardware, Plumbing, and Heating was located on the north side of Lockport Street. Jones came to the area as a tinner and opened a shop in 1890. The tinner shop developed into Jones Hardware, which would operate in Plainfield for over 80 years. In the 1895 *Will County Directory*, the business is listed as Jones and Capps Hardware. John Richard "J.R." Jones married Elizabeth Capps of Chicago, and they had a daughter, Elizabeth, and a son, Richard Ira Jones. After the death of his wife, J.R. married Grace Patterson and had a daughter, also named Grace. J.R. died in 1924. His son was known as Ira and continued the business. Pictured at left, Ira was a member of the 313th Engineers of the 88th Division, serving in France during World War I. He served on the Plainfield School District 202 Board of Education from 1936 to 1972 and was president for his last 15 years. Richard Ira Jones Middle School in Plainfield is named for him.

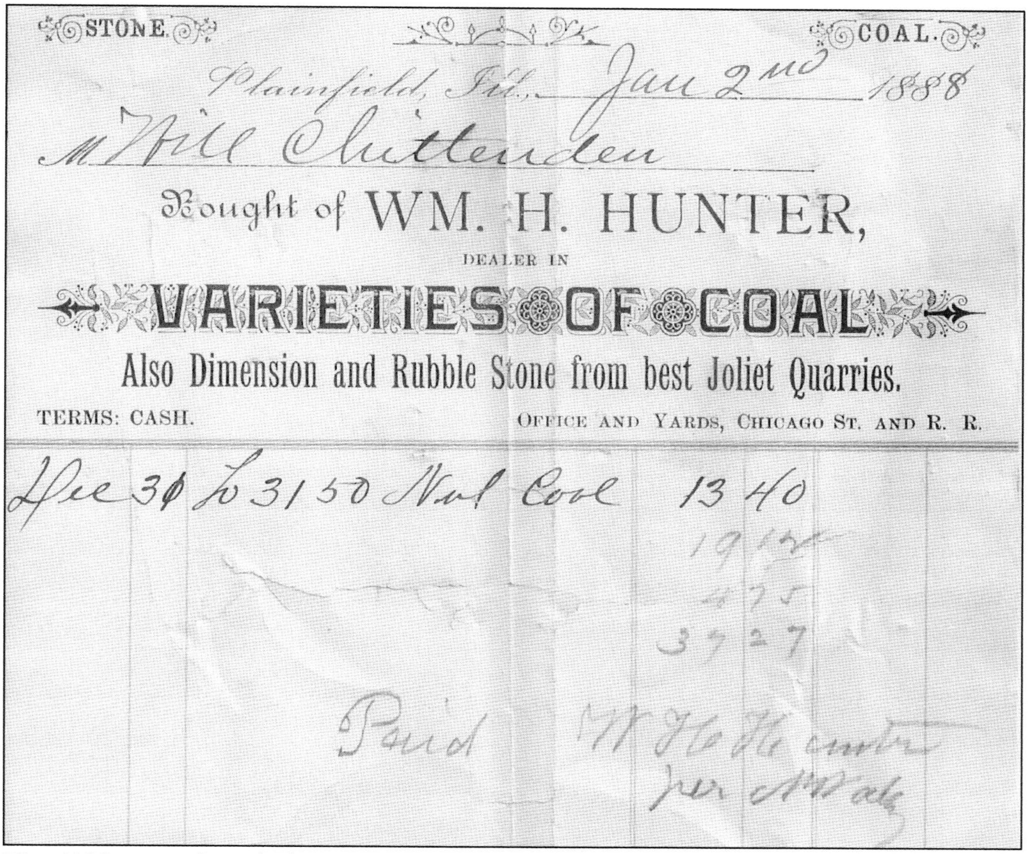

STONE. COAL.

Plainfield, Ill., Jan 2nd 1888

M Will Chittenden

Bought of WM. H. HUNTER,

DEALER IN

VARIETIES OF COAL

Also Dimension and Rubble Stone from best Joliet Quarries.

TERMS: CASH. Office and Yards, Chicago St. and R. R.

Dec 30 To 3150 Nut Coal 13 40

Paid

This 1888 receipt from dealer W.H. Hunter notes that he offers coal and stone at Chicago Street and the railroad. The business advertised stone from the Joliet quarries. The stone quarries of Plainfield were also of considerable size and furnished a fair amount of building stone for local use in barns and homes. The piece of 1889 letterhead below is from A.J. McCreery, dealer in coal. It appears that McCreery bought out Wm. Hunter. The letterhead is signed by A.J. McCreery. The office and yards were on Chicago Street at the railroad. In the 1895 *Will County Directory*, A.J. McCreery is listed as a grocer in Plainfield. His father, Joseph, came to Plainfield in 1846 and owned 250 acres in Plainfield Township. Joseph and his wife, Abigail, had 12 children.

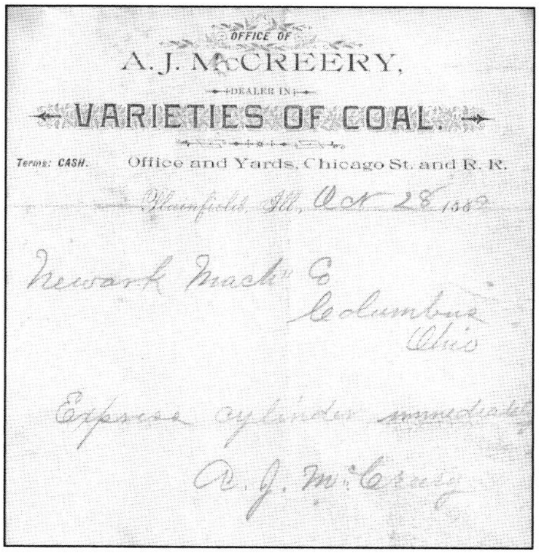

OFFICE OF

A.J. McCREERY,

DEALER IN

VARIETIES OF COAL.

Terms: CASH. Office and Yards, Chicago St. and R. R.

Plainfield, Ill., Oct 28 1889

Newark Mach Co
Columbus
Ohio

Express cylinder immediately

A. J. McCreery

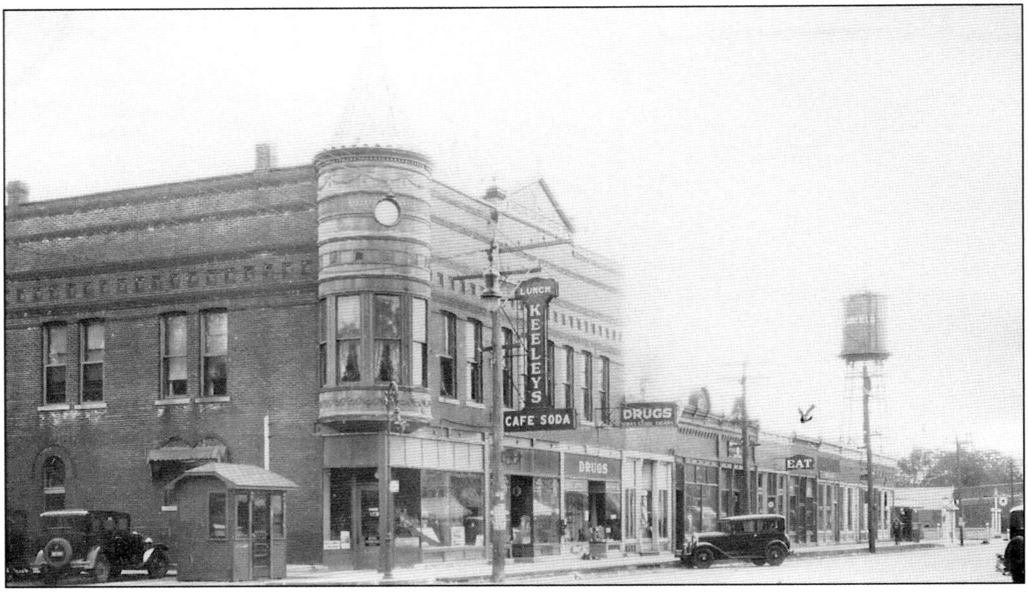

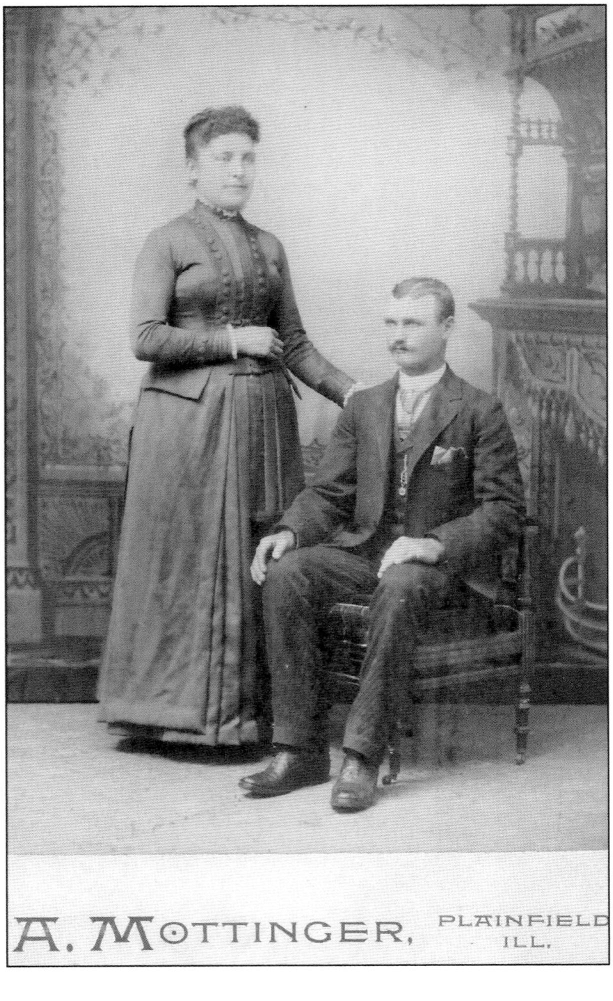

A.H. Mottinger was the photographer who occupied a portion of the opera house building during the 1890s fire. In addition to his plates and negatives that were lost in the fire, his insurance claim included three bicycles belonging to him and his two brothers. He stated they were stored in his gallery, awaiting the spring. The bank in the building had a fireproof vault. When the vault was opened after the fire, it was found that not even a paper was colored from the effects of the heat. All was safe—no pun intended. The bank and A.E. Mottinger's photography studio temporarily moved to H.H. Newton's Furniture Store. It was reported that I.E. Clippinger, owner of the opera house building, was willing and even anxious to rebuild, and if the tenants were to agree to return, construction would begin at once.

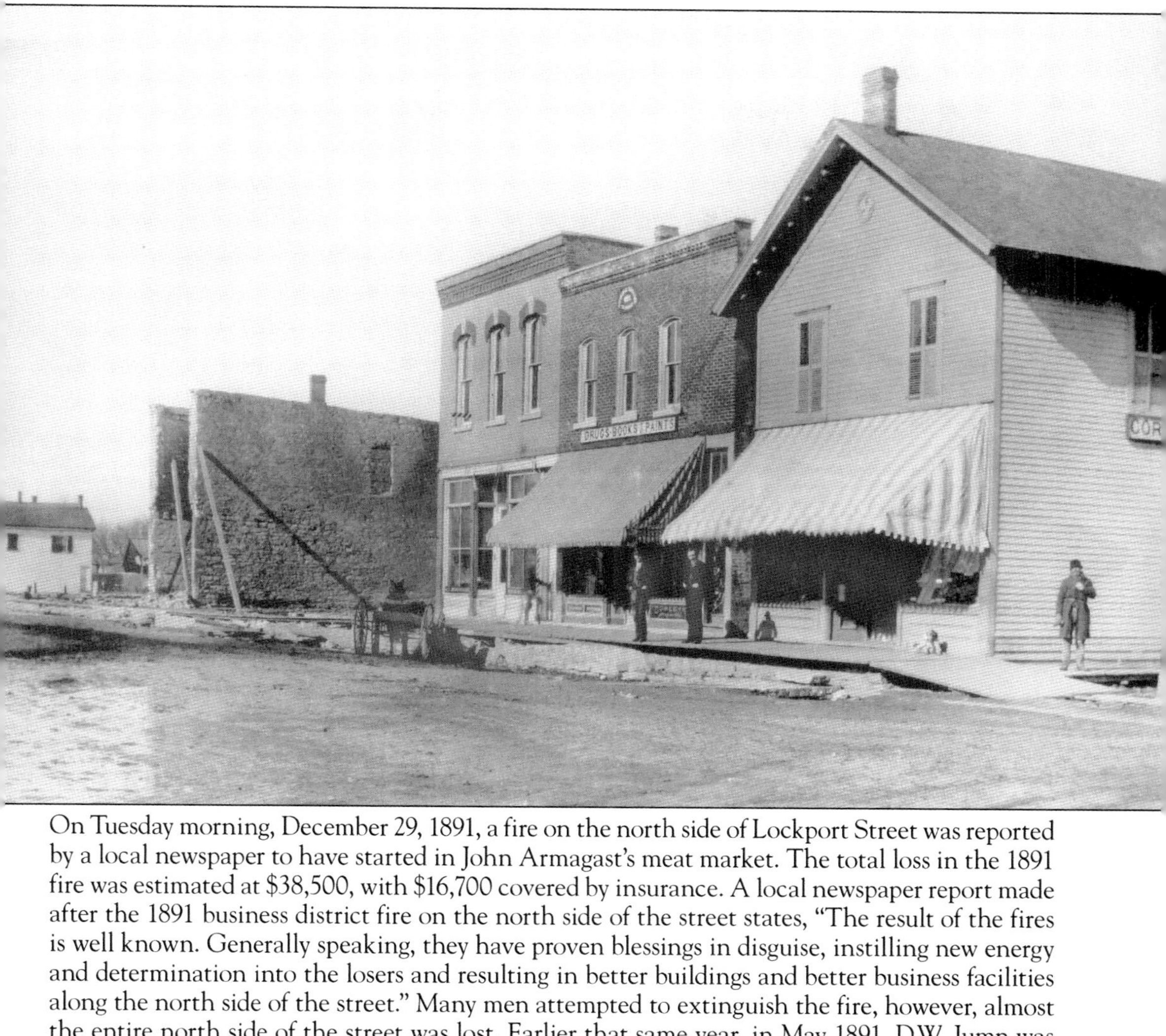

On Tuesday morning, December 29, 1891, a fire on the north side of Lockport Street was reported by a local newspaper to have started in John Armagast's meat market. The total loss in the 1891 fire was estimated at $38,500, with $16,700 covered by insurance. A local newspaper report made after the 1891 business district fire on the north side of the street states, "The result of the fires is well known. Generally speaking, they have proven blessings in disguise, instilling new energy and determination into the losers and resulting in better buildings and better business facilities along the north side of the street." Many men attempted to extinguish the fire, however, almost the entire north side of the street was lost. Earlier that same year, in May 1891, D.W. Jump was appointed a committee of one to look into fire dangers in the village.

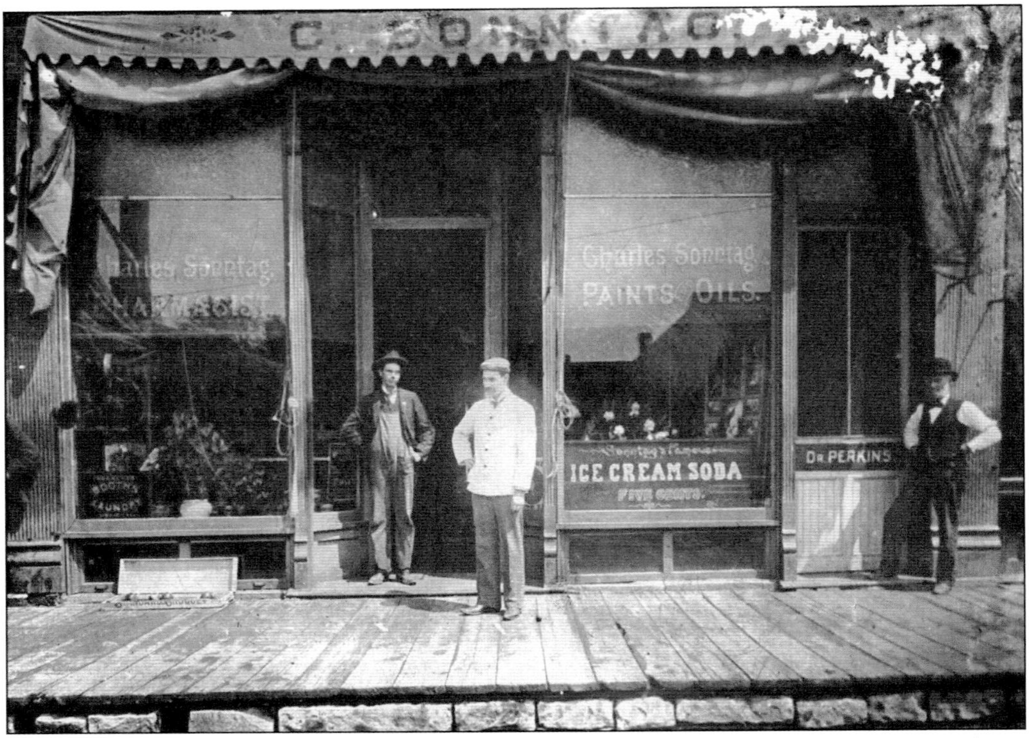

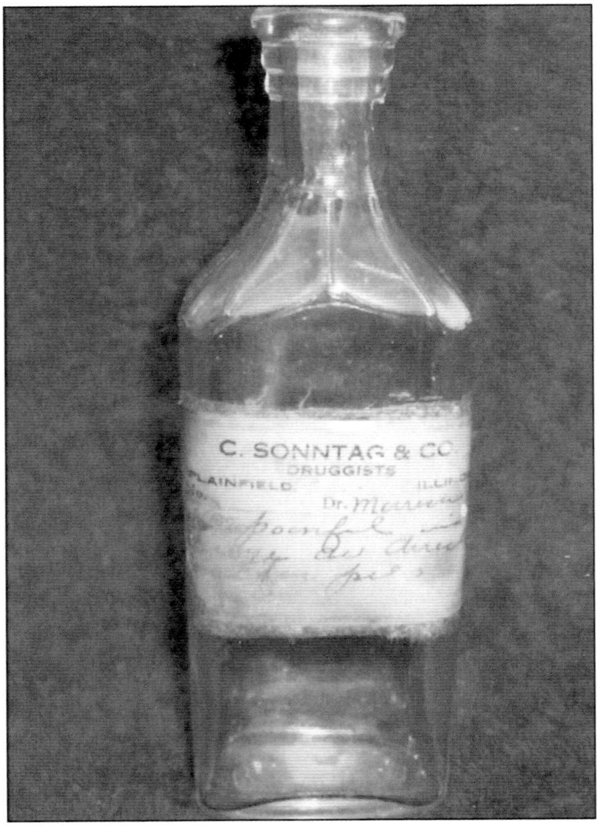

Plainfield is one of a few towns that claim to be the home of the original ice cream sundae. A local belief is that Plainfield druggist Charles Sonntag created an ice cream dish "after the urgings of patrons to serve something different." His syrup topping over a dish of ice cream was named the "Sonntag." Since *Sonntag* means "Sunday" in German, the name was translated to Sunday and later spelled *sundae*. The window in this photograph advertises that Sonntag is a pharmacist and sells paints and oils in addition to his famous ice cream soda. The paper label on this early pharmaceutical bottle reads, "C. Sonntag & Company, Plainfield, Illinois." These bottles were normally sealed with a cork, and a few have survived with the label intact.

A.J. Perkins, MD, began studying medicine at age 15. He came to Plainfield in 1865 after graduating from medical school at the Eclectic Medical Institute in Cincinnati, Ohio. He was a member of the Plainfield school board in addition to being president of the Plainfield town board for several years. In 1897, Dr. Perkins built a gas plant in town that furnished light to an entire town block.

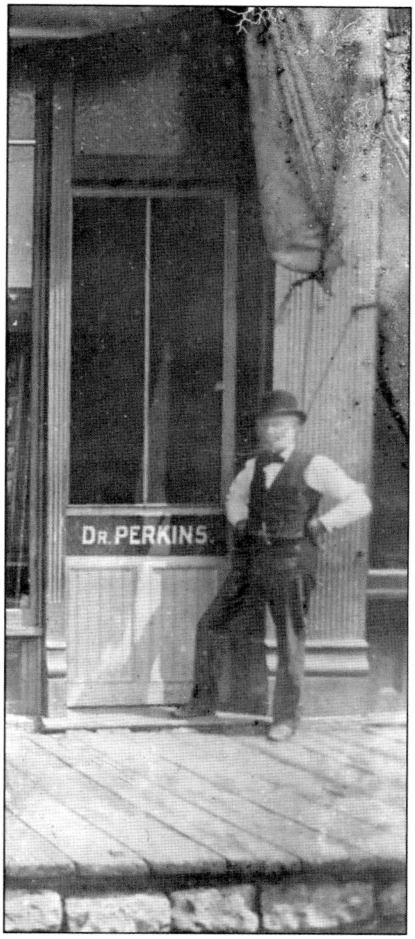

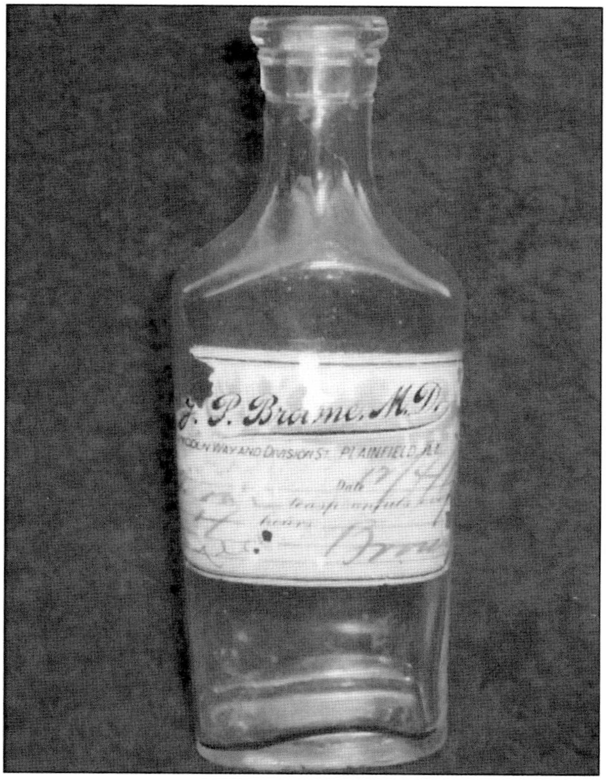

The paper label on this early Plainfield pharmaceutical bottle reads, "J.P. Browne, MD." He was located at Lincoln Way and Division Streets. This intersection is now known as Route 30 and Route 59. The bottle is dated December 4, 1911. Even though there may have been more at the time, the 1918 *Reliable Directory of Will County Farmers and Breeders Book* lists Dr. Browne as one of three physicians in the village of Plainfield. He was also the Plainfield school administrator from 1893 until 1901.

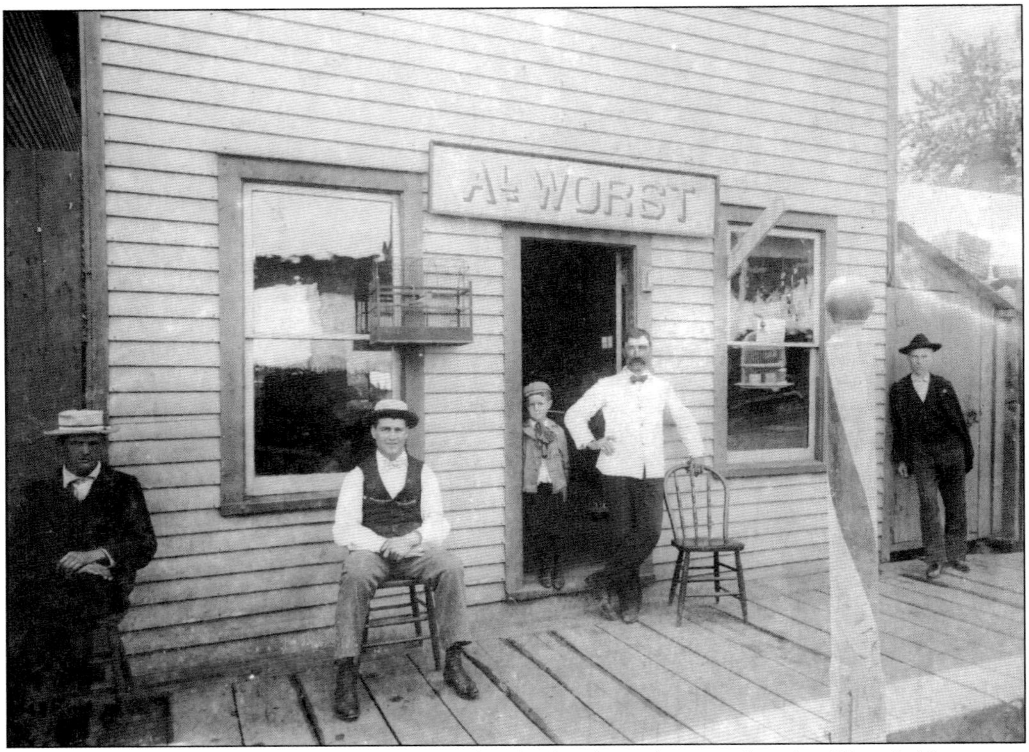

Albert Worst is pictured above in front of his barbershop along with a few Plainfield patrons and a unique wooden barber pole out front. He opened his shop in 1881. At the time, being the "Worst" barber shop in Plainfield did not mean a person got a bad haircut. To this day, the shop remains in the family. Worst was the great-grandfather of the current owner, Don Kinley. The shop is now named the Lincoln Way Barber Shop after the Lincoln Highway, which was the first transcontinental highway. Below, the photograph is labeled, "Lincoln Way, Plainfield, Ill." On the right is the Plainfield State Bank, with Allen's Texaco Garage just down the street. The Congregational Church is on the left, or on the north side, of the street in this photograph.

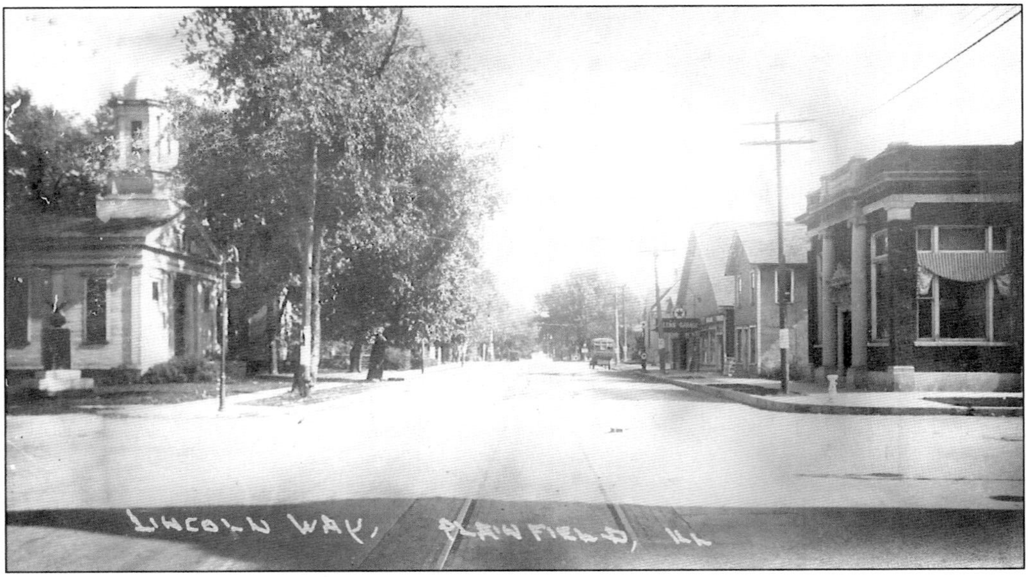

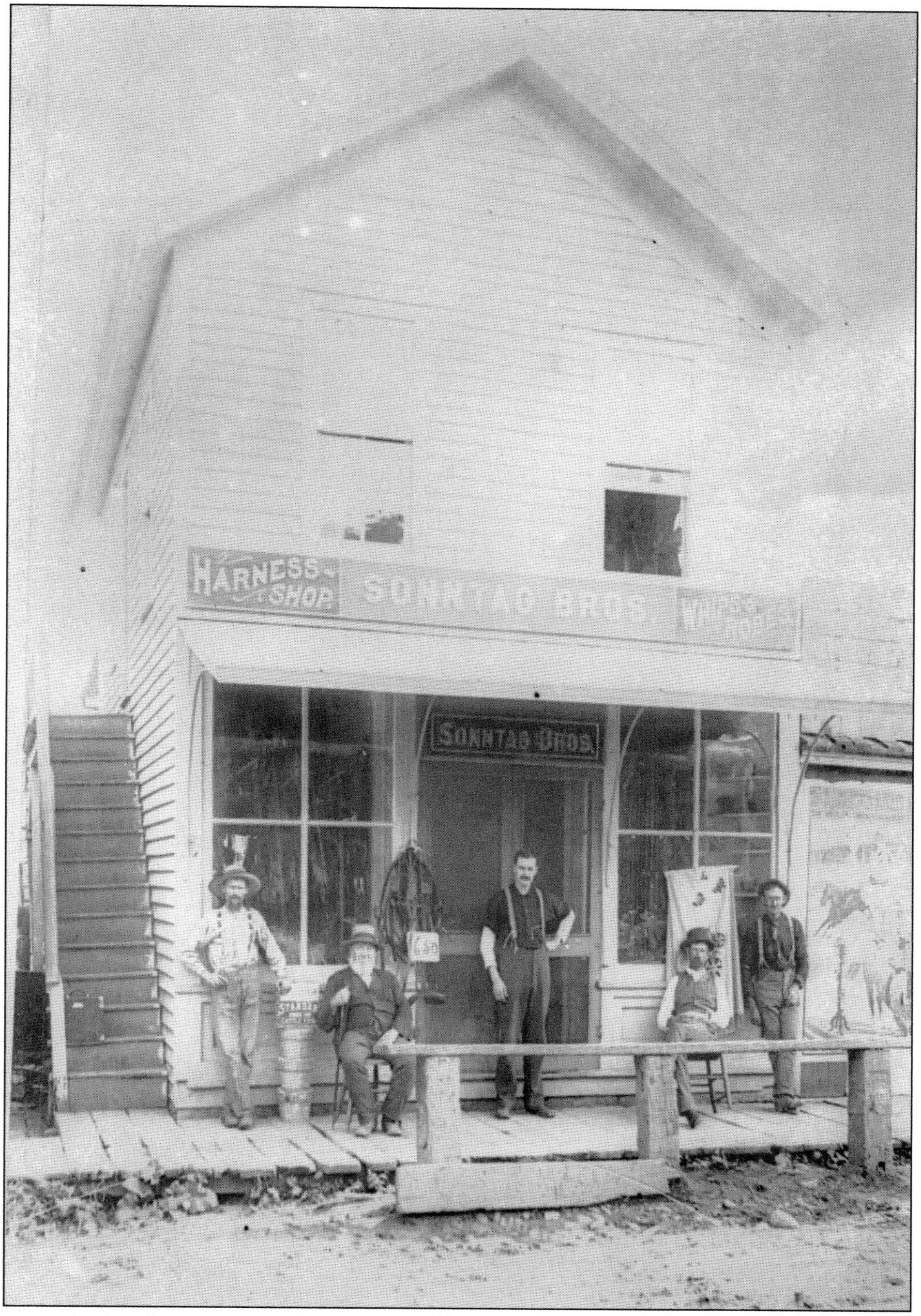

Albert and John Sonntag owned the Sonntag Brothers Harness Shop. The store was on Lincoln Way, also known as Lockport Street. John was born in 1853 and was four years older than Albert. Both brothers died in 1934 and are buried in the Plainfield Township Cemetery. Their last name is sometimes spelled Sontag on township records, even though the sign above the store clearly has "Sonntag" on it. The shop advertised saddle, collars, whips, robes, blankets, combs, and all other articles usually found in a first-class harness shop. It also sold Globe Oil Company's Celebrated Diamond Black Leather Oil.

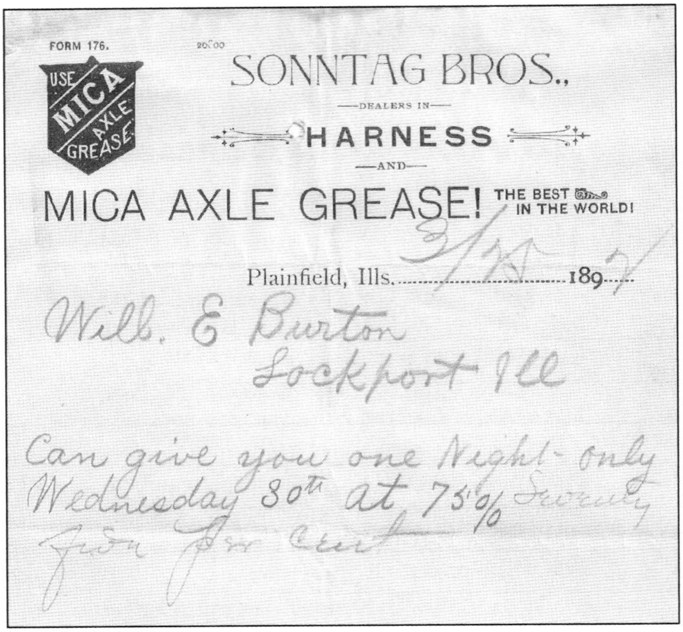

FORM 176.

USE MICA AXLE GREASE

SONNTAG BROS.,

DEALERS IN

HARNESS

AND

MICA AXLE GREASE! THE BEST IN THE WORLD!

Plainfield, Ills. 1897

Will. E Burton
Lockport Ill

Can give you one Night only
Wednesday 30th at 75% Seventy
five per cent

This 1892 letterhead is from Sonntag Brothers Harness Shop, which also carried Mica axle grease. This grease was used for the horse carriage wheels and axles. Albert and John Sonntag are listed in the 1895 *Will County Directory* as owners of the harness shop. In the 1927–1928 city directory, they are still registered as harness makers. Albert is listed as living on Chicago Street in Plainfield. John and his wife, Mary, were living on Lincoln Way, which is also known as Lockport Street. Their harness shop was located on Lincoln Way.

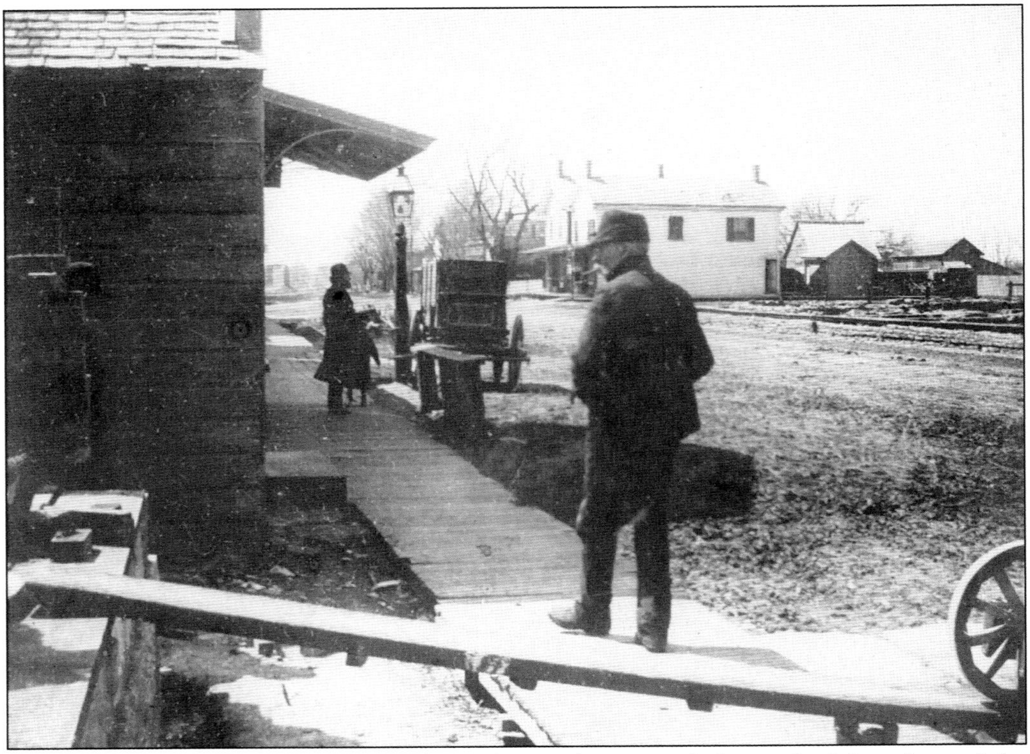

This photograph, looking west on Lockport Street, shows a gaslight on the left in front of the building. The board appears to be a ramp, possibly for something being built. The timber from Plainfield's woods was often sawed into boards, hauled to Chicago, and used to construct frame houses. The first bridge in the township was built across the DuPage River and was made of wood. The timber came from early settler Lorin Burdick. In the 1870 census, Plainfield Township had about 800 inhabitants.

Benjamin P. Whitson and his wife, Mary Emma, operated a meat market in Plainfield in the early 1900s. The caption under the print on this calendar reads, "Now, wouldn't you be the Iceman?" Benjamin was born in 1858 and died in 1932. Mary Emma was born in 1859 and passed away in 1915. Both are buried in the Plainfield Township Cemetery.

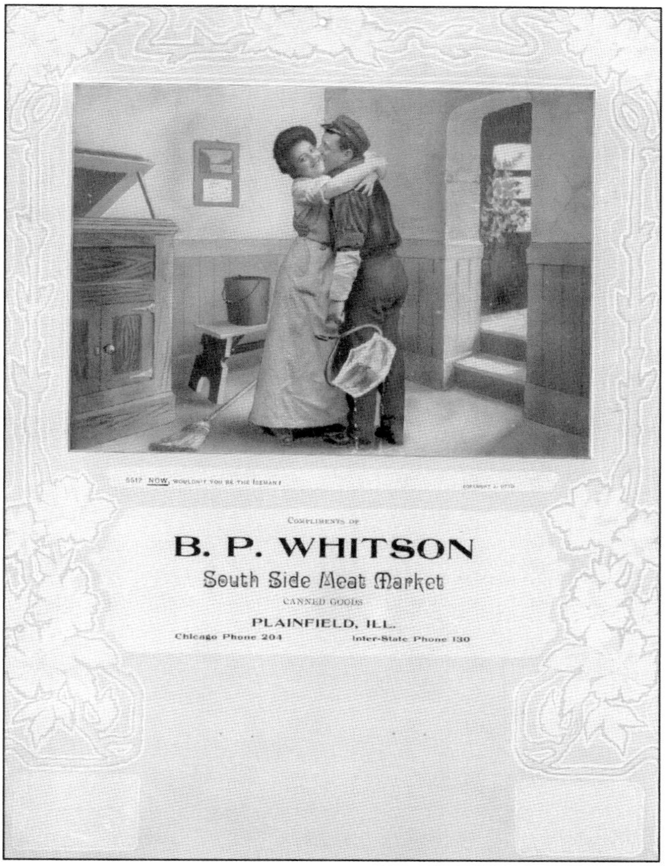

The Meyer Bakery and Whitson Meat Market are pictured on the south side of Lockport Street in this winter 1908 photograph. It is difficult to see the women standing inside the business looking outside, as the men pose for this photograph. Neither business is listed four years later in the 1912 *Plainfield Business Directory.*

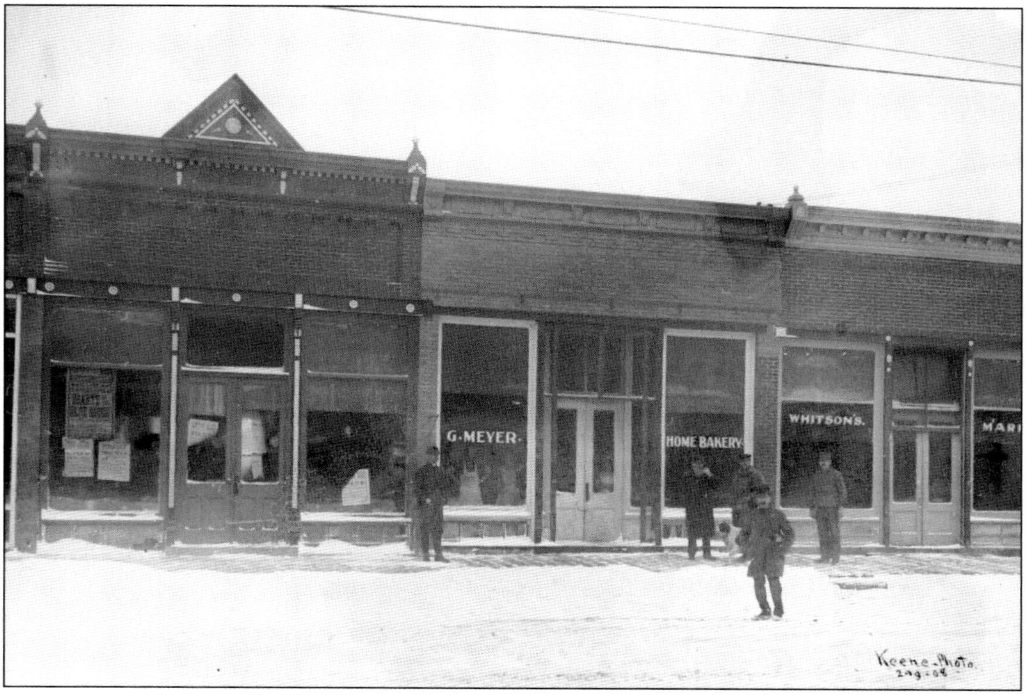

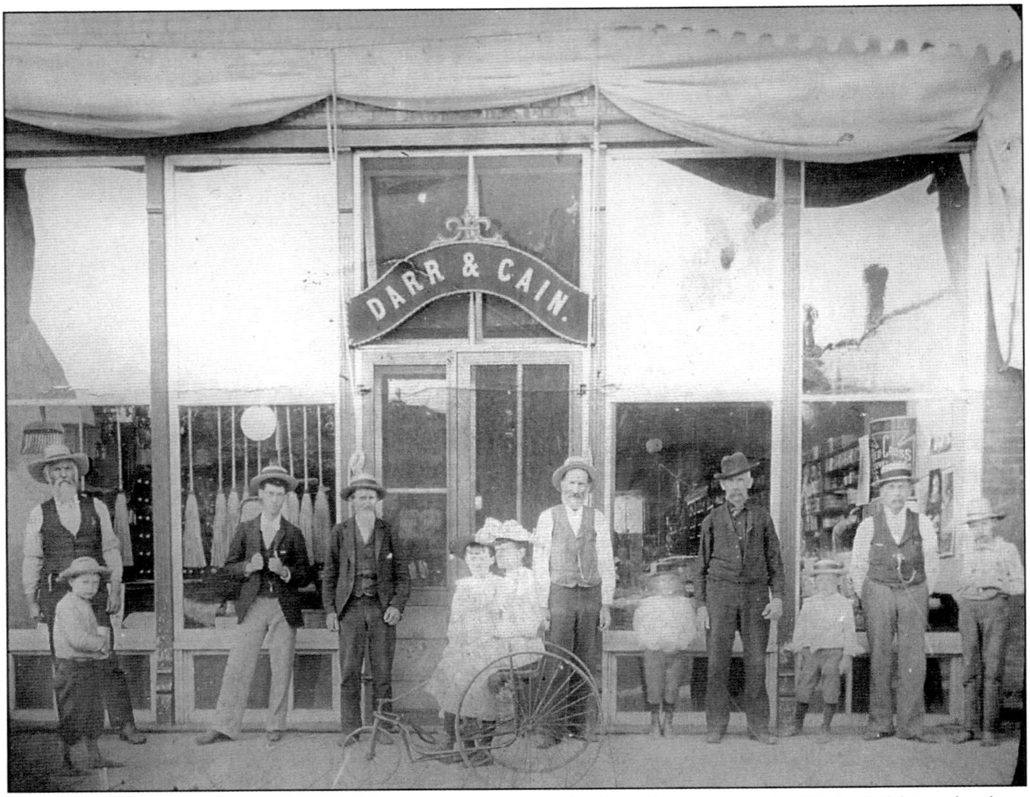

David Darr and his partner, William Cain, operated a hardware store in Plainfield in the late 1800s. After losing the store in the 1891 fire on the north side of Lockport Street, they moved across the street and reopened. Darr and Cain were Union soldiers and mustered into the 100th Illinois Infantry on August 1, 1862. Adults pictured are, from left to right, Charles Geist, John Overman, James Smiley, Cain, Ben Whitley, and Darr. Margaret Erwin is on the tricycle, and the other children are unknown.

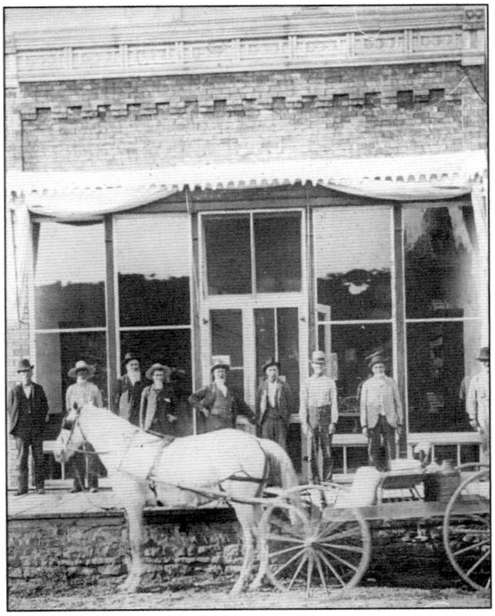

This is the same Plainfield storefront shown above. At the time of this photograph, the owners were David Darr and Adam Spangler. Capt. Ed McAllister mustered Plainfield resident Spangler into the 10th Illinois Infantry in 1861. Pictured from left to right are unidentified, unidentified, John Van Horne, James Smiley, Spangler, Darr, Jonas Bronk, Nate Waltz, and Fred Burgstahler.

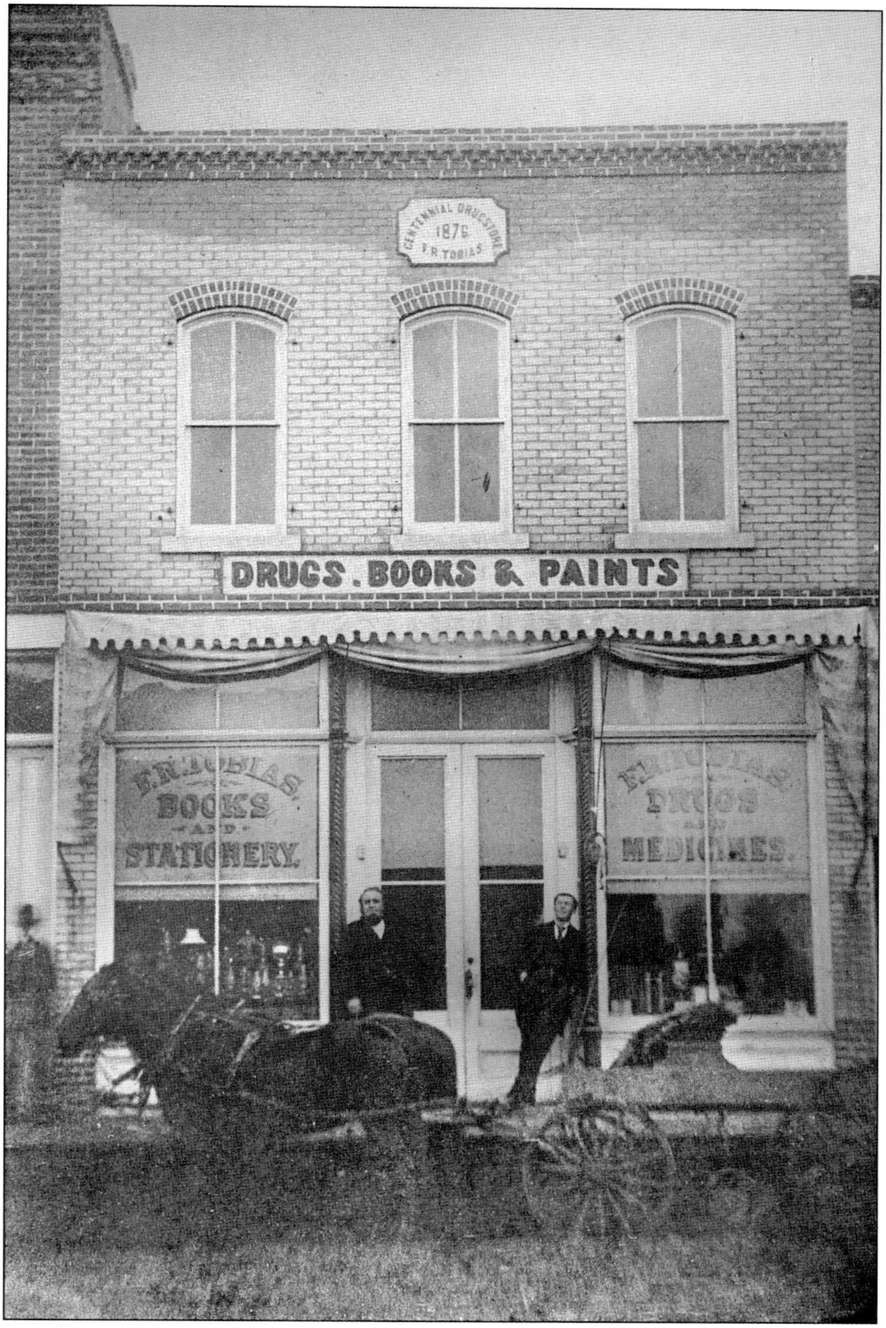

The F.R. Tobias Centennial Drugstore was built in 1876. The store sold medicines, drugs, books, stationery, and paints. The building survived the fire of 1891 that destroyed much of the north side of Lockport Street in Plainfield. Franklin R. Tobias was born in Pennsylvania on June 16, 1823. He was married to Caroline Steele from Chillicothe, Ohio, and had four children. Their daughter Elizabeth married Alfred Hartong. An 1873–1876 *Plainfield Business Directory* lists both the Tobias Drugstore and the Clippenger and Mills Drugstore in Plainfield. The F.R. Tobias building remains standing today on Lockport Street. There is a Franklin "B." Tobias listed on the Civil War Muster Rolls from Plainfield who joined the 132nd Illinois infantry at the age of 20.

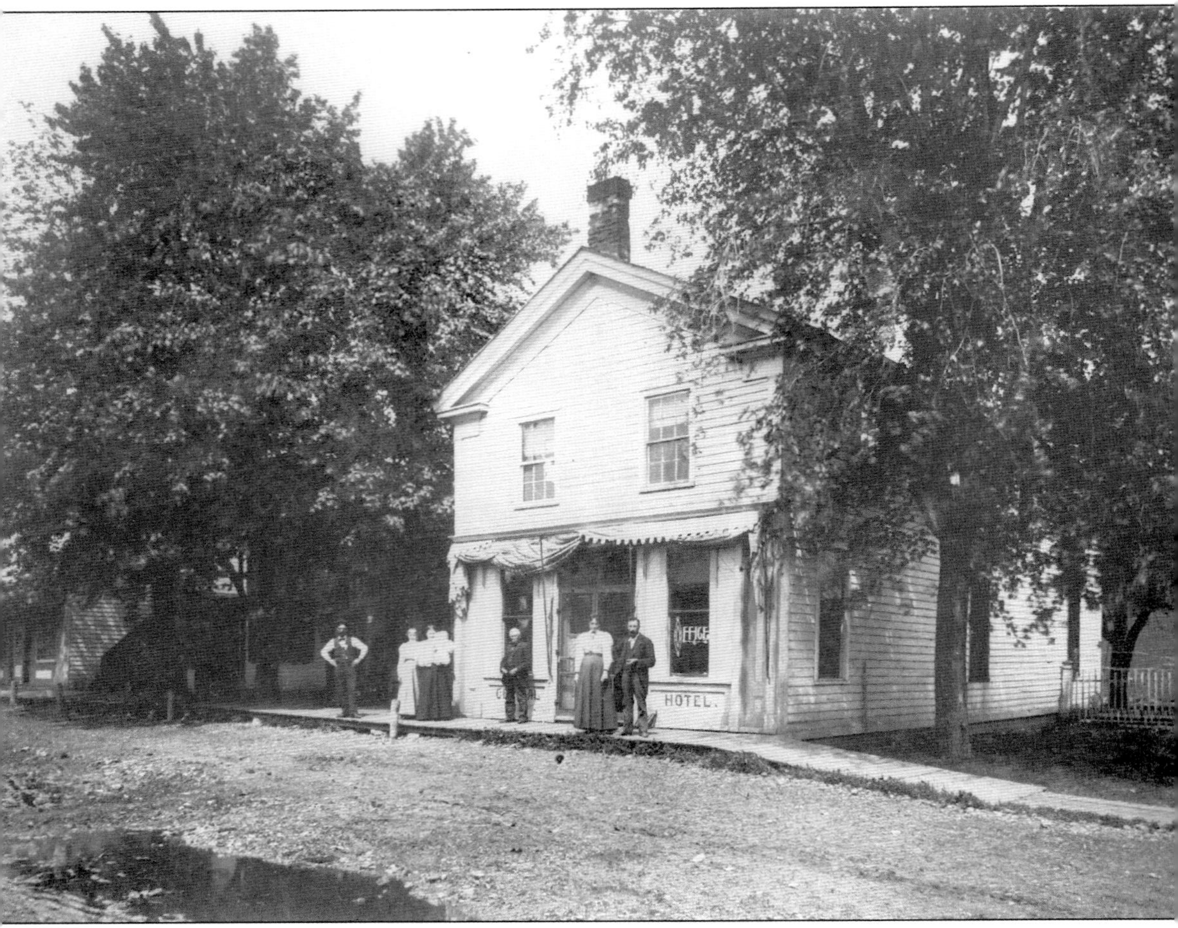

In this photograph of the Central Hotel, a man and some women are standing near the front door with other residents to the left. James W. Beggs ran a hotel in Naperville for seven years before purchasing the Central Hotel in Plainfield. It was said that Beggs was "a man of genial and accommodating disposition, as a landlord, he was very popular, and the traveling public made his place their headquarters." He also ran a stagecoach line to Joliet. Beggs was elected mayor of Plainfield in 1899 and was the Plainfield postmaster for two terms. The hotel was later owned by a host of other people, including a Mr. Hentz, "Humpy" Flagg, Archie McLaughlin, Joe Pollard, George Tuttle, Will Lund, and John Lynch.

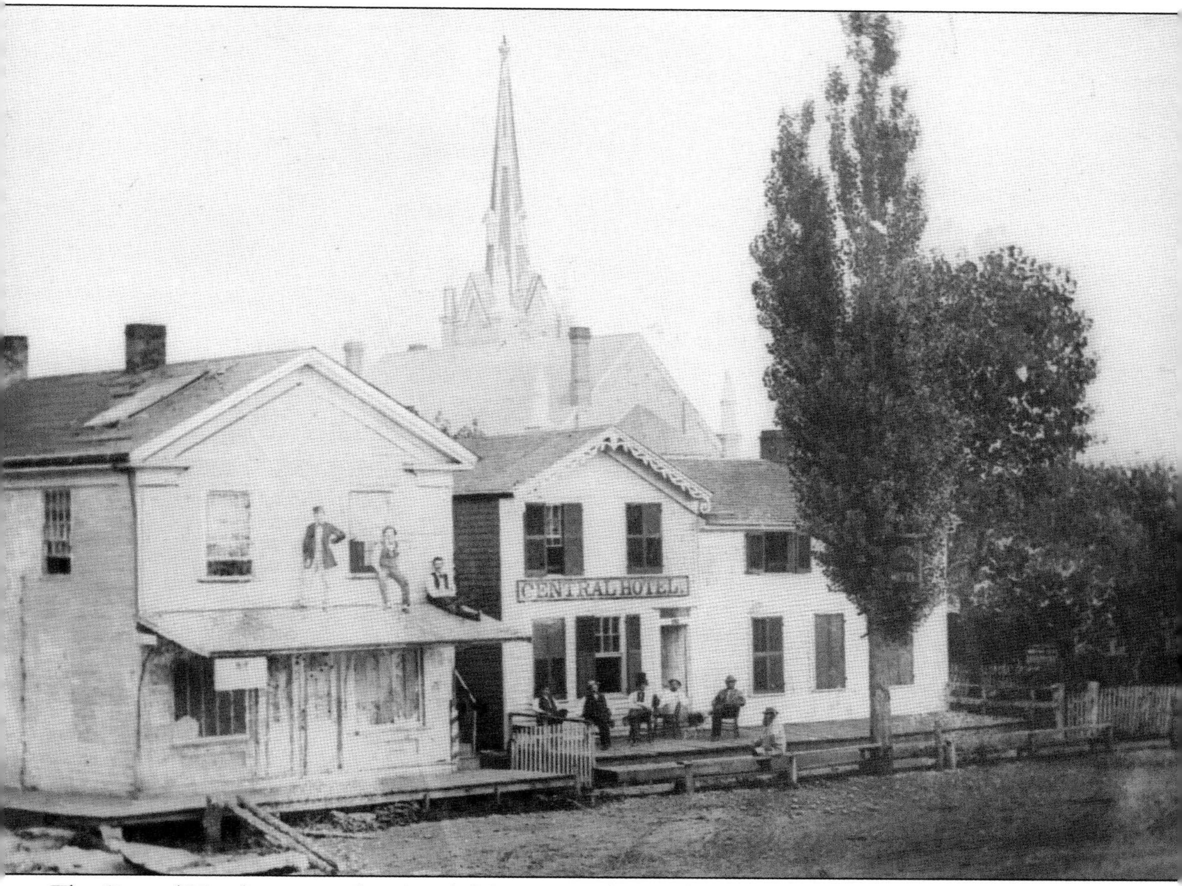

The Central Hotel is pictured in this A. Mottinger cabinet photograph. Several people are shown posing, including the men on the awning of the building to the left. Built in 1845 as a home on Des Plaines Street and owned by Root Kent, the house was purchased by James W. Beggs in 1865 and turned into the Central Hotel. Around 1870, the Chittenden Store building at Division and Commercial Streets was physically moved and added on to the Central Hotel. Beggs operated the hotel for 25 years. He was born in March 5, 1835, and died on February 28, 1906. Beggs was married to Emerette Clary from Palmyra, New York, who died in 1900 at the age of 58.

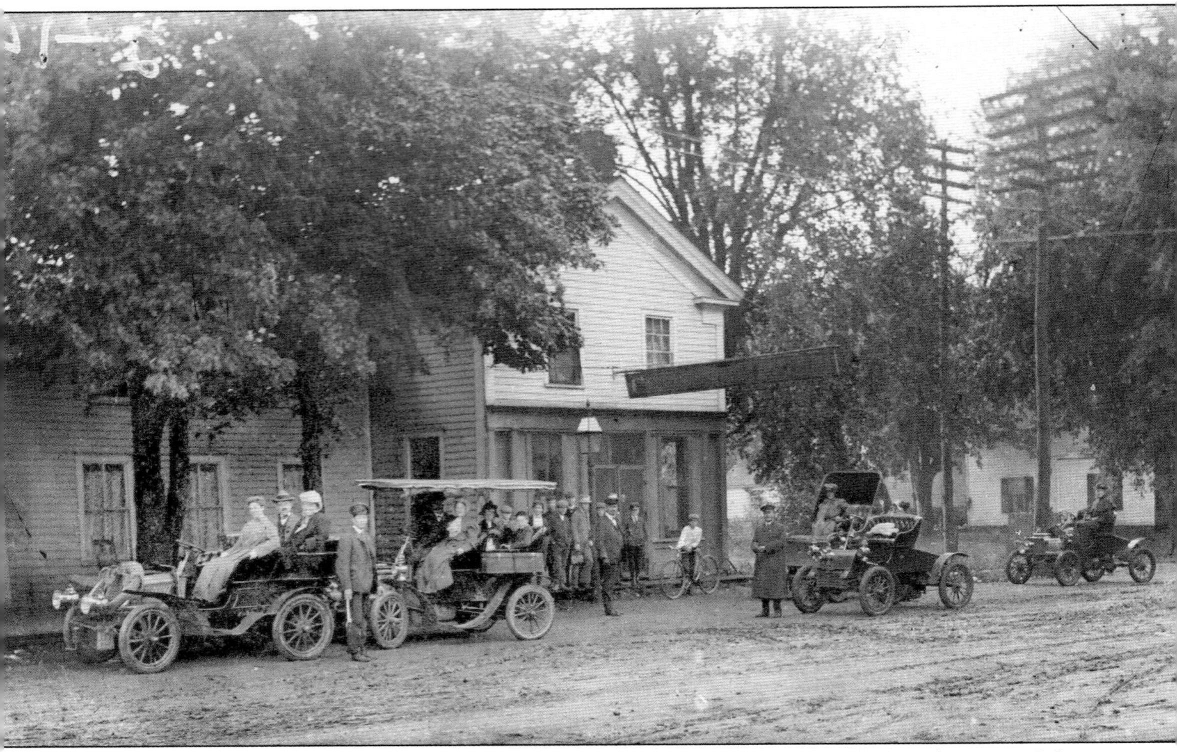

The Central Hotel in Plainfield has a host of early vehicles parked in front. The cars of this era were crank-start, as is evident with the car on the left. The hotel had numerous owners between 1890 and 1920. In the 1890s, Illinois congressman Joe Cannon and Sen. Billy Mason stayed at the hotel when in town. The hotel closed around 1920, and the south end of the building was used as a hatchery for about six years. The McArthur Hatchery was moved to the McArthur Farm northeast of Plainfield, and the hotel property was sold to Paul Birthisel of Park Ridge, Illinois. The Central Hotel was torn down in 1945.

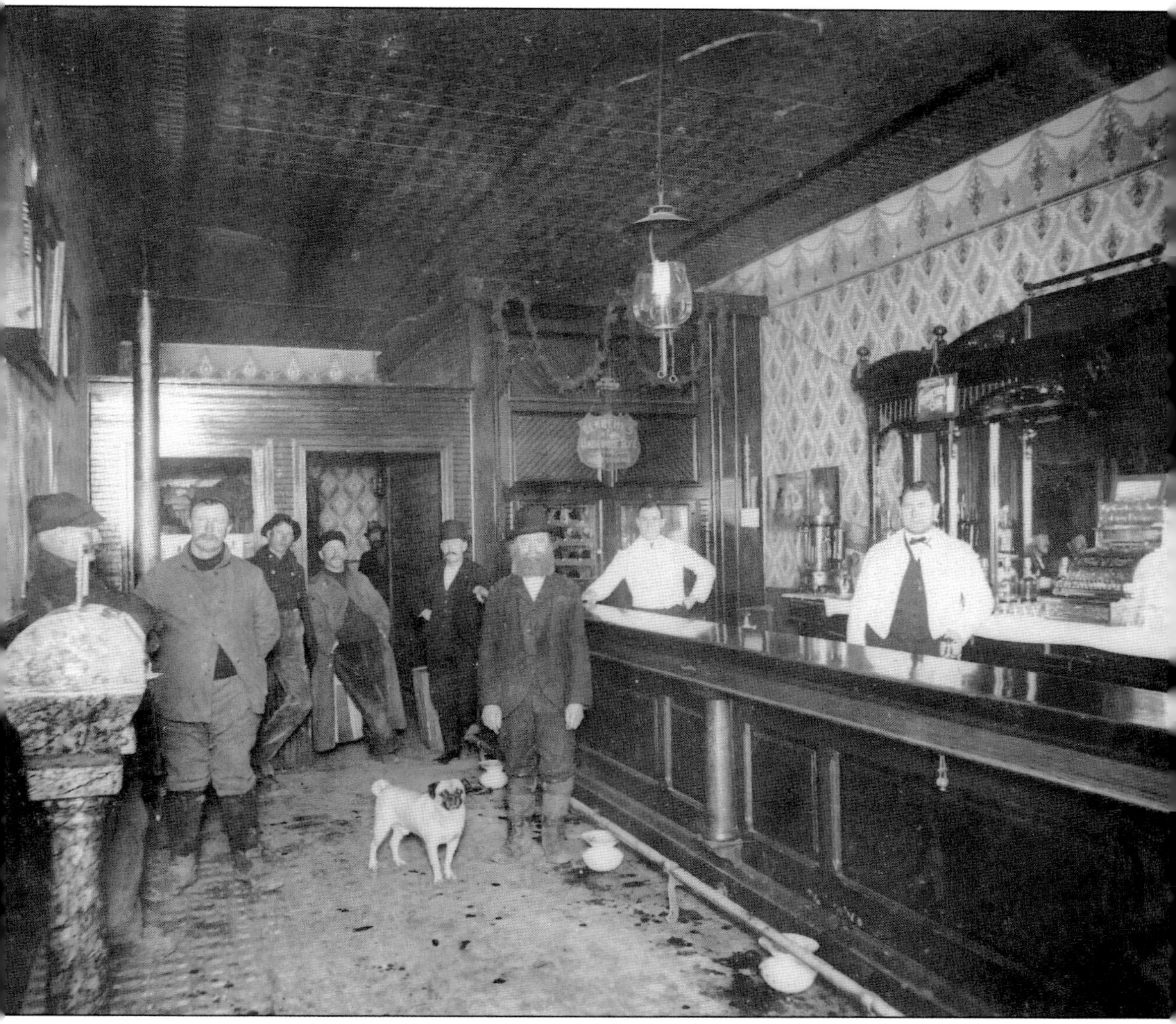

This photograph shows the interior of the John Powell Saloon in Plainfield. Note the spittoons on the floor, where all of the chewing tobacco that missed its target has landed. Pictured behind the bar are John Powell and William Metzger. Standing, from left to right, are Dan King, Frank Day, Bart Stopp, Barney Wright, John Needham, and Christ Shaffer. The dog is Peggie the pug. It was said that a few churchmen were in the saloon at the time of the photograph, but they had ducked into the back room. In this case, the saloon does not have tables and stools, so everyone is standing. During this time period, men often drank straight rye or bourbon. There were often no fancy cocktails or drinks served at the saloons. Many saloons were dance hall saloons or billiards or gambling saloons. In this case, the John Powell Saloon is just a plain drinking saloon. Outside, there were wooden sidewalks, hitching posts, and a dusty street in front of the building.

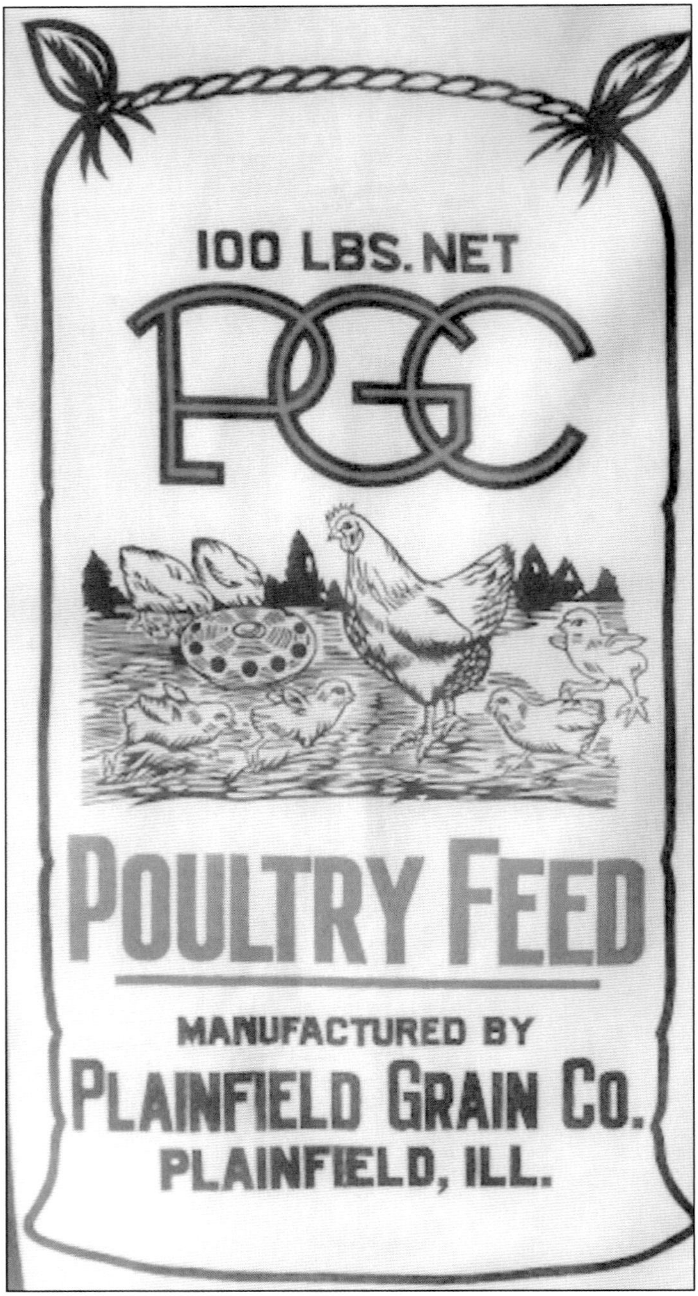

The early Plainfield Grain Company also sold poultry feed, as advertised on this 100-pound feedbag. The 1911 Plainfield Grain Company Bylaws (revised in 1915) state under section one that "the company exists for the purpose of buying and selling farm grains, seeds, lumber and coal with the principal office located at Plainfield, Illinois." Section two of the bylaws states that the company would have 1,500 shares of stock at $50 each, or $75,000 total. It also states that no one could own more than 10 shares. Each director would be allowed $2 compensation for each meeting he attended or for each day necessarily employed in service for the grain company. When reviewing the annual books, the director's compensation would be increased to $3 per day.

This beautiful 1905 tin advertisement is from of Kersten and Smiley. The advertising image is titled "Carnation Girl." Kersten and Smiley owned some of the grain elevators in the area including one on the south side of Main Street (Route 126), just east of the railroad tracks. James Smiley passed away sometime between 1904 and 1911. The elevator then became part of the Plainfield Grain Company. Some information also documents the name with a spelling of *Kirsten*.

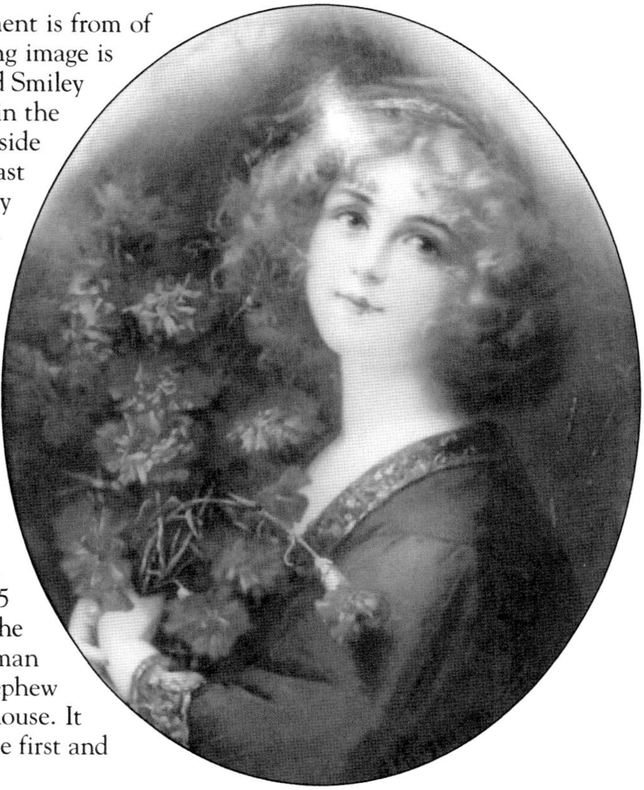

Dr. E.C. Hoffman and his wife are pictured in their very early, chain-driven car. Doctor Hoffman is listed as a dentist in Plainfield in the 1895 *Will County Directory*. According to the Miles Hartong research files, Hoffman built this car with the help of his nephew in a structure south of the opera house. It is noted in his files that this was the first and only car ever built in Plainfield.

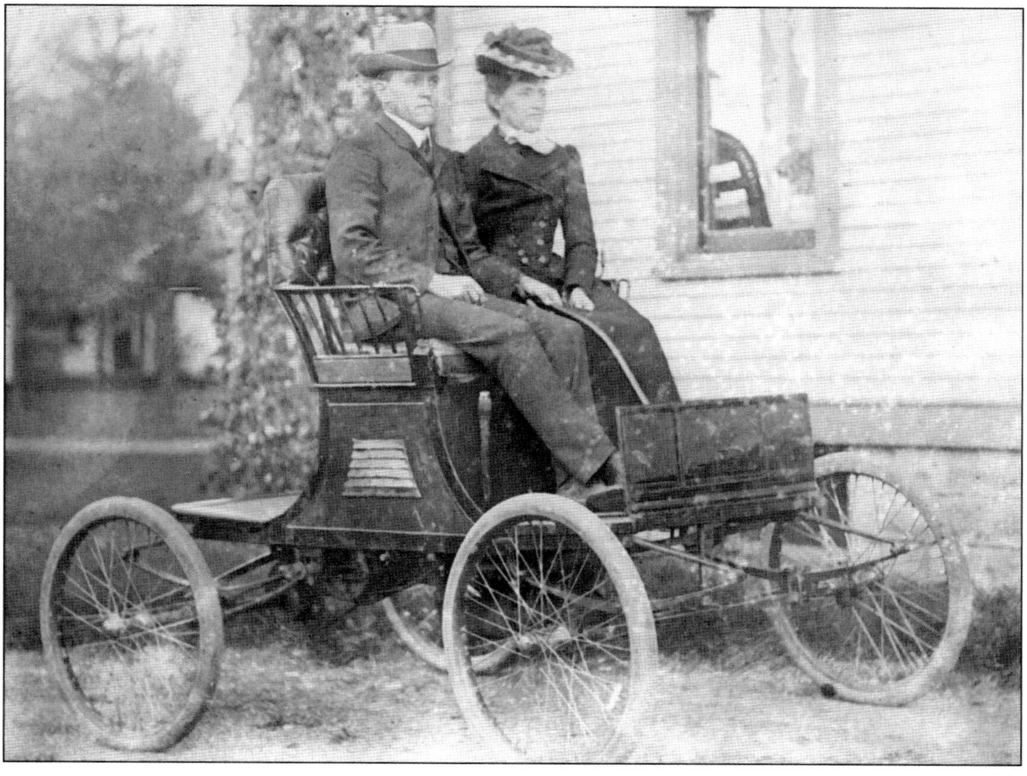

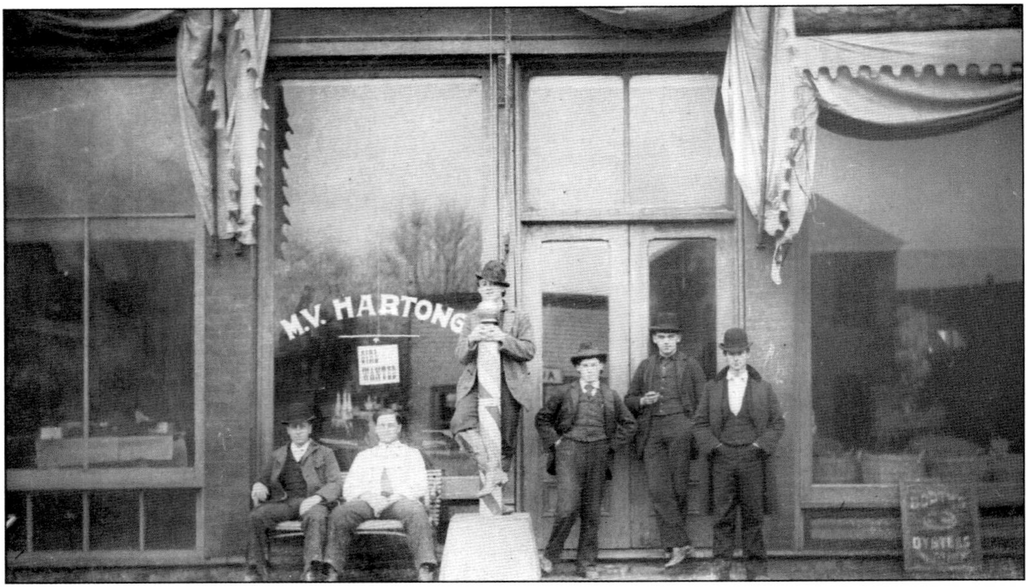

The M.V. Hartong Barbershop has a sign—"Girl Wanted"—hanging in the front window. One young fellow has climbed up on the unusual wooden barber's pole outside of the barbershop. Miles V. Hartong was born in 1870 and passed away in 1950. He is listed in various city directories as a barber (1895), plumber (1912), and garage owner (1927). Hartong even operated a restaurant at Electric Park and was also a local historian. He took photographs and notes of his findings, later using them in historical lectures that he presented over the years. He was known for his handmade bows, arrows, and knives. Below is an 1888 advertising receipt to Marvin and Blakely for $3. It is signed Corbin and Chittenden, who owned a store in town. Ulysses Blakely owned the *Enterprise* newspaper for 47 years.

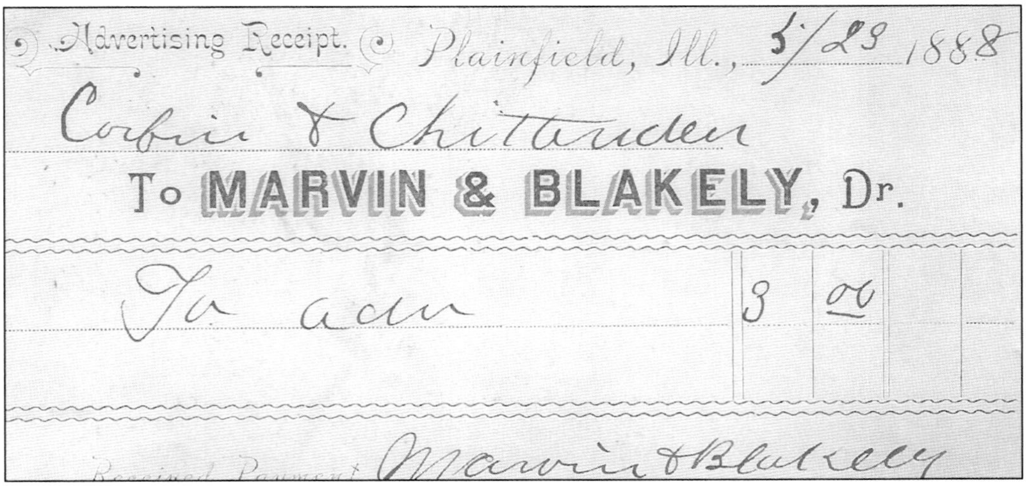
Advertising Receipt. Plainfield, Ill., 5/29 1888

Corbin & Chittenden

To MARVIN & BLAKELY, Dr.

To adv 3 00

Received Payment Marvin & Blakely

Dr. John C. Owens was born on January 3, 1857, in Western Township of Oneida County, New York. After receiving his medical degree from Syracuse University College of Medicine in 1882, he moved to Joliet, Illinois. He had specialized in diseases of the eye. A year later, he moved to Plainfield. In 1888, Dr. Owens opened a drugstore to complement his already established medical office. At one point, he also opened a jewelry store. Owens was a member of the Modern Woodsmen of America. He married his wife, Mary (below) in 1883. Mary's parents, Hiram and Mary Jane Hitchcock, were early settlers of Grundy County. The Owenses owned a 200-acre farm in Na-au-Say Township in Kendall County, Illinois. Mary passed away in 1928.

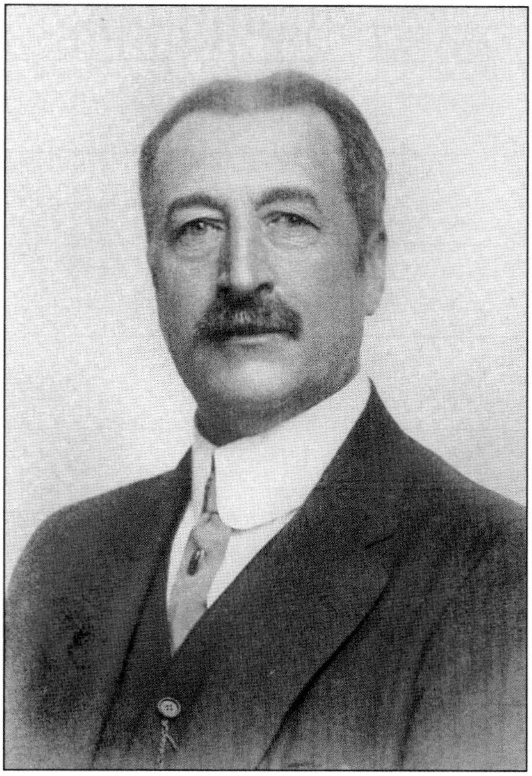

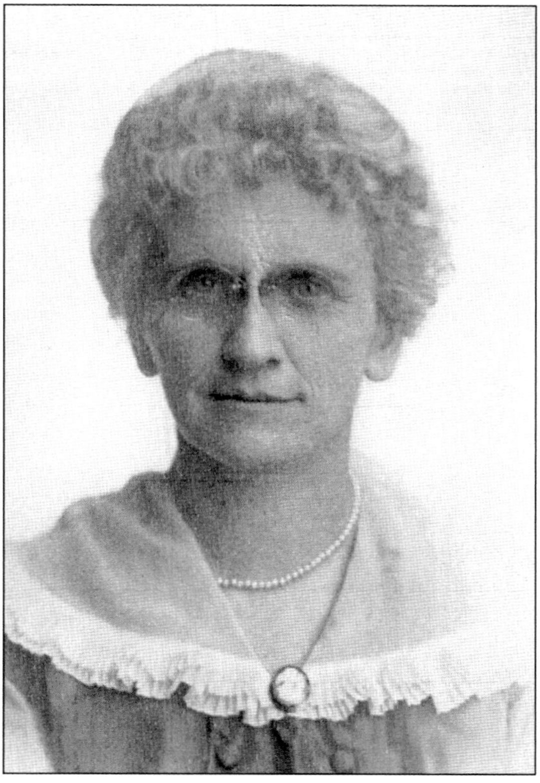

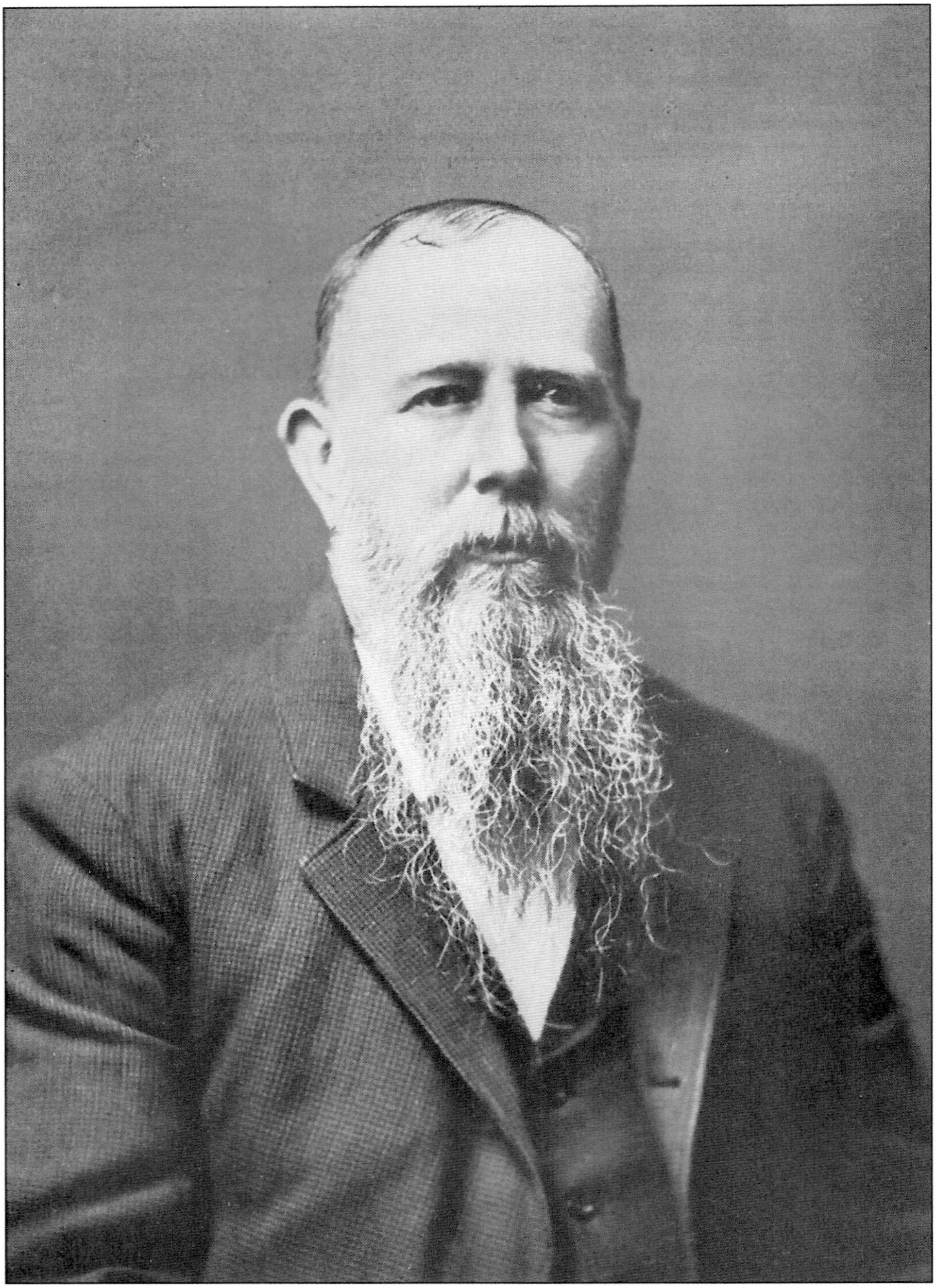

David W. Jump, MD, was engaged in practice in Plainfield directly after graduating from the University of Michigan in March 1872. He was both a physician and a surgeon. Dr. Jump was born on August 24, 1847, in Ohio. He was married to Alice Watkins on November 13, 1873. Alice was born in Plainfield, where her father was a pioneer farmer. In addition to his medical practice, Dr. Jump owned a drugstore in town for many years, where the younger of his two sons worked as a clerk. Dr. Jump was a member of the Ancient Free and Accepted Masons Lodge No. 536 of Plainfield. He was also a Plainfield school director for many years.

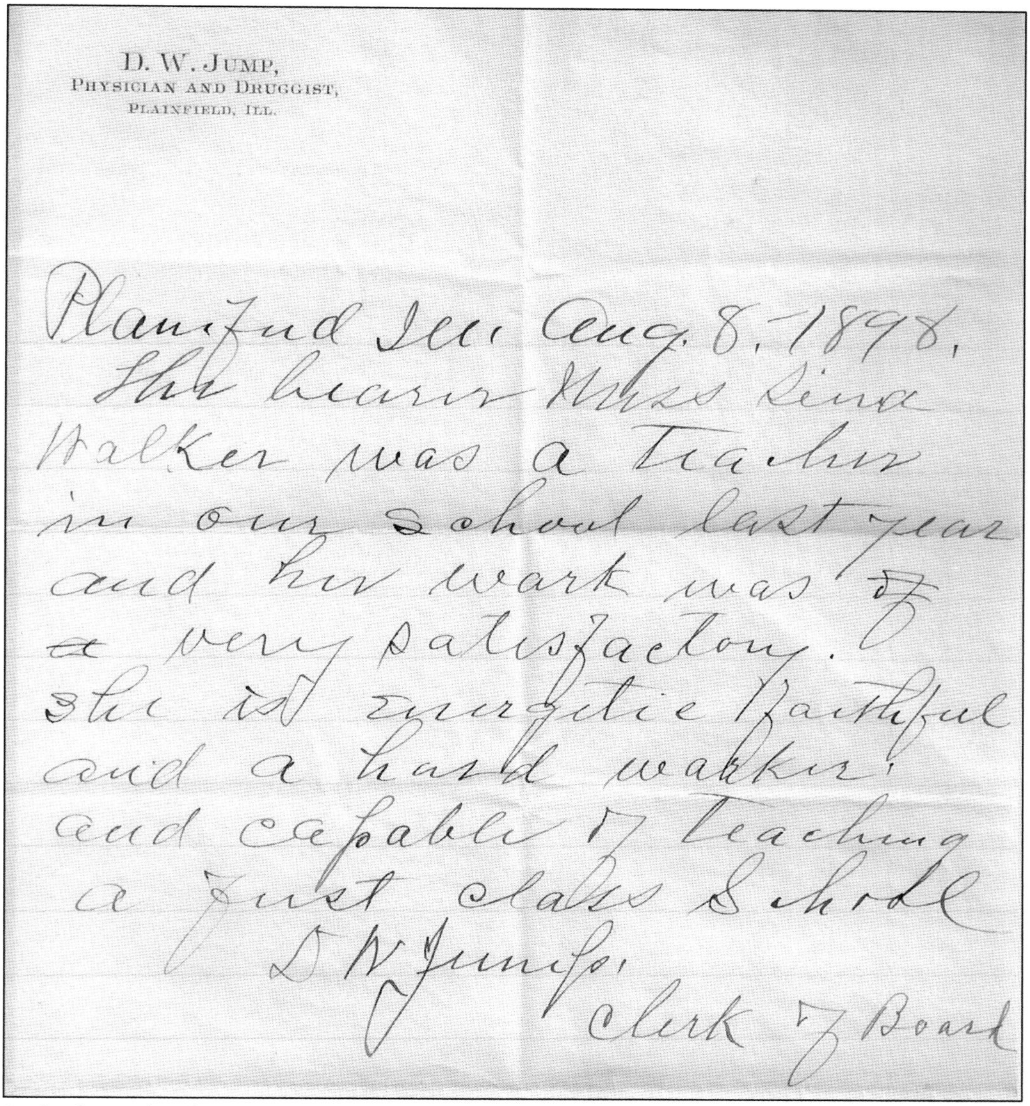

D. W. JUMP,
PHYSICIAN AND DRUGGIST,
PLAINFIELD, ILL.

Plainfield Ill Aug. 8. 1898.
The bearer Miss Lina Walker was a teacher in our school last year and her work was of very satisfactory. She is energetic faithful and a hard worker and capable of teaching a first class School
D W Jump.
Clerk of Board

In this letter dated August 8, 1898, Dr. D.W. Jump writes that the previous year, Lina Walker was a teacher in the Plainfield schools. He tells that her work was satisfactory and that she is energetic, faithful, and a hard worker. She is capable of teaching at a first-class school, according to Jump. It is signed by D.W. Jump, Clerk of Board. Walker is listed as one of the four graduates of the first class of the three-year high school in Plainfield in 1891. In the 1891 graduation program, Walker is listed as speaking on the "Essay and Valedictory on the Character of the Puritans." Jump's son, Clyde, of the class of 1893, also is listed in the program as presenting the "Declamation on Tyranny of Labor." Walker would later become Mrs. Harry Pike of Plainfield.

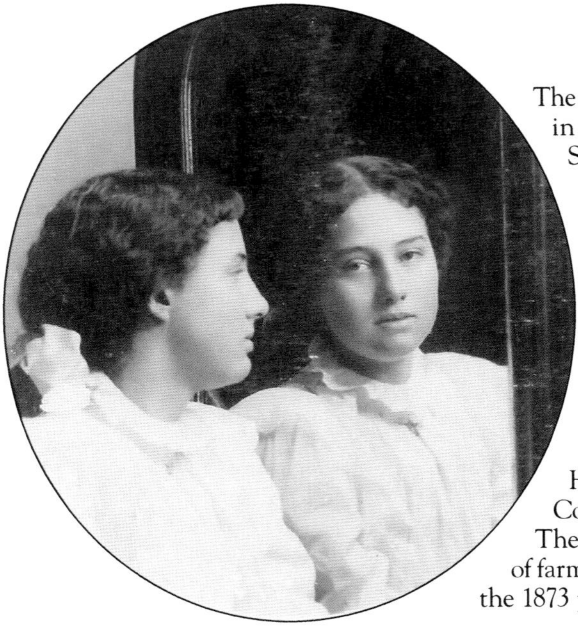

The Mottinger Photography Studio was located in the opera house building on Lockport Street. It was owned and operated by Almon H. Mottinger. A.H. Mottinger Photography Studio took a majority of the early Plainfield cabinet photographs. The left photograph is an example of early trick photography, by collecting the photograph while the young girl is looking in the mirror. George and Caroline Mottinger came to Will County in 1845, purchasing land in Plainfield Township. L.H. Mottinger was, at one time, the Will County sheriff. His brother A.E. Mottinger served as Will County chief deputy sheriff under his brother. The Mottinger families owned several pieces of farmland northeast and east of the village, per the 1873 plat map of Will County.

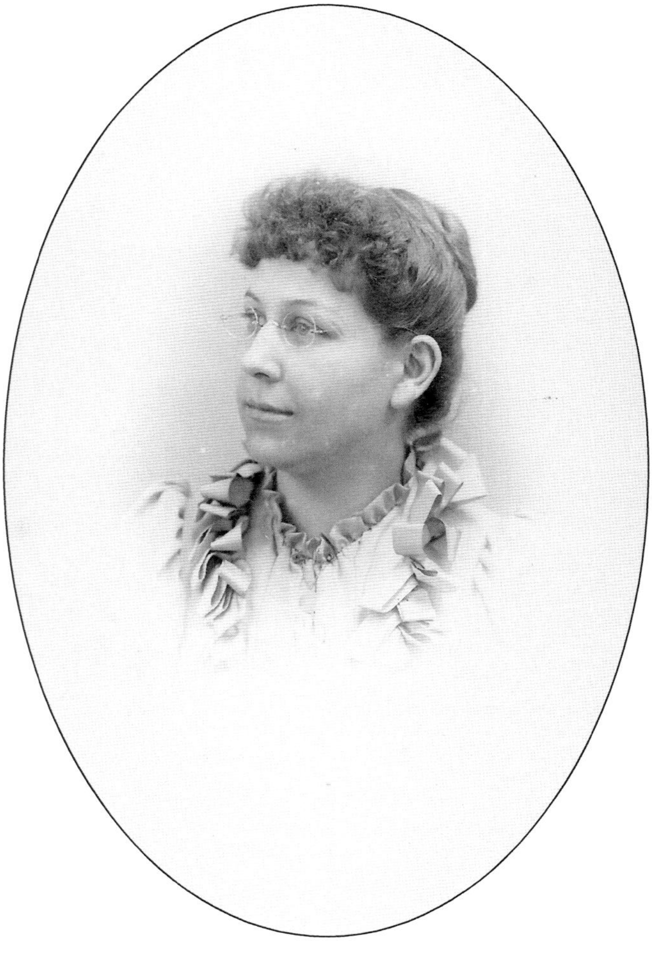

George B. Luce and Son were the undertakers, funeral directors, and dealers in furniture in Plainfield. This was common during a time when caskets were made of wood, as was most furniture. The business also advertised motor services for funerals in some of its early advertisements. The other option was probably horse-drawn funerals. The 1924 phone book lists the undertaking business as located on Lockport Street, with George living on Division Street.

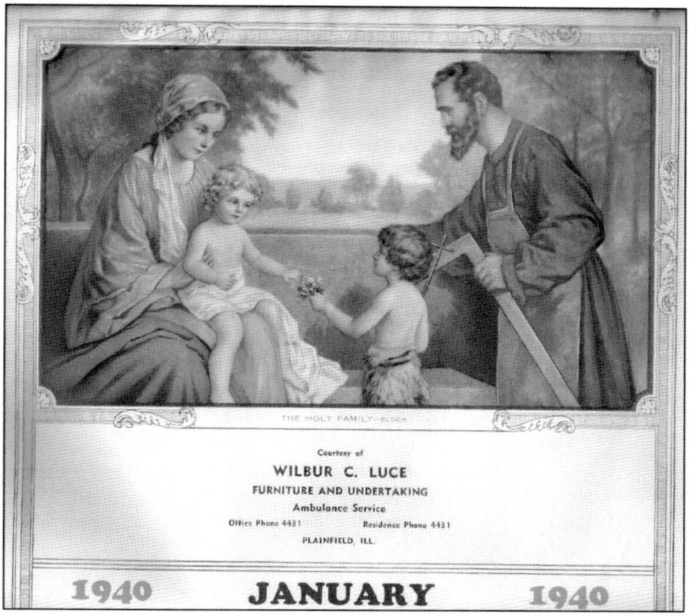

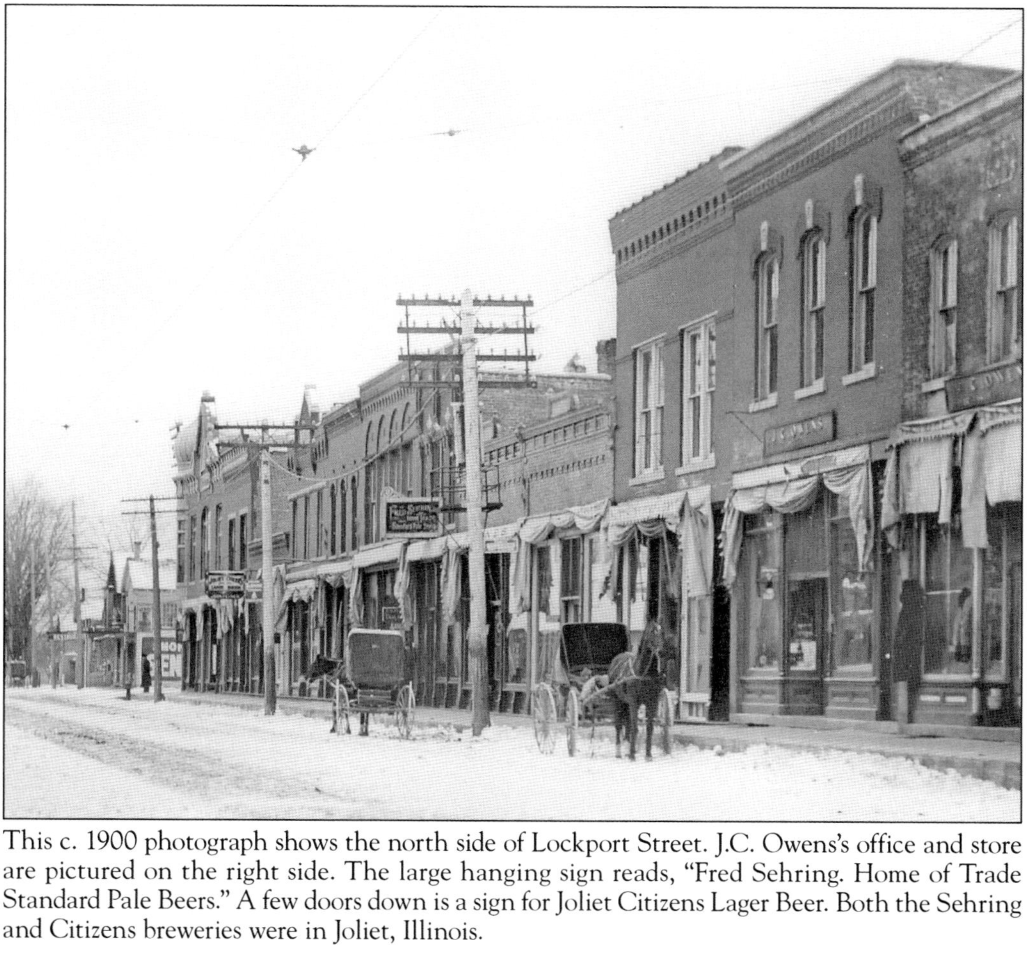

This c. 1900 photograph shows the north side of Lockport Street. J.C. Owens's office and store are pictured on the right side. The large hanging sign reads, "Fred Sehring. Home of Trade Standard Pale Beers." A few doors down is a sign for Joliet Citizens Lager Beer. Both the Sehring and Citizens breweries were in Joliet, Illinois.

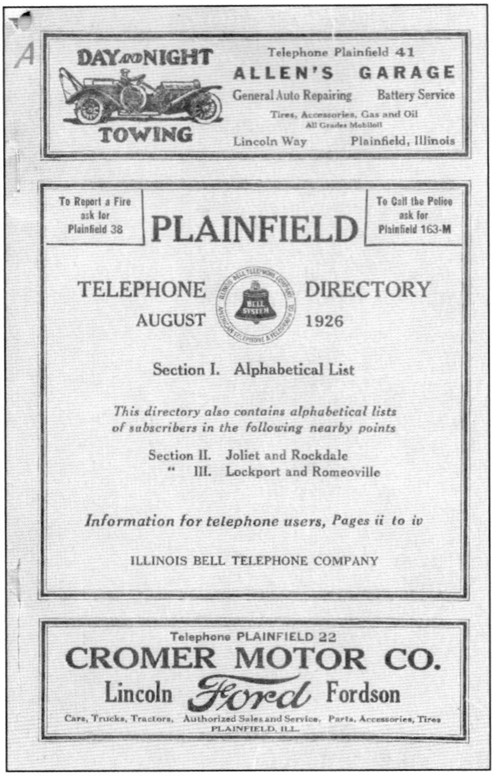

The 1926 Plainfield, Illinois, phone book has a grand total of four and a half pages of resident listings. It also has listings for Joliet, Lockport, and Rockdale, which are indicated as toll calls. It features Allen's Garage on the front cover, which is advertising day and night towing. Allen's Garage was located on Lincoln Way, better known as US Route 30. The Cromer Motor Company sold Lincoln and Ford cars and Fordson tractors. The back cover of the phone book features an advertisement for Owen's Confectionery and Restaurant for ice cream and homemade pies, located on Lincoln Way. Also on the back are ads for J.R. Jones Hardware Store, selling Moore's Furnaces, which were manufactured in nearby Joliet, Illinois, and the Reuben H. Donnelley Corp., which published telephone directories.

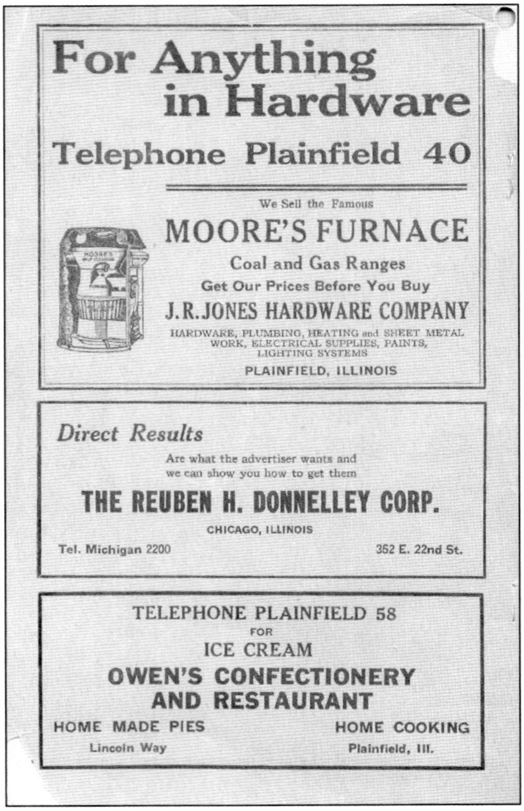

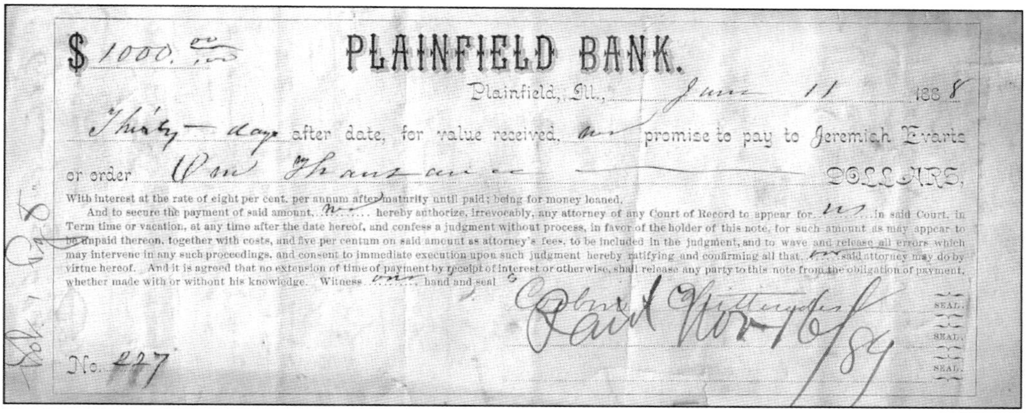
$1000.00/100 PLAINFIELD BANK.

Plainfield, Ill., June 11 1888

Thirty days after date, for value received, we promise to pay to Jeremiah Evarts or order One Thousand DOLLARS,

With interest at the rate of eight per cent. per annum after maturity until paid; being for money loaned.

And to secure the payment of said amount, we hereby authorize, irrevocably, any attorney of any Court of Record to appear for us in said Court, in Term time or vacation, at any time after the date hereof, and confess a judgment without process, in favor of the holder of this note, for such amount as may appear to be unpaid thereon, together with costs, and five per centum on said amount as attorney's fees, to be included in the judgment, and to wave and release all errors which may intervene in any such proceedings, and consent to immediate execution upon such judgment hereby ratifying and confirming all that our said attorney may do by virtue hereof. And it is agreed that no extension of time of payment by receipt of interest or otherwise, shall release any party to this note from the obligation of payment, whether made with or without his knowledge. Witness our hand and seal

SEAL. SEAL. SEAL.

Paid Nov 16/89

No. 227

The Plainfield Bank document above is dated 1888 and promises to pay Jeremiah Evarts $1,000. The interest rate was eight percent. Corbin and Chittenden, early business owners in Plainfield, signed it. Evarts was a Civil War veteran who started the first bank in Plainfield, originally known as the Evarts Private Bank, in 1887. The Evarts Private Bank burned within a year. The Plainfield State Bank was founded in 1913 in the Robertson Building at 159 Lockport Street. In 1915, two and a half years later, a new bank building, pictured below, was erected about a block east on the south side of Lockport Street. In 1940, it became the Plainfield National Bank. In 1959, the bank was given a complete remodeling, both inside and outside.

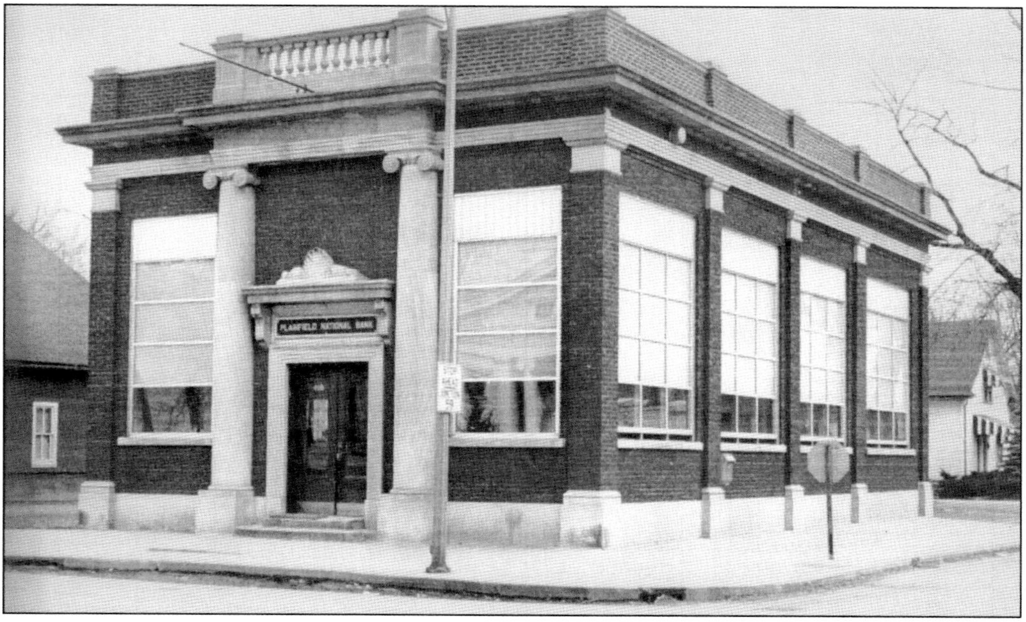

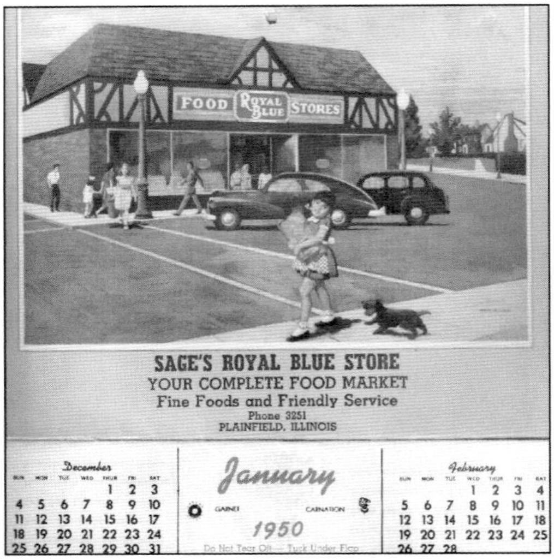

Sage's Royal Blue Store was an independently owned food market. It was located at 508 Lockport Street in Plainfield. As shown on this 1950 calendar, the store had a four-digit phone number, 3251. The store's motto was "Where to find them." Before the large grocery chains became popular, small, independent grocery stores were common in communities. Most villages the size of Plainfield would have had several small, independently owned stores.

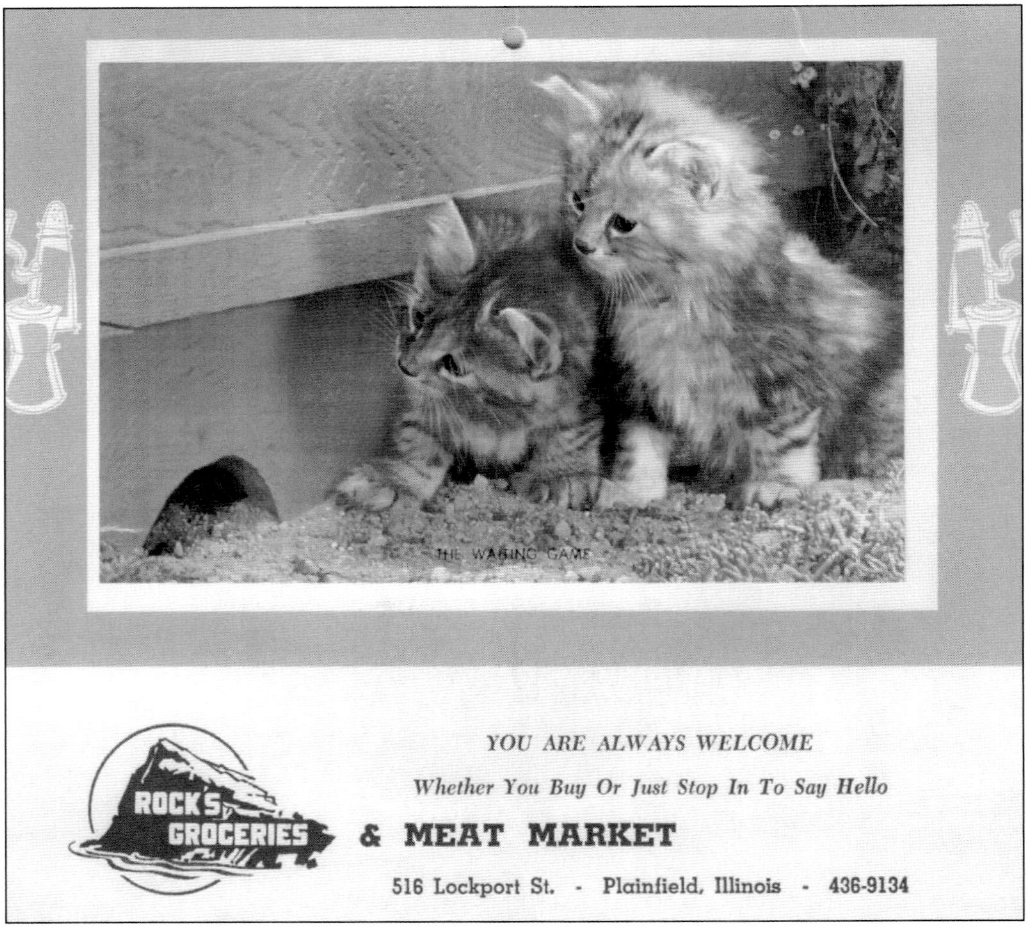

Rock's Groceries and Meat Market, along with Rock's Deli on Lockport Street, was a favorite in Plainfield for many years. Many high school students in Plainfield visited the deli, which was known for beef sandwiches and sodas. The owner, Richard "Dick" Rock, was also the mayor of Plainfield from 1997–2004.

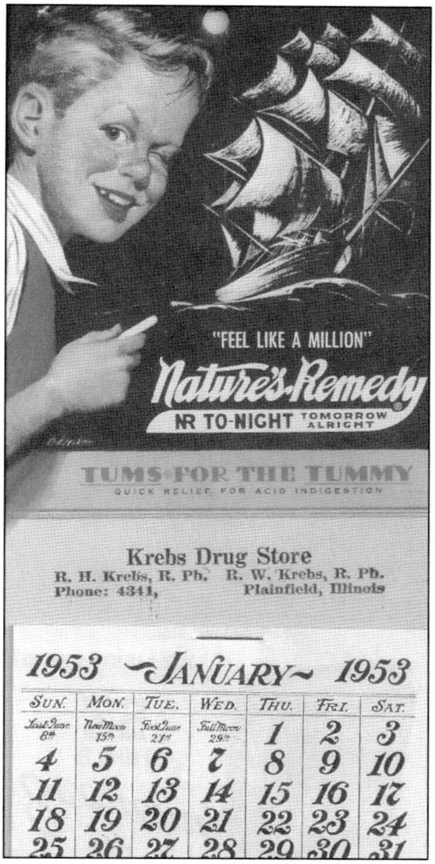

This 1953 calendar advertises both Krebs Drug Store and Tums. The drugstore operated in the village of Plainfield for over 80 years and is listed in the 1926 Plainfield Telephone Directory as Krebs Bros. Drugs, with the phone number 49. It was located at 505 Lockport Street. The store was purchased in 1986 by the Milligan family and closed for business in 2002. Below is a photograph of the interior of Burkes Drugstore in 1959. It was at 520 Lockport Street.

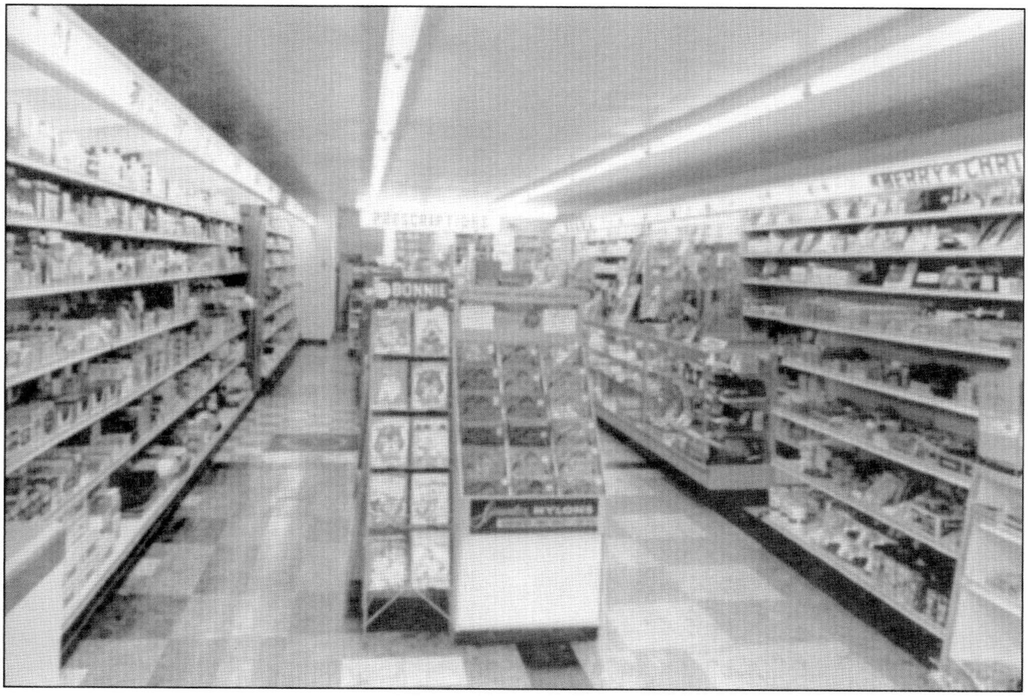

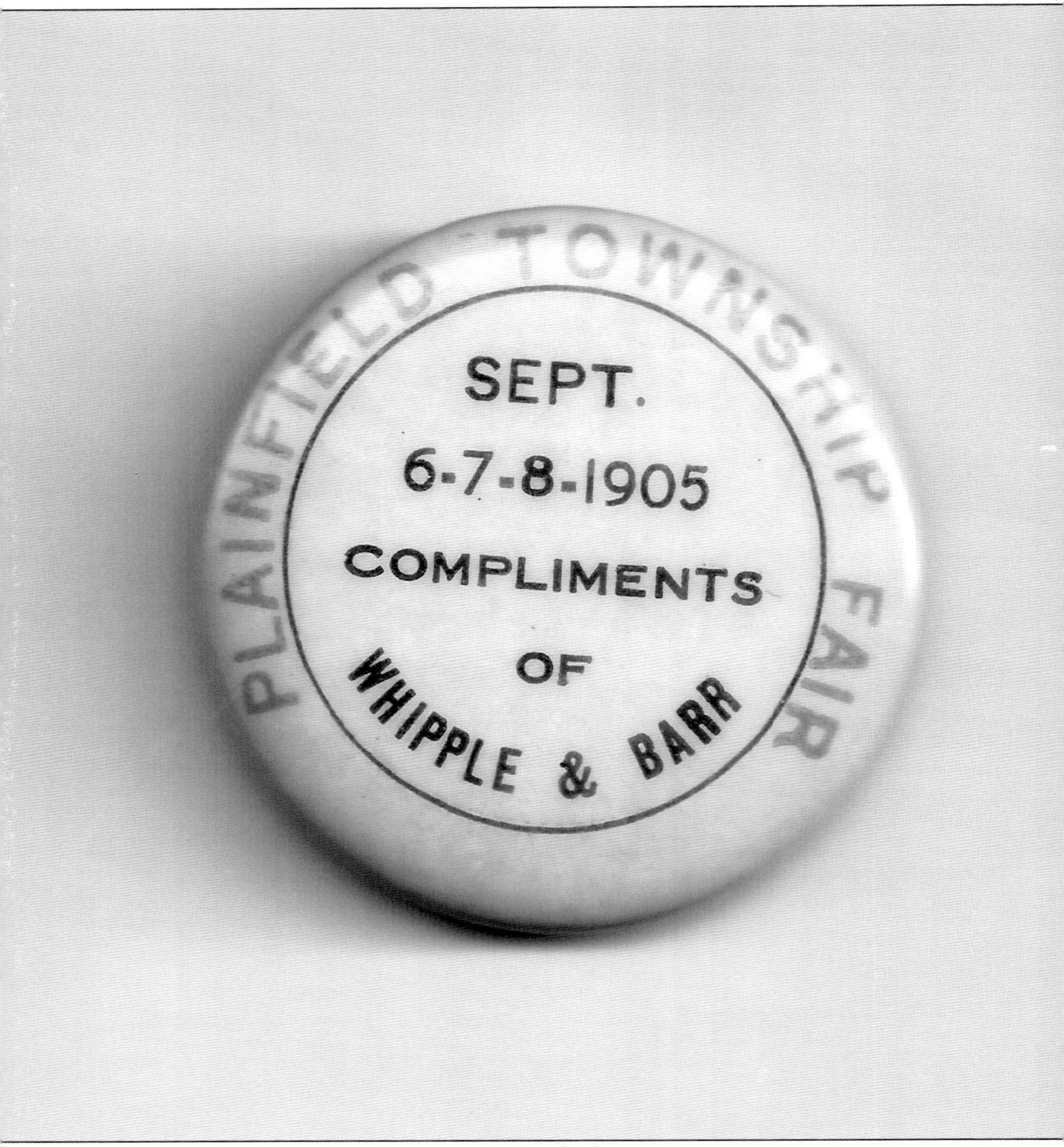

This button is from the September 1905 Plainfield Township Fair. These fairs often included pie-eating contests, a grain show, and a ladies' baking contest. The Plainfield Township Fairs were held the first week of September at Electric Park. This button is compliments of Whipple & Barr, the owners of three grain elevators, located in Plainfield, Caton Farm, and Frontenac. Levi Whipple and Charles V. Barr were married to sisters. The Barr home still stands at 15022 Bartlett Street in Plainfield. Whipple was a charter member of the Knights of Pythias lodge in Plainfield. Levi's son Lester owned a hardware store in Plainfield, while his son Chester was associated with the grain elevator.

This 1925 racing program is from the Plainfield Motor Speedway, located at the far east end of Ottawa Street. The inside of the program reads, "Official Program and Score Book / Second Annual Automobile Racing Season at Plainfield Motor Speedway / Plainfield, Illinois (near Joliet) / Under Management of Plainfield Motor Speedway Association." The program has several photographs of racecar drivers, including famous veterans of the Indy 500. One such driver who came to Plainfield to race was Cliff Woodbury, the 1929 Indy 500 pole sitter.

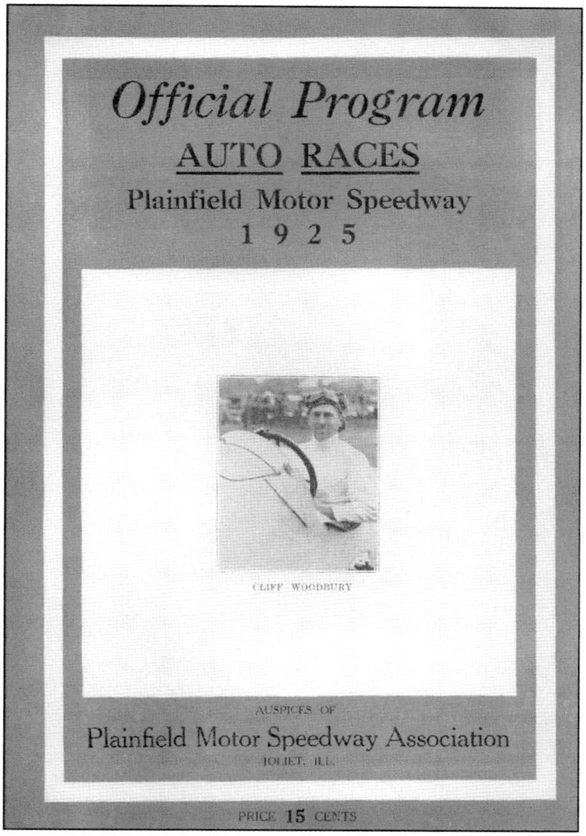
Official Program

AUTO RACES

Plainfield Motor Speedway

1 9 2 5

CLIFF WOODBURY

AUSPICES OF

Plainfield Motor Speedway Association

JOLIET, ILL.

PRICE 15 CENTS

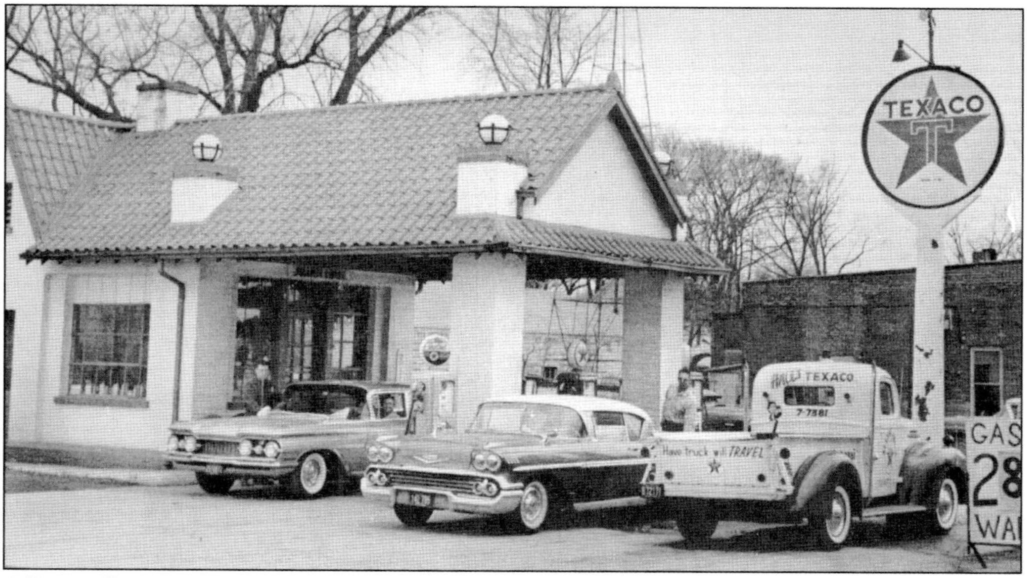

Allen Hall's Texaco service station was located on Lockport Street. The tailgate on the pickup reads, "Have Truck will Travel," while the sign in the corner announces, "Gas War / 28¢." Allen and his wife, Marie, drove a Plainfield school bus for many years and were well liked by all the schoolchildren who rode the bus. This building still stands and is listed in the National Register of Historic Places.

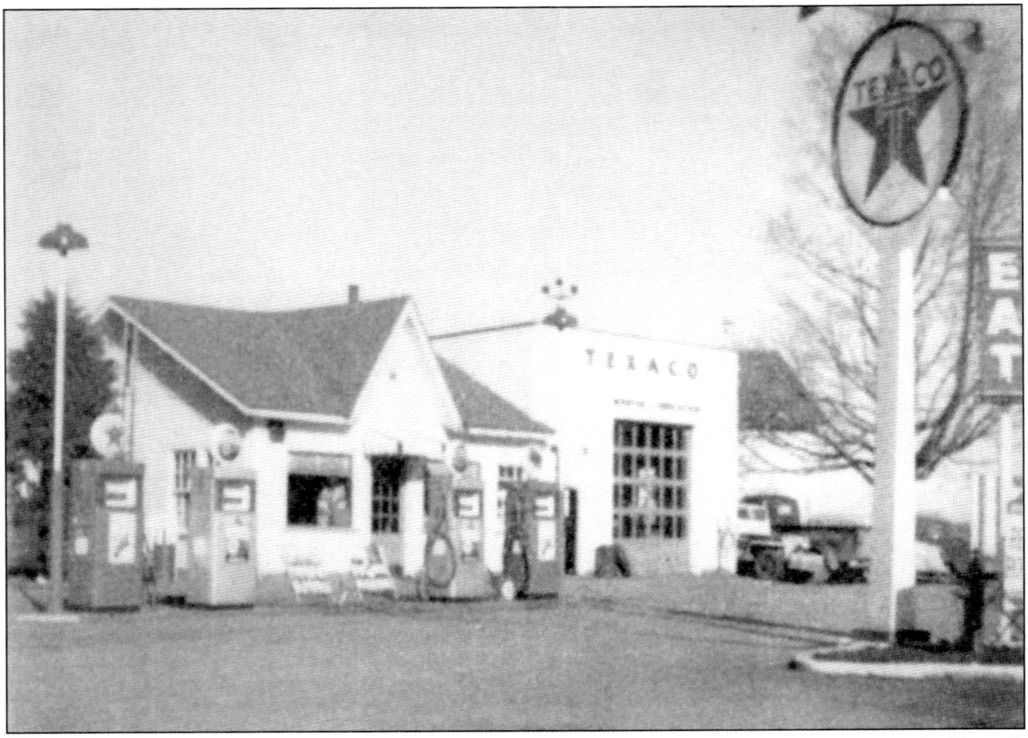

Bleck's Texaco Service Station, shown above, was located at 900 Division Street in Plainfield, with the phone number 7-9392. Bill Bleck and his wife, Lillian, owned and operated this gas station for many years. The station owners advertised and offered prompt and courteous service. The structure also housed the Maple View Coffee Shop. Pictured below is Al Morel's Mobil gasoline station at the southwest corner of Routes 59 and 126. This station was later owned and operated by Jerry and Ann Taylor of Plainfield. Note the Mobil Pegasus logos that are mounted on the outside walls of the station. (Below, courtesy of Jerry and Ann Taylor.)

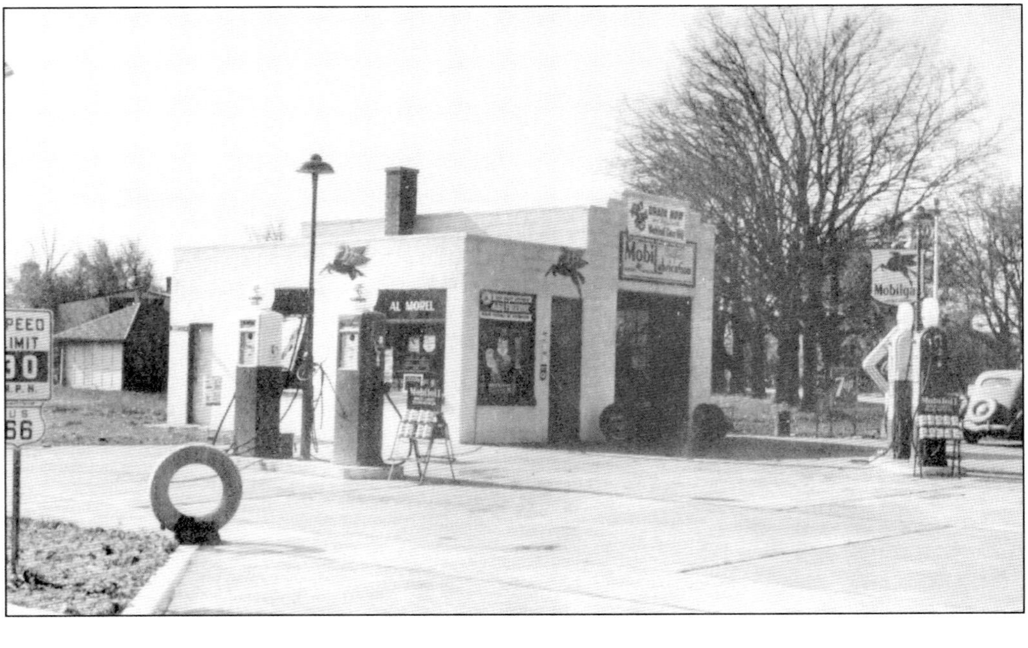

Three

Leisure Time

Plainfield's Electric Park, located on both sides of the DuPage River, was developed by the Joliet, Plainfield & Aurora Railway through the Fisher Construction Company. A dam on the DuPage River had created a boating area 150 feet wide and a mile in length, where one could enjoy a paddleboat ride on the *Mary Lee*. There was swimming, fishing, boat rentals, and, for the adventurous, a toboggan slide that would launch one into the river. Hot air balloon ascensions were a common occurrence at the park. On July 26, 1911, while performing a stunt with his balloon at a height of 700 feet, Prof. Harry Darnell fell to his death into the DuPage River. An auditorium with a seating capacity of 3,500 and a stage that held a large pipe organ were constructed at the park. Also on the grounds was a dancing pavilion, a two-lane bowling alley, a restaurant, a bathhouse, and boathouse. A wooden roller coaster stood at the park for many years as well. One could also play ball at the ballpark or at the athletic grounds, which were equipped with a grandstand. There was a riding gallery as well as bandstands where one could relax to a band or orchestra concert, two or three evenings a week. One of the unique features of the park was the various-sized cottages constructed with canvas sides. Folks could rent these cottages by the week, month, or season. For a 10-day period in late July and early August, the Will County Chautauqua held its annual event at the park. Electric Park was also home to the Plainfield Fair, which drew crowds from miles away. Exhibits were held in the auditorium. Winners received ribbons in the baking and sewing categories. In 1923, the park closed as the result of the Joliet, Plainfield & Aurora Railway going out of business. The auditorium was later reopened and served as a popular roller-skating rink for several years before it closed. In 1990, the auditorium was destroyed as a result of the tornado.

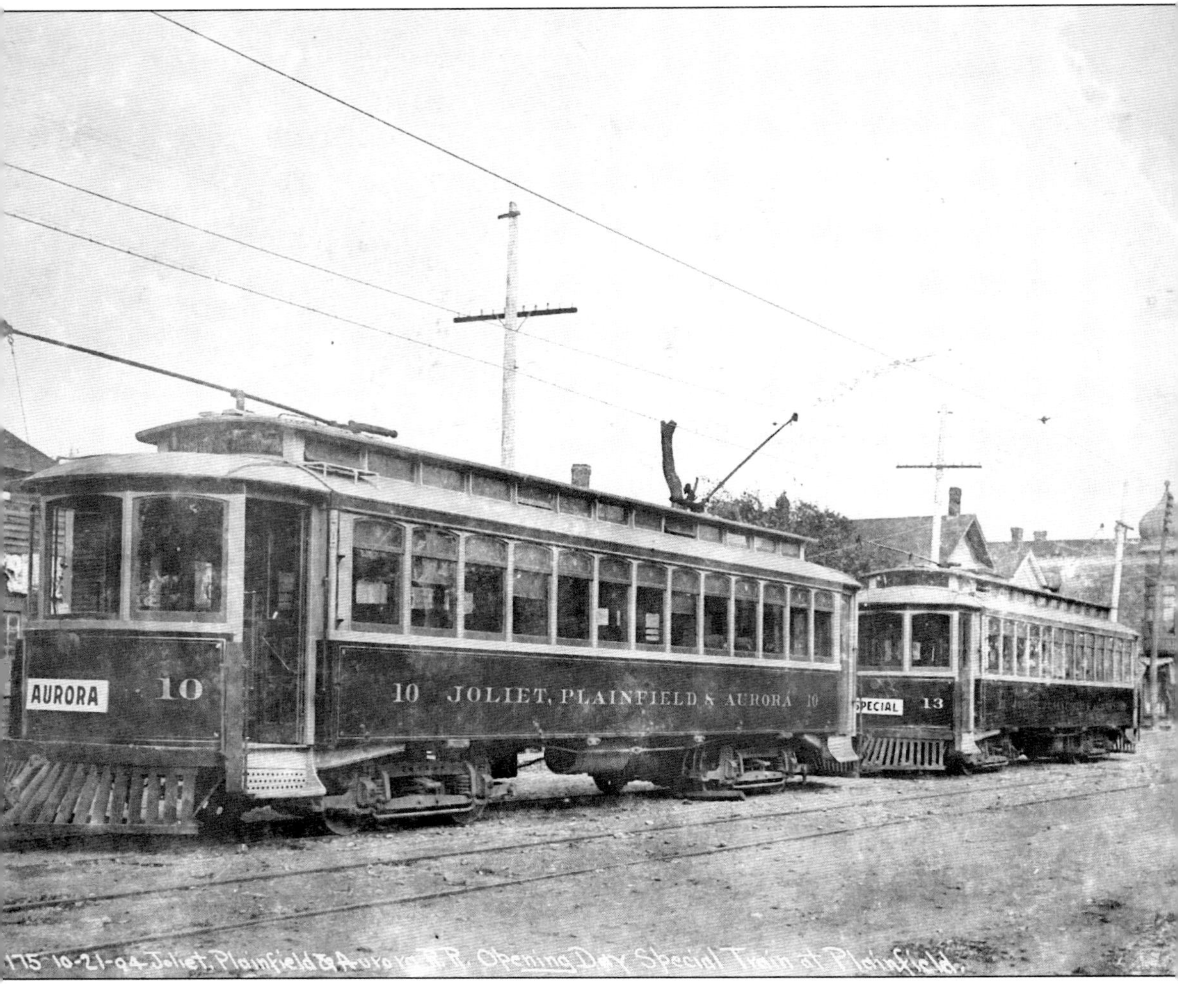

This photograph of the special train for the Joliet, Plainfield & Aurora Railway shows Plainfield on opening day of Electric Park on October 21, 1904. It was later said that this day was the dawn of a new era for Plainfield. The town had been transformed into a thriving suburban town known all over northern Illinois. The park was originally intended as a picnic grounds for trolley line excursionists. It soon became an ideal summer resort, where folks could spend a few weeks, months, or the entire summer season. The Fisher Company of Joliet had built the Joliet, Plainfield & Aurora line. The company claimed, "The railway was not only strictly first class in every respect, but superior to the average electric railroad, and equal to the best that had yet been produced in 1904."

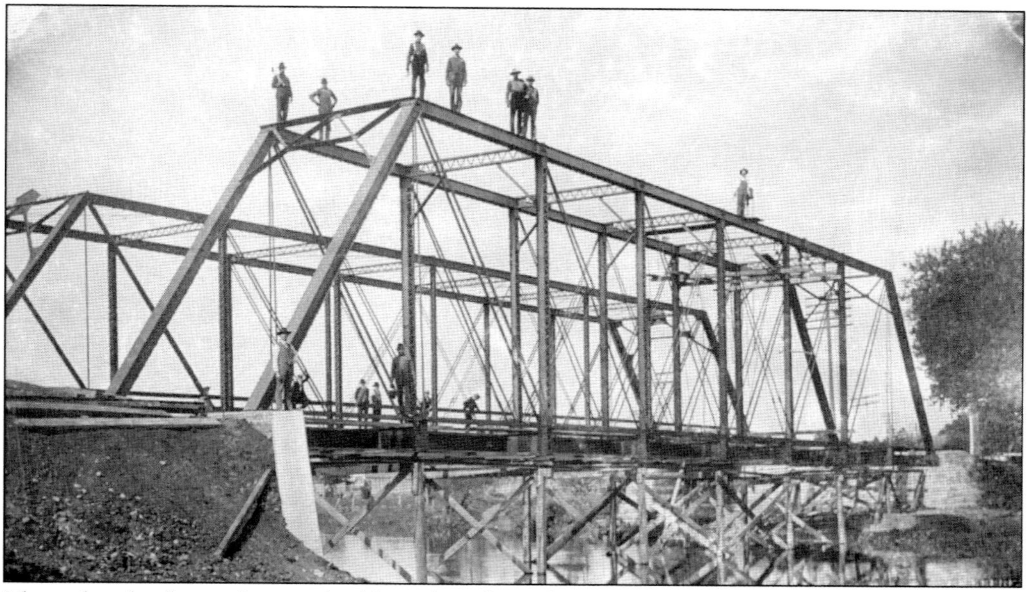

These daredevils are the men building the Joliet, Plainfield & Aurora Railway trolley bridges at Electric Park. The man on the left even carries his hammer on top of the bridge with him for the photograph. The Fisher Construction Company was a corporation organized for the purpose of building a line between Plainfield and Joliet. The company was composed of H.A. Fisher (president), F.E. Stoddard (secretary), and Lee D. Fisher (chief engineer).

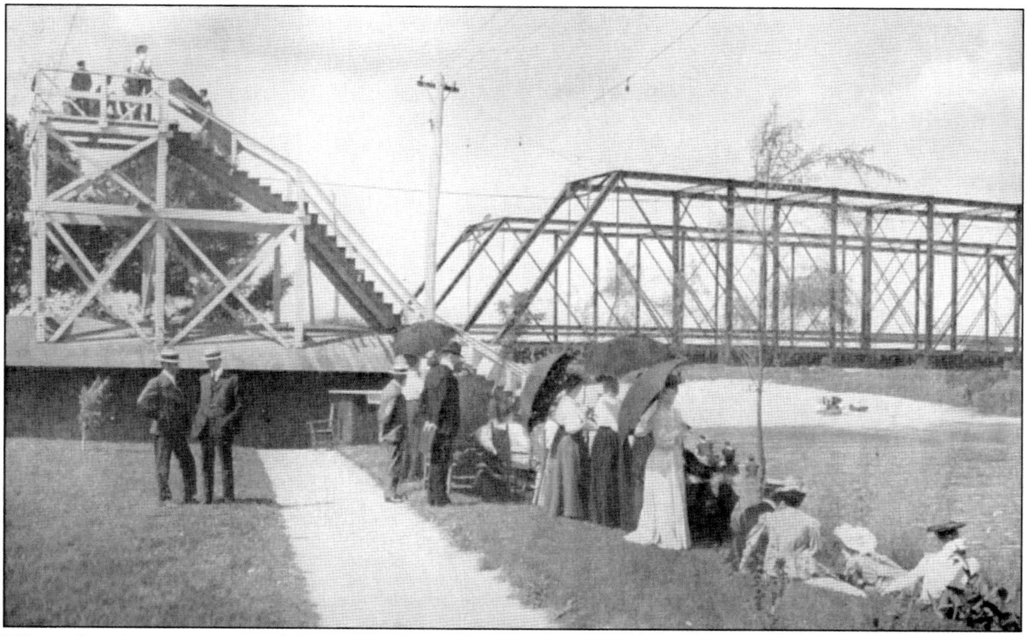

These families are pictured enjoying the park. Children are on top of the, slide while the mothers carry umbrellas, shading themselves from the sun. After the park opened in 1904, it often catered to the various local companies. The railway rented private train cars to bring employees out to the park for company picnics. Some of these special cars were very plush and even had carpeting. The building of this railway line resulted in an increase of business to the merchants of both Plainfield and Joliet.

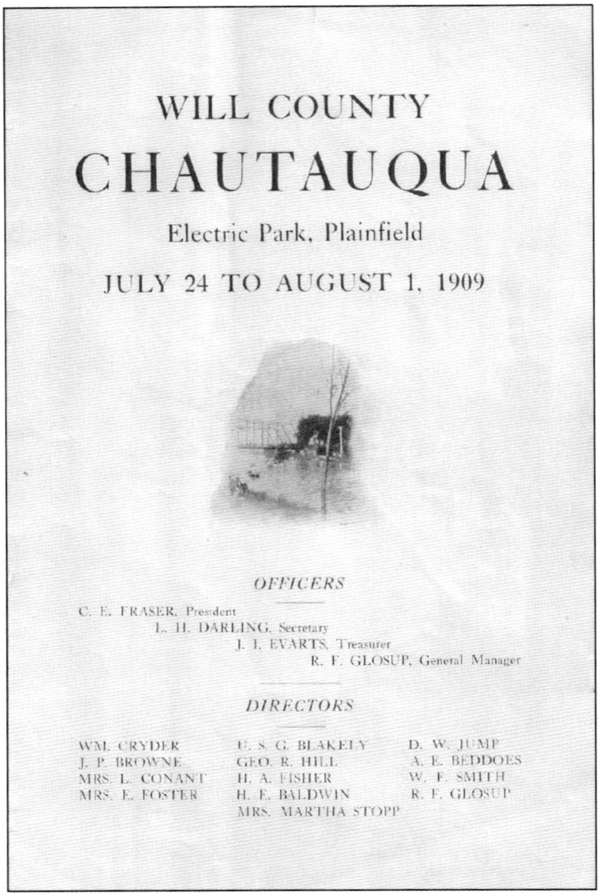

WILL COUNTY

CHAUTAUQUA

Electric Park, Plainfield

JULY 24 TO AUGUST 1, 1909

OFFICERS

C. E. FRASER, President
L. H. DARLING, Secretary
J. I. EVARTS, Treasurer
R. F. GLOSUP, General Manager

DIRECTORS

WM. CRYDER	U. S. G. BLAKELY	D. W. JUMP
J. P. BROWNE	GEO. R. HILL	A. E. BEDDOES
MRS. L. CONANT	H. A. FISHER	W. F. SMITH
MRS. E. FOSTER	H. E. BALDWIN	R. F. GLOSUP
	MRS. MARTHA STOPP	

This is a program for the fourth annual Will County Chautauqua, held from July 24 to August 1, 1909, at Electric Park in Plainfield. It advertises that no better talent will be heard anywhere than has been secured for this event. Included in the program's list of entertainment is the Apollo Quartette and Bell Ringers, Tahan the White Indian, the Chicago Ladies Orchestra, and Dr. Lena Sadler. Sadler lectured to woman only on their health and was assisted by a trained nurse. Below is a photograph of the auditorium where events were held during the Chautauqua session.

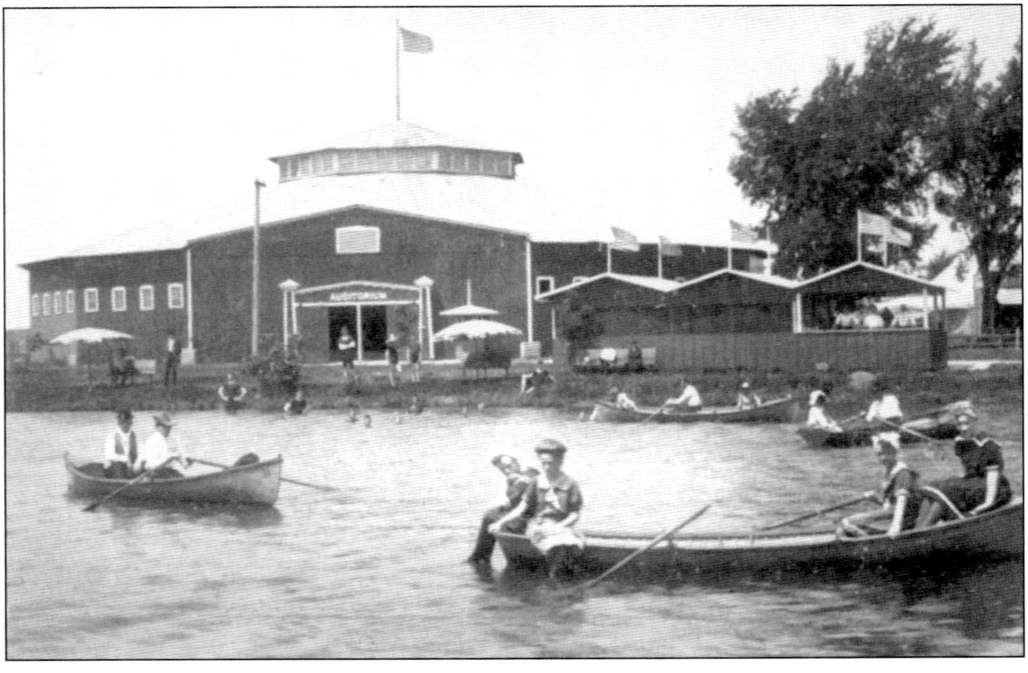

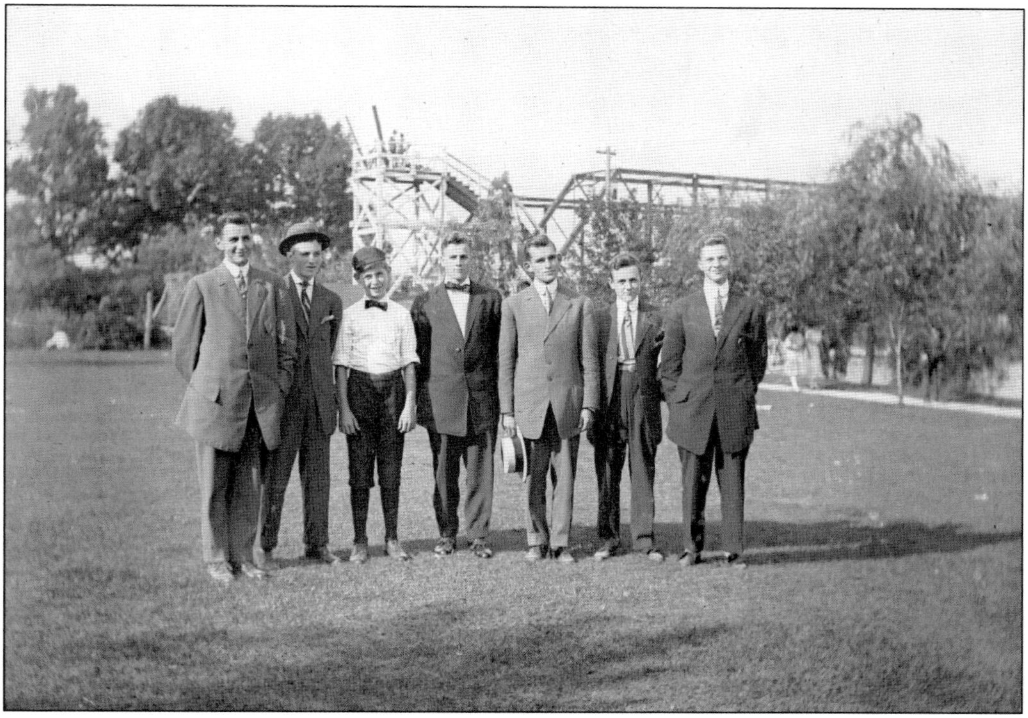

These young men are perhaps employees of Electric Park. They all are wearing suits and ties, with the exception of the third boy from the left, who is sporting a bow tie and knickers. The park employed several young men who worked in various jobs. In the background are the tops of the trolley bridges and of the toboggan slide. A few people are standing at the top of the toboggan ride as they wait to slide into the DuPage River.

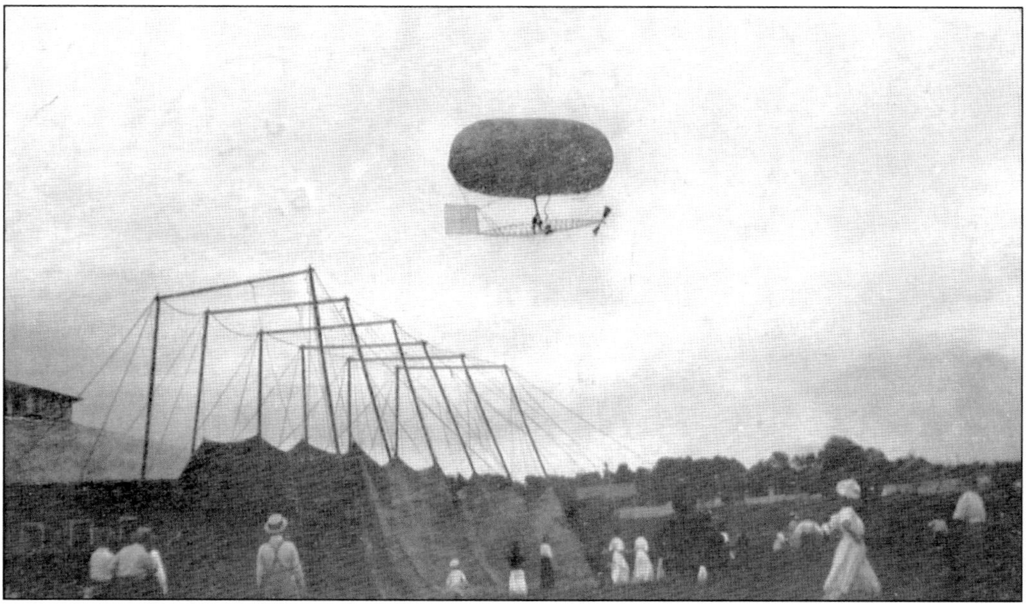

Hot air balloons were a popular attraction at the park. The structure on the ground in this photograph holds the balloon down as it is filled. On July 26, 1911, balloonist Harry Darnell fell to his death into the DuPage River. He is buried in the Plainfield Township Cemetery.

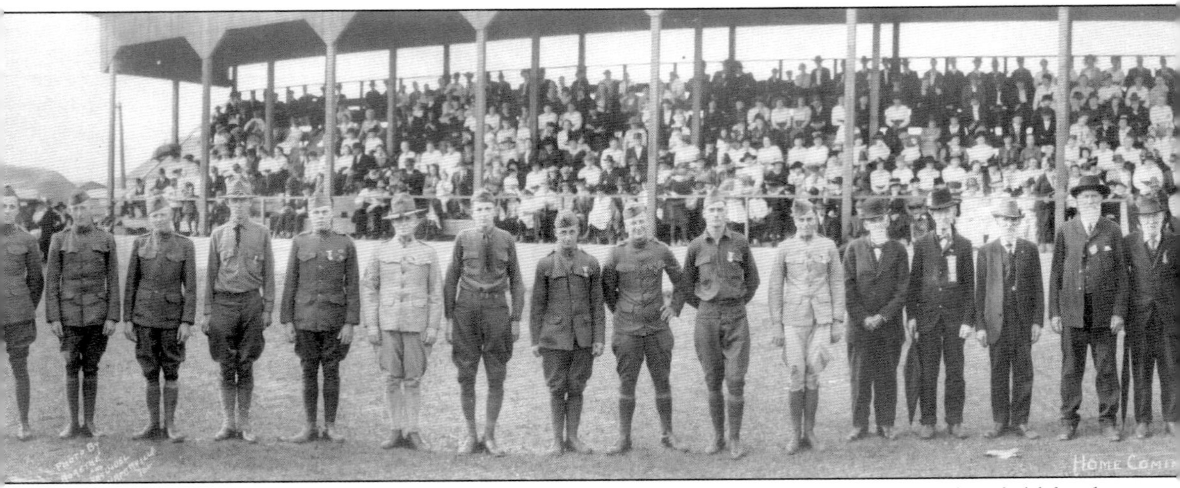

The grandstand is filled with spectators on October 1, 1919, at Electric Park in Plainfield for this panoramic photograph titled "Home Coming Soldiers and Sailors." It includes Plainfield veterans of the Civil War, Spanish-American War, and World War I. Several of the Civil War veterans have Grand Army of the Republic badges and ribbons pinned to their chests. They are, from left to right, Ira Jones, A. Loscheider, Robert Bill, Clinton King, Archie Meyers, Clarence Brown, Ralph Russell, Walter Mather, Lester Shaw, Otto Annis, Ray Annis, Walter Burch, Emanuel

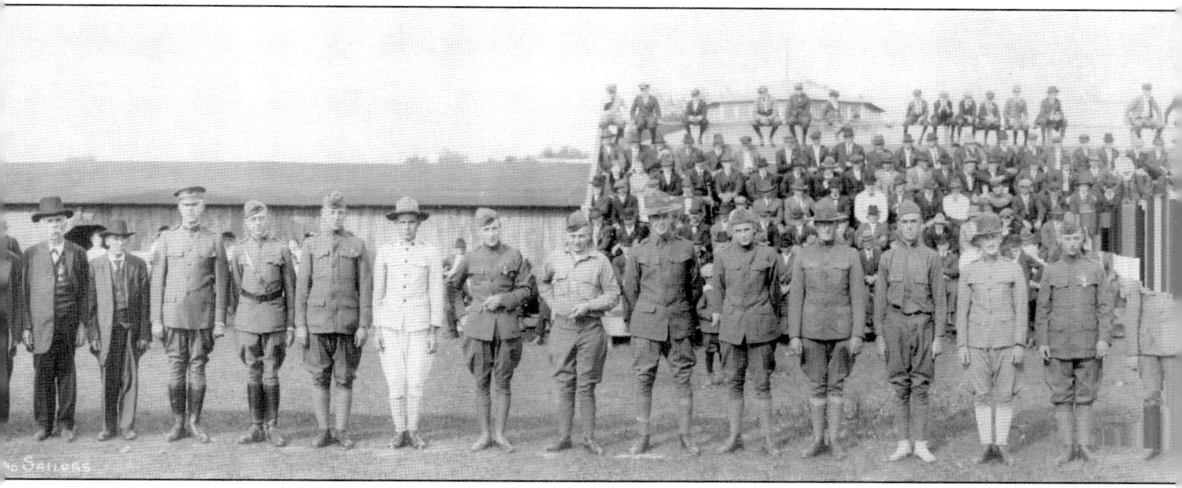

Brown, John Lyman, John Bragaw, William Cain, William Austin, Anson Keene, John McLauglin, Chris Steafbold, Dr. Ryden, Robert Bradley, Ray Falkenberg, Ed Countryman, Tracy Kazar, Oscar Schwanke, Carlton Steigle, Milton Sonntag, Walter Boner, Herman Worst, David Fairweather, Frank Wright, and Sam Macaluso. There is a monument at Settlers Park in Plainfield with the names of all the Civil War, Spanish-American War, and World War I veterans from Plainfield.

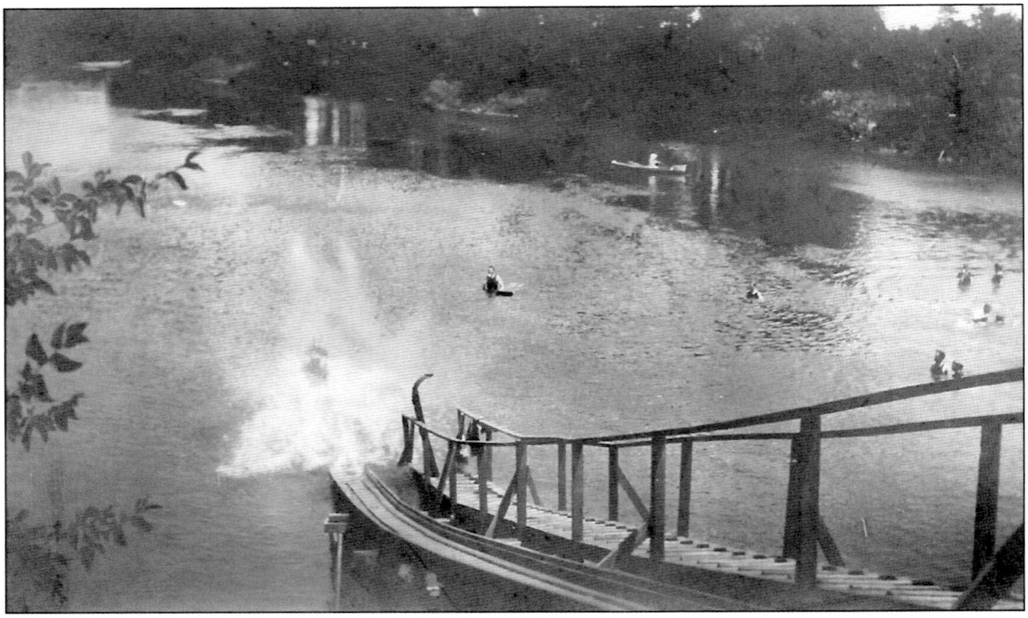

The photograph above shows the view going down the slide into the DuPage River at Electric Park. One ad reads, "Electric Park is a delightful summer resort with Chautauqua grounds on the DuPage River. A clean stream for boating, fishing and bathing, pure air and restfulness are the features at the park. The pavilion, seating 3,500 people, contains a pipe organ, and the Will County Chautauqua holds its meetings here. Liquors are prohibited. Family cottages are equipped with gas, electric lights and water." In the photograph below, some girls are about to go boating on the mighty DuPage River. White dresses and hair bows were the normal attire while at Electric Park during this time period.

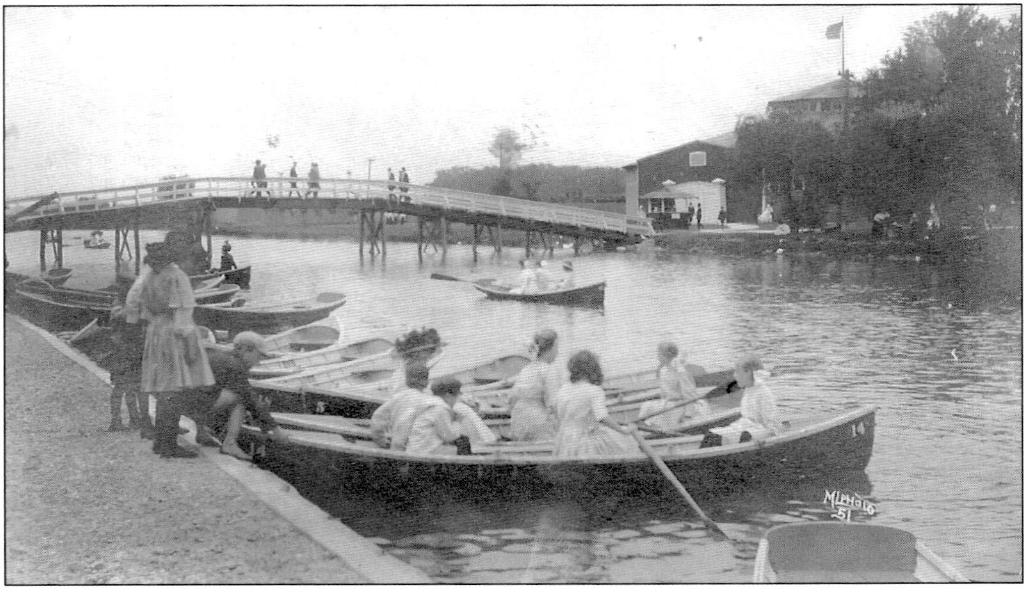

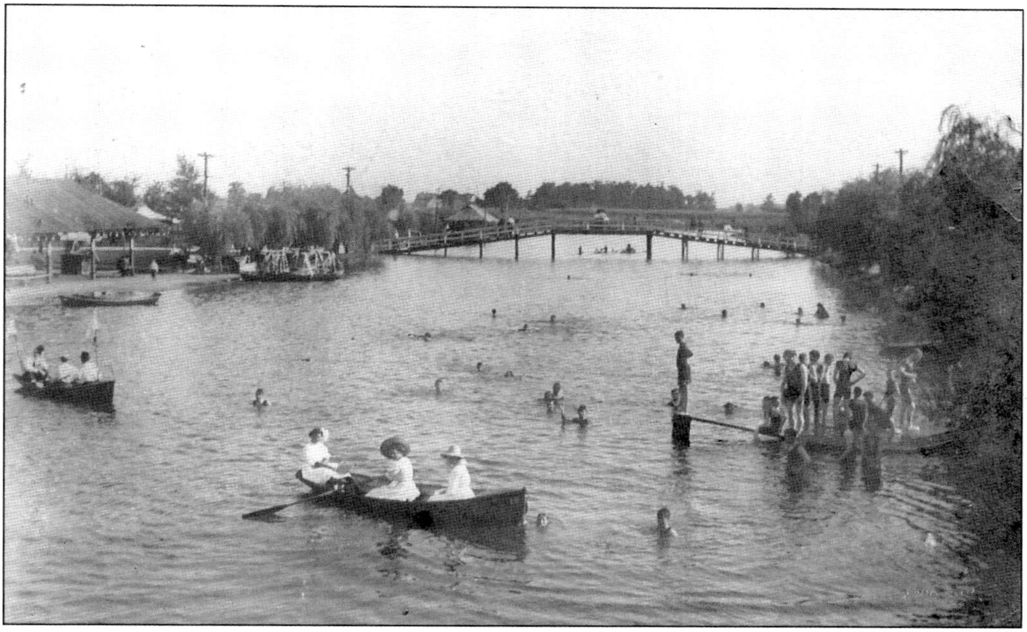

The footbridge at Electric Park can be seen in the background of this photograph. The ladies in the boat are enjoying the day on the DuPage River in their long, white, cotton dresses and floppy hats of the time. On the back, dated July 7, 1909, is written, "Came over here for a time, can you find me in the picture? Look under the water, L.H." It was postmarked in Plainfield and sent to Michigan. Numerous bathers are to the right in the photograph. The boathouse is pictured in the distance on the left, which is on the east side of the DuPage River. This advertisement from the June 1931 issue of *Joliet Magazine* is for Jimmie Green and His Orchestra playing for the De La Salle Welcome Dance. De La Salle was a boys' high school started in 1918 that would later become Joliet Catholic High School.

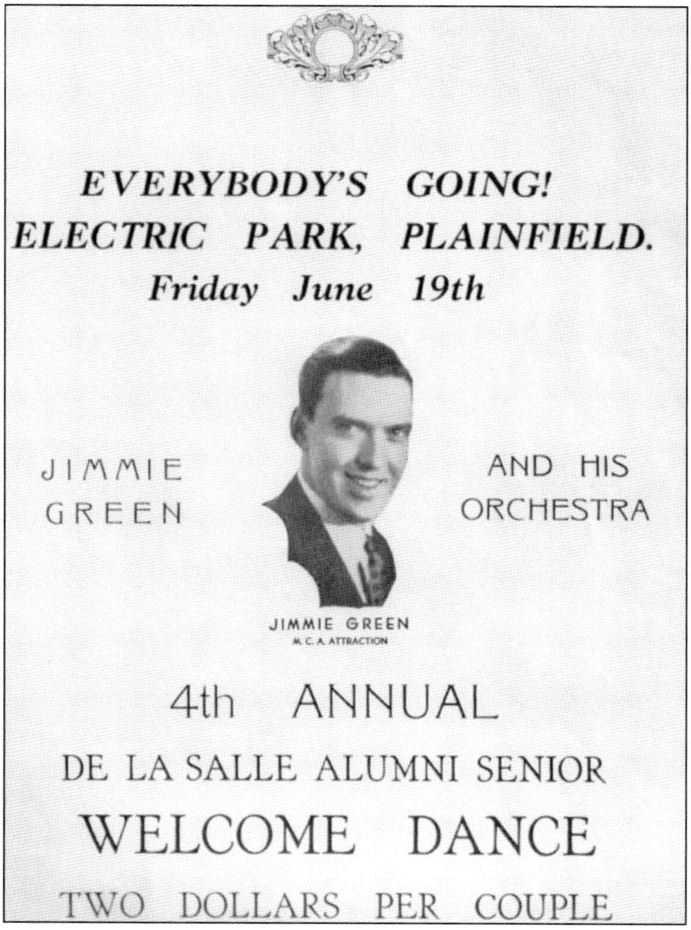

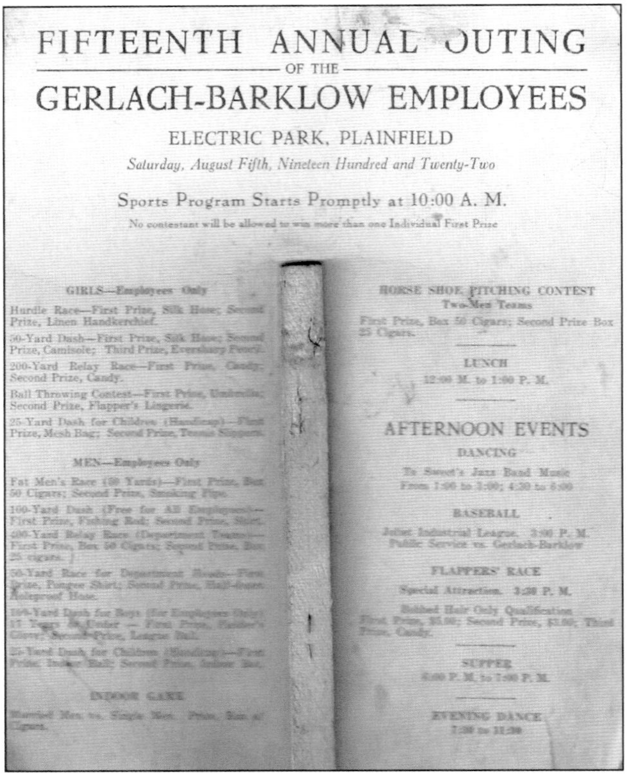

FIFTEENTH ANNUAL OUTING

OF THE

GERLACH-BARKLOW EMPLOYEES

ELECTRIC PARK, PLAINFIELD

Saturday, August Fifth, Nineteen Hundred and Twenty-Two

Sports Program Starts Promptly at 10:00 A. M.

No contestant will be allowed to win more than one Individual First Prize

GIRLS—Employees Only

Hurdle Race—First Prize, Silk Hose; Second Prize, Linen Handkerchief.

50-Yard Dash—First Prize, Silk Hose; Second Prize, Camisole; Third Prize, Eversharp Pencil.

200-Yard Relay Race—First Prize, Candy; Second Prize, Candy.

Ball Throwing Contest—First Prize, Umbrella; Second Prize, Flapper's Lingerie.

25-Yard Dash for Children (Handicap)—First Prize, Mesh Bag; Second Prize, Tennis Slippers.

MEN—Employees Only

Fat Men's Race (50 Yards)—First Prize, Box 50 Cigars; Second Prize, Smoking Pipe.

[illegible]

INDOOR GAME

[illegible]

HORSE SHOE PITCHING CONTEST
Two-Men Teams

First Prize, Box 50 Cigars; Second Prize Box 25 Cigars.

LUNCH
12:00 M. to 1:00 P. M.

AFTERNOON EVENTS

DANCING

[illegible]

BASEBALL

[illegible]

FLAPPERS' RACE

Special Attraction. [illegible] P. M.

Bobbed Hair Only Qualification
[illegible]

SUPPER
[illegible]

EVENING DANCE
[illegible]

The back of this fan advertises the 15th Annual Outing for Gerlach Barklow Employees on August 5, 1922. Several local companies held their company picnics at Electric Park. Girls' and men's employee-only hurdle and 25- and 50-yard-dash races were held. First and second prizes for the girls were silk hose and a linen handkerchief. The prizes for the men were a box of 50 or 25 cigars. The only qualification for the flapper's race was for a girl to have bobbed hair. The girls' ball-throwing contest prize was flapper's lingerie or an umbrella. The front of the fan has an image by Zula Kenyon, a famous woman artist from the Gerlach Barklow Calendar Company in nearby Joliet.

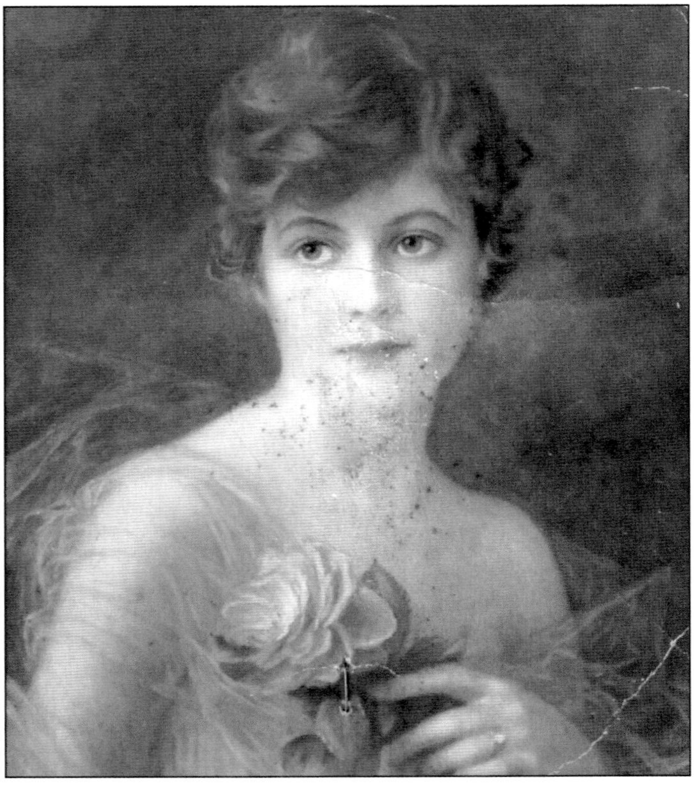

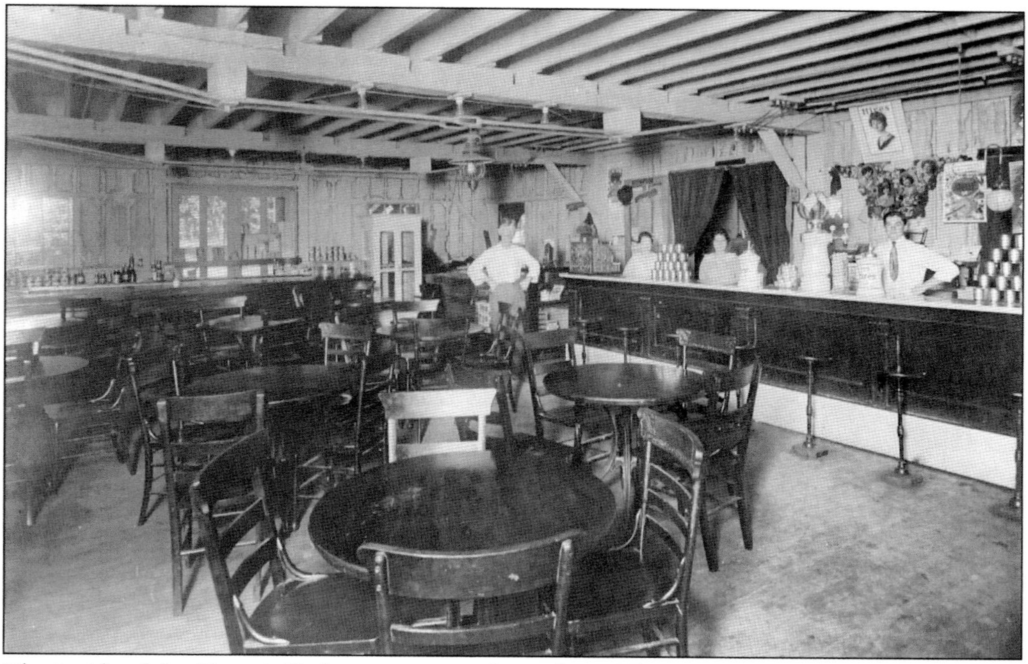

The inside of the Electric Park restaurant is shown here. The restaurant, dining hall, and boat docks as well as the cottages were on the east side of the DuPage River. Note the Hires root beer sign hanging above the soda bar. Alcohol was prohibited at the park, as was smoking and spitting. The dance hall, bathhouse, bowling alley, and auditorium were on the west side of the DuPage River. An early Electric Park brochure advertises that the park has "absolutely pure country air, laden with the order of clover blossoms, the honey suckle and violet. The evenings and nights are cool, free from mosquitoes and other disagreeable insects." Below, the back cover of the park program shows a bird's-eye view of the location of various buildings at the park.

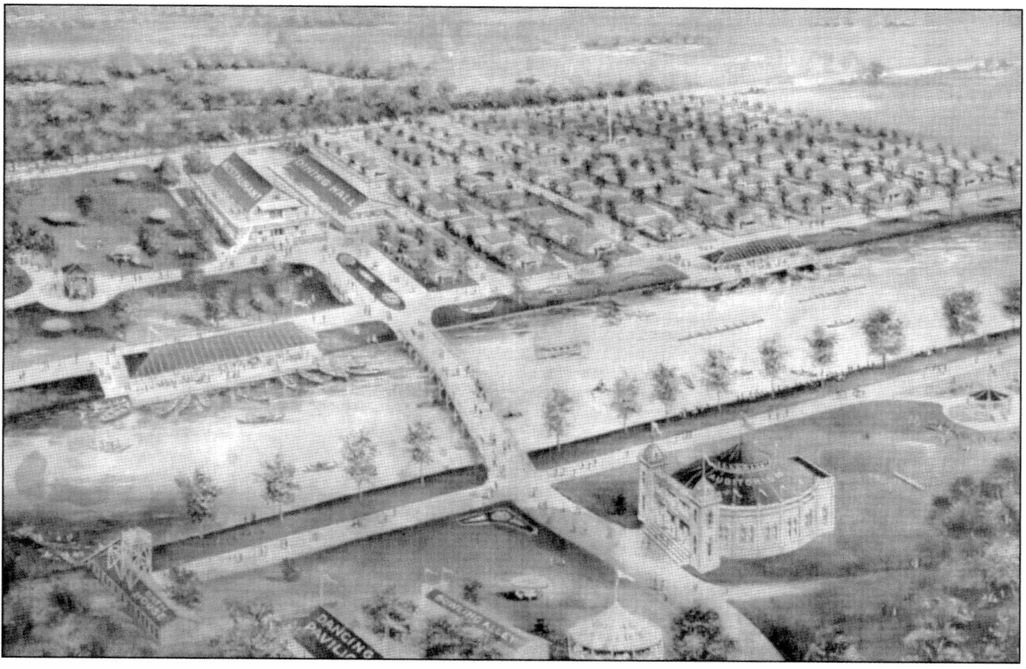

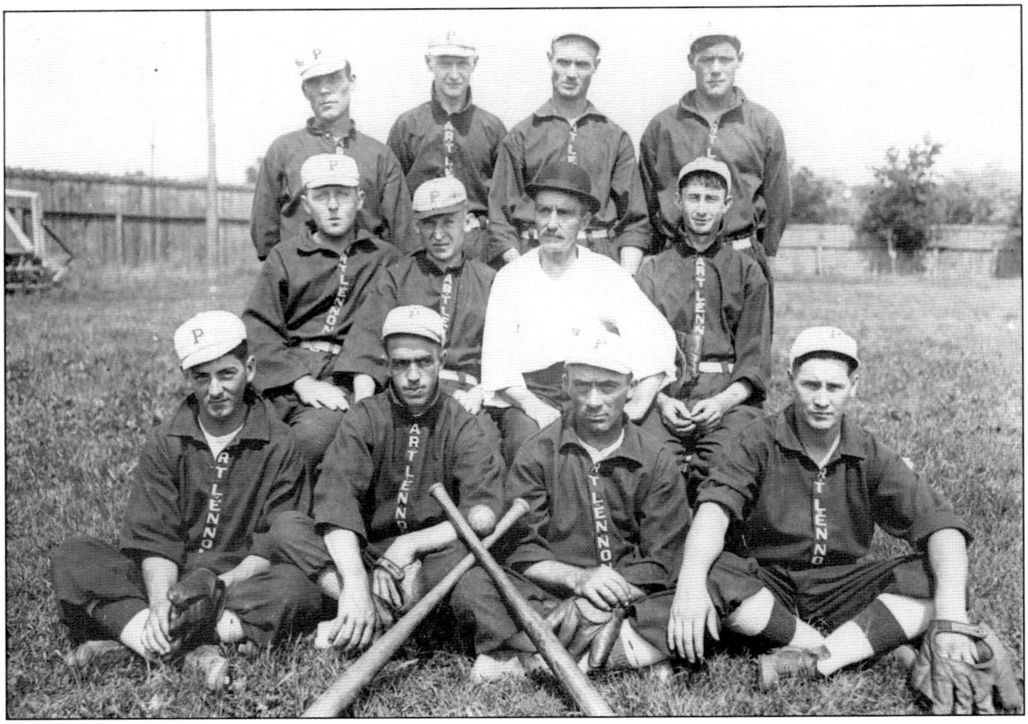

Art Lennon sponsored this early baseball team, pictured for a team photograph at Electric Park. The Lennon Wallpaper Company was located in Joliet, Illinois. Note the "P" emblem on players' hats. Over the years, several company-sponsored teams in the Joliet Industrial League played at Electric Park. In some cases, various local companies would hire an employee just because he was a very good baseball player. These local companies and their teams were very competitive.

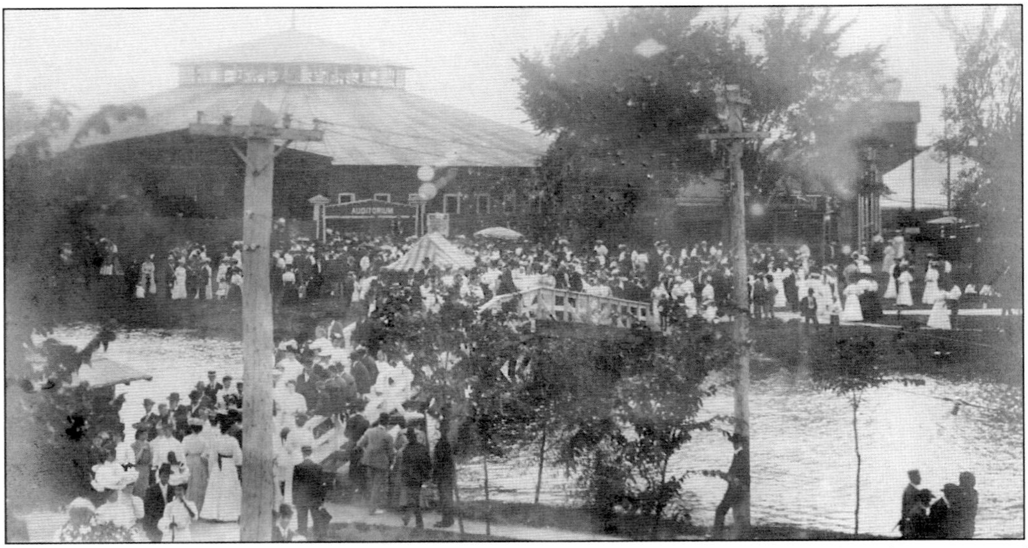

Crowds of people would attend Electric Park. This photograph was probably taken during one of the Chautauqua fairs. The 1909 Chautauqua program advertises, "The cost is a mere bagatelle, at sixteen cents a day for entertainment. If you cannot attend one of the entertainment sessions, loan the ticket to a friend."

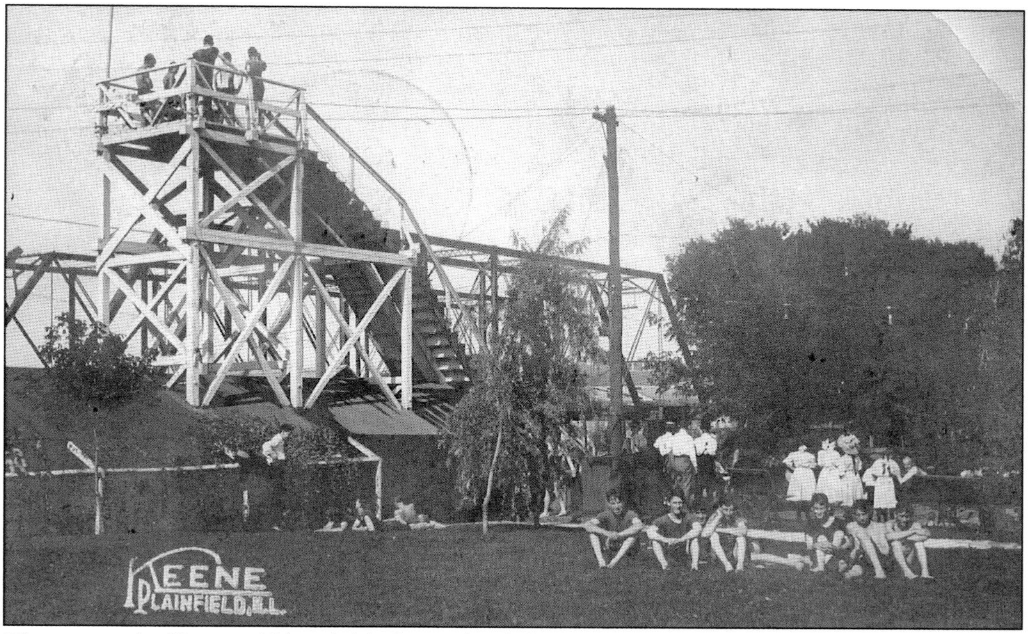

This image, by Keene of Plainfield, shows the slide to the river as well the trolley bridges in the background. Posing in front are some handsome boys in their bathing suits, while young girls in fancy dresses watch the action from the slide into the DuPage River. This real-photo postcard was postmarked in 1908 from Plainfield and only sent as far as Joliet. The sender writes, "The sunset is just grand tonight. I am out on the river watching it and enjoying it immensely." Below, this postcard shows an early automobile coming down the dirt street near the trolley depot at Electric Park. In an early Electric Park brochure, one of the park rules states, "Campers must retire by 10:30 p.m., and should not indulge in loud or boisterous language in the cottages, as it prohibits those who wish to retire early the rest they are entitled."

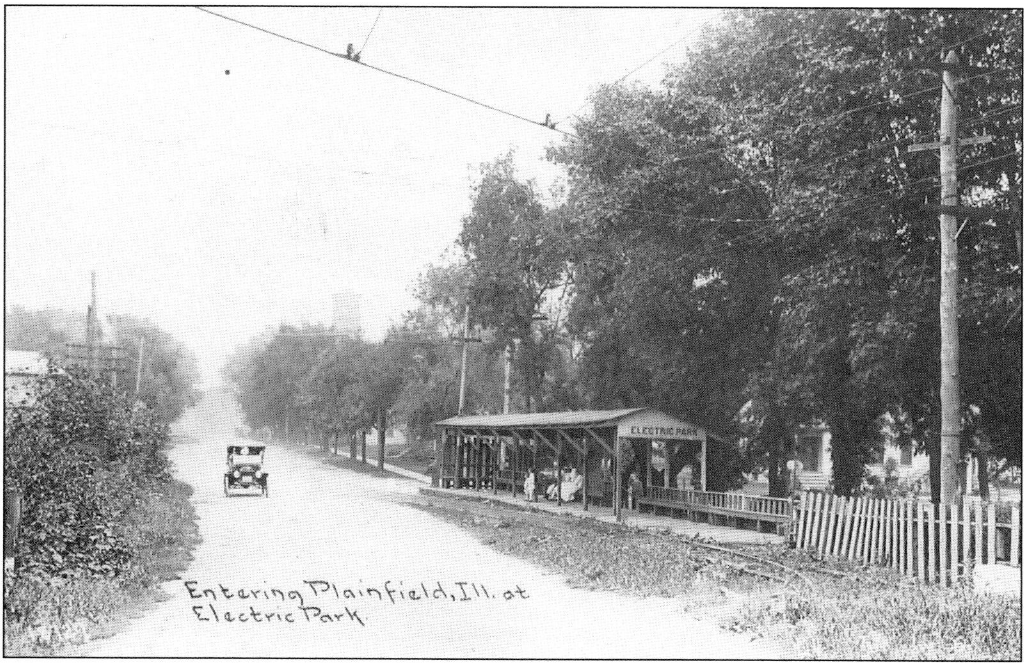

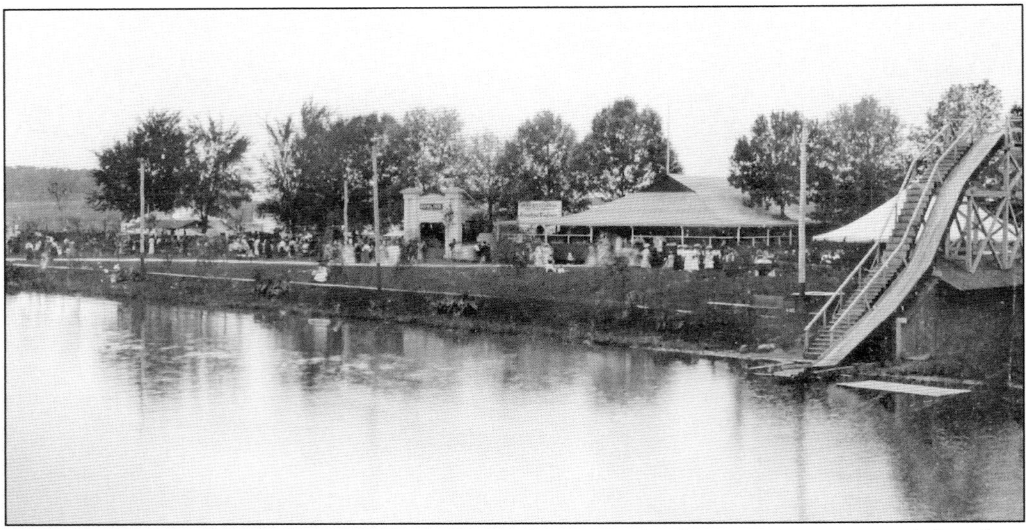

The sign just to the left of the Dance Hall at Electric Park advertises International Gasoline Engines. Above the arch, a sign reads, "Bowling." The dance hall floor measured 40 feet by 120 feet. Note the tree growing through the dance hall roof on the right. Bands from all over the Chicago area, including those from Joliet, played at Electric Park. The bowling alley had two lanes. Electric Park advertised "excellent alleys, kept in first class condition, with an attendant always in charge."

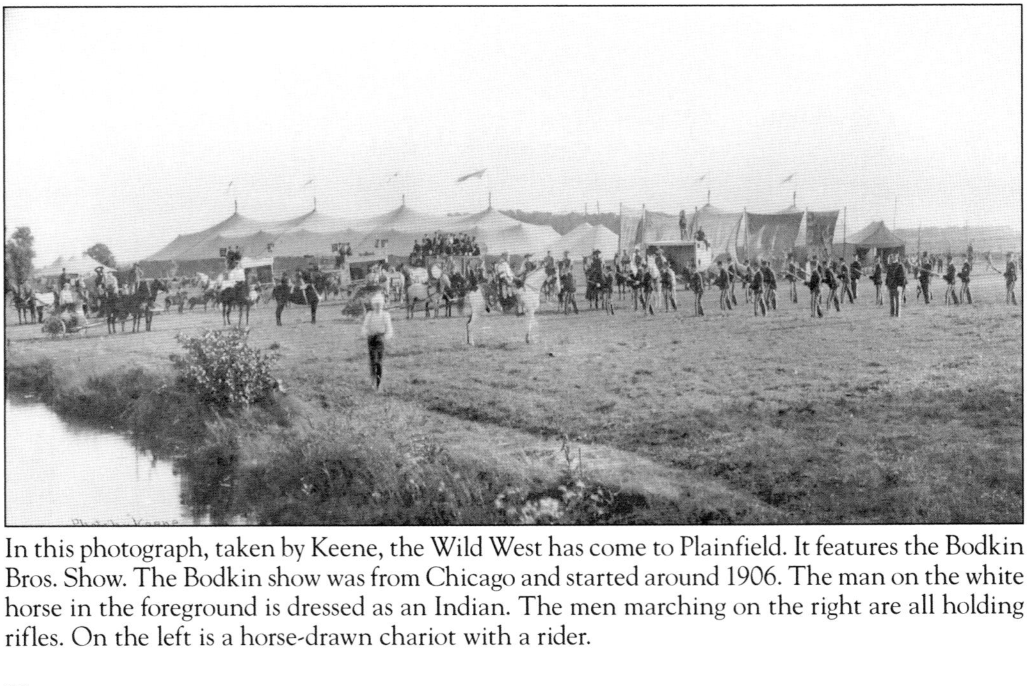

In this photograph, taken by Keene, the Wild West has come to Plainfield. It features the Bodkin Bros. Show. The Bodkin show was from Chicago and started around 1906. The man on the white horse in the foreground is dressed as an Indian. The men marching on the right are all holding rifles. On the left is a horse-drawn chariot with a rider.

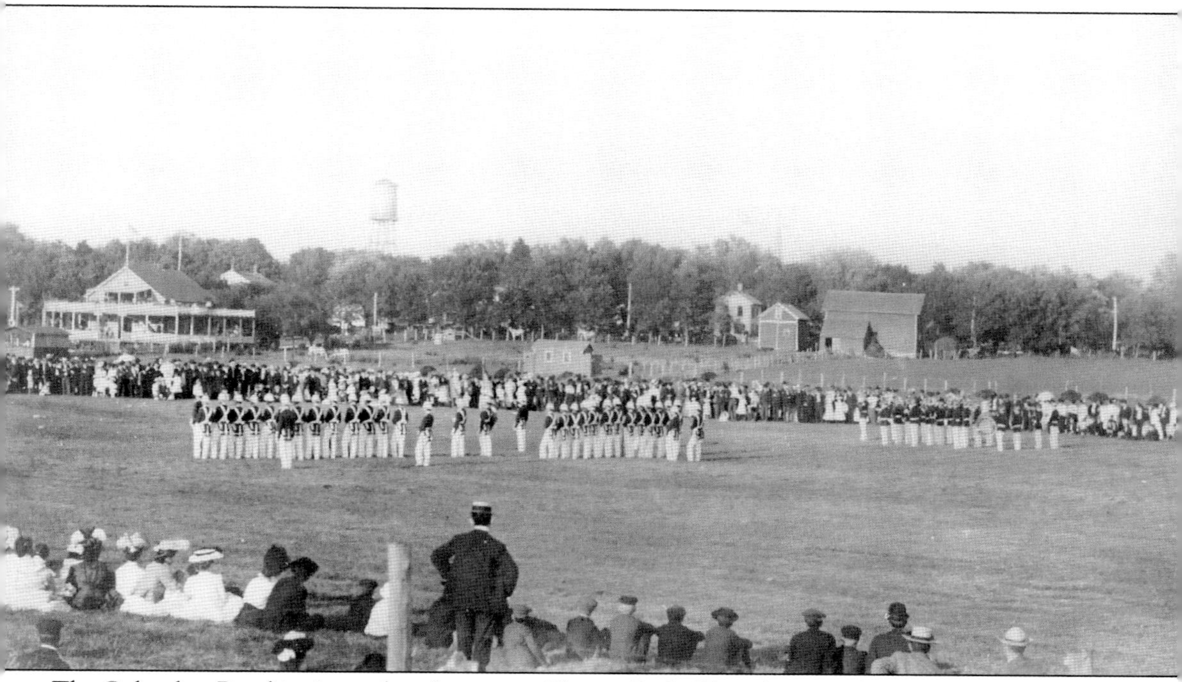

The Columbus Band is pictured performing at Electric Park. This photograph was taken looking east toward downtown with the water tower in the background. The large, two-story building on the left is the park's restaurant. On the right are a farmhouse, large barns, and a few horses grazing in the pasture. Electric Park was situated within the actual village of Plainfield. One ad in an Electric Park brochure reads, "The town of Plainfield is beautifully laid out and inhabited by a class of people who has secured a competence in agriculture and mercantile pursuits. They have selected Plainfield as the most beautiful and in all respects the most enjoyable to live. There are five churches, one of which is supplied with a chime of bells, said to be the finest in the state."

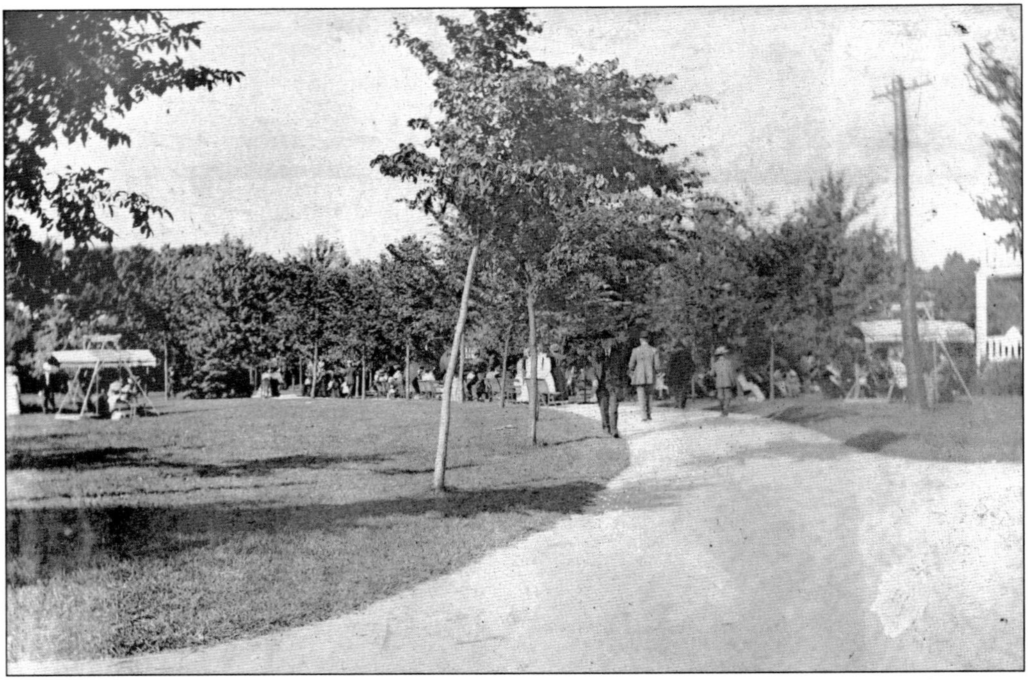

Photographs of center walkways in Electric Park are rare. Photographers often snapped pictures of boaters and bathers in the river, but they rarely captured the internal section of the park. According to an early Electric Park brochure, the park had "giant elm and maple trees of original forest growth, affording the most inviting resting places along the sloping river banks, and the disciples of Izaak Walton may reveal in such piscatorial pleasures as few localities can offer." In 1923, the park was sold. The east side, where the cottages were located, was divided into lots and sold. In the 1930s, roller-skating began in the auditorium and continued for decades. The auditorium was on the west side of the river.

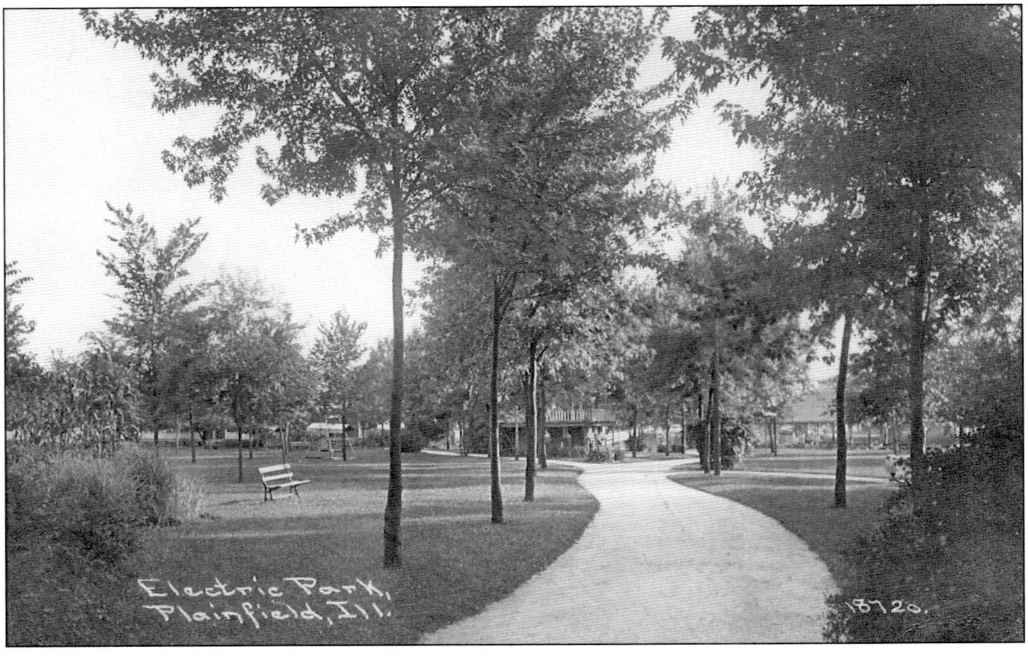

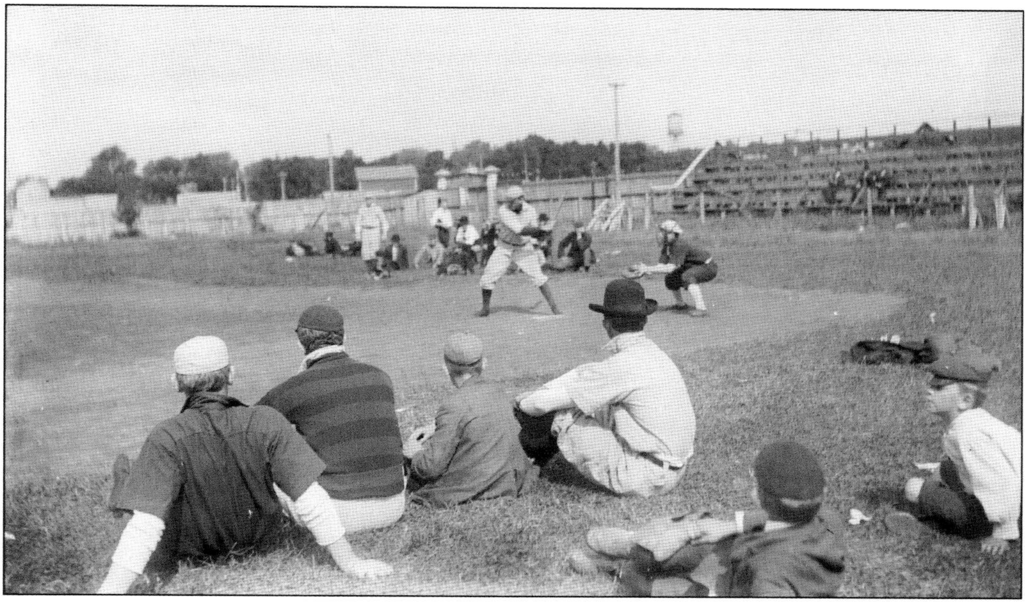

An Electric Park program advertises: "The Park is provided with an excellent ball park with a large grandstand and one-sixth mile athletic track, and thoroughly equipped for all athletic sports. This feature of the park attracts a good many interesting events and assists materially in making up the season's program. Students from high schools in all cities of northern Illinois meet here for their annual competitive events." Above, these boys are wearing their various hats and enjoying a game at the park. Below, the grandstands are filled with spectators for this baseball game at the park. The auditorium is pictured in the background.

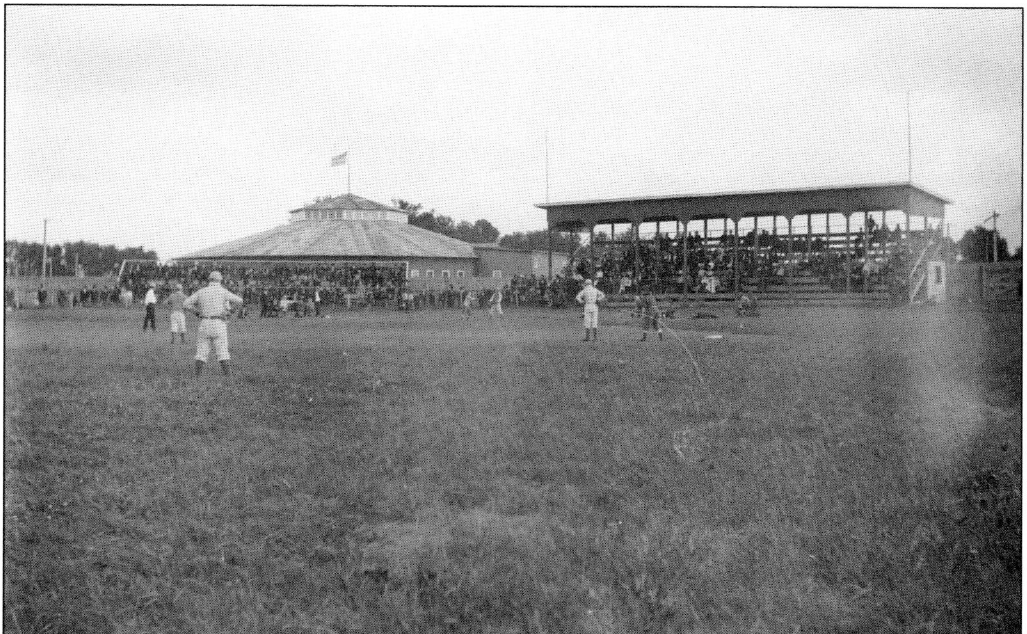

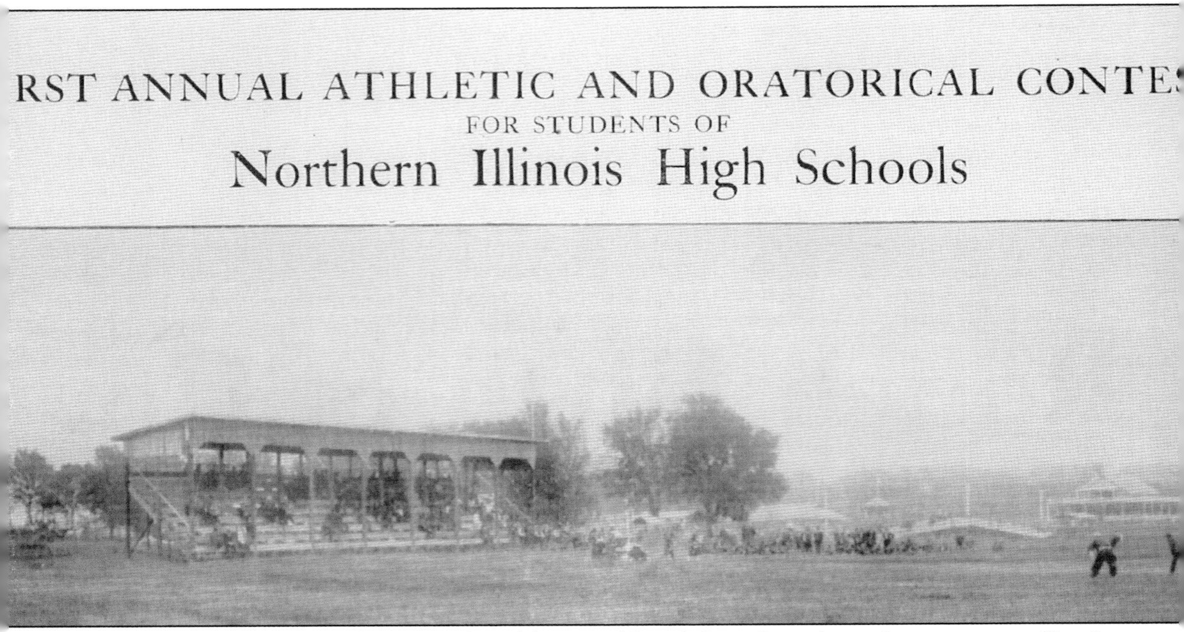

This postcard of the Electric Park Athletic Field and Grandstand was for a contest offered to students of high schools in northern Illinois in 1906. The event included not only a picnic and athletic contest in the afternoon, but also an oratorical and elocutionary contest at the new, $10,000 auditorium in the evening. It mentions that a large number of medals will be awarded. The athletic field track was one sixth of a mile long. Students from various high schools in northern Illinois met annually at Electric Park for many years to compete in athletic events. The participants could travel by automobile or by electric railway to the park. The railway offered travel to Joliet every half hour on weekends and hourly on weekdays.

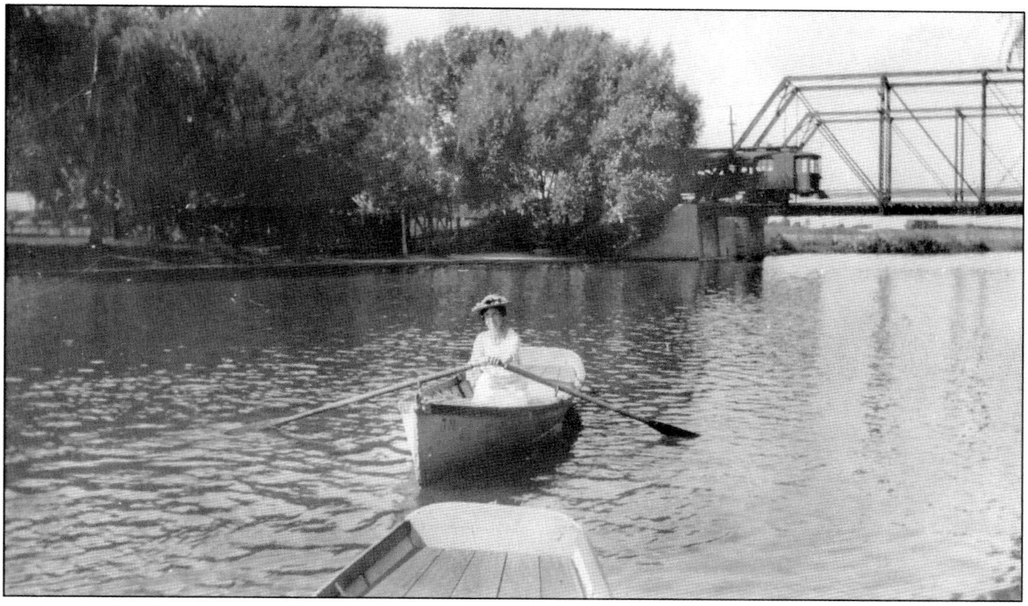

This lady in her fancy, flowered hat is rowing boat no. 59 down the DuPage River. The trolley train is just passing over the river on the bridge. An early Electric Park brochure advertises safe boating and bathing due to the uniform depth of the DuPage River. It was only four to five feet, which was perfectly safe for ladies and children. It advertised, "In four years since the opening of the park, not an accident of any kind has happened on the river. It is a veritable paradise for children. They take care of themselves and get rosy cheeks and are so perfectly well to enjoy themselves to the very limit every hour they are awake."

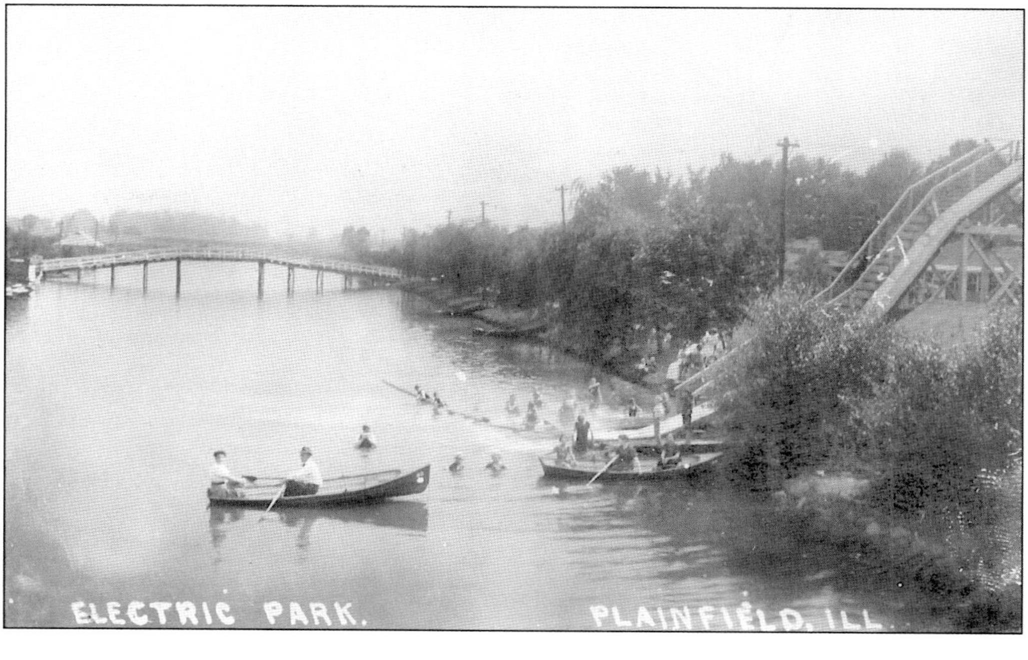

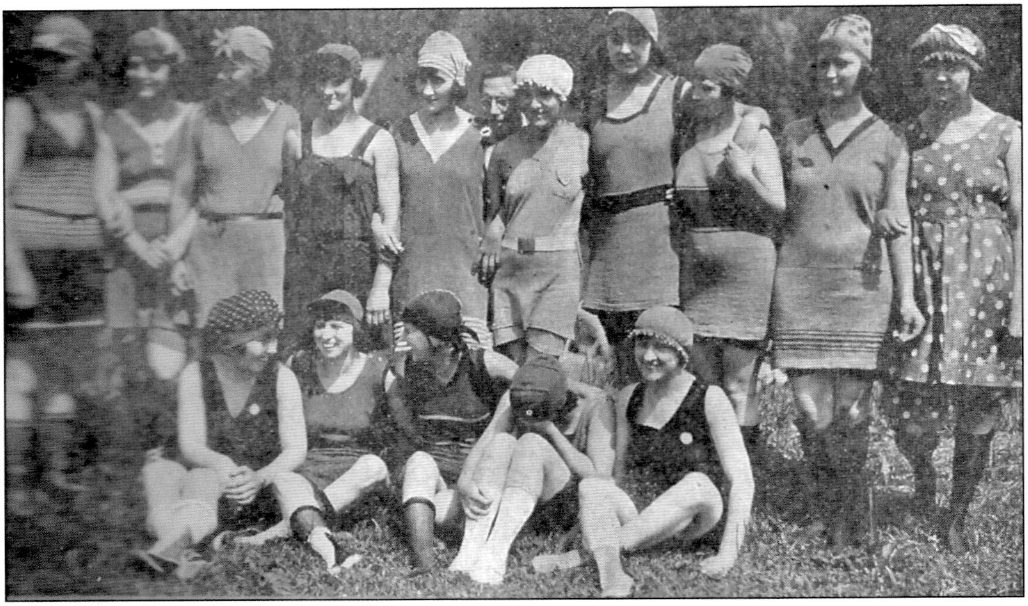

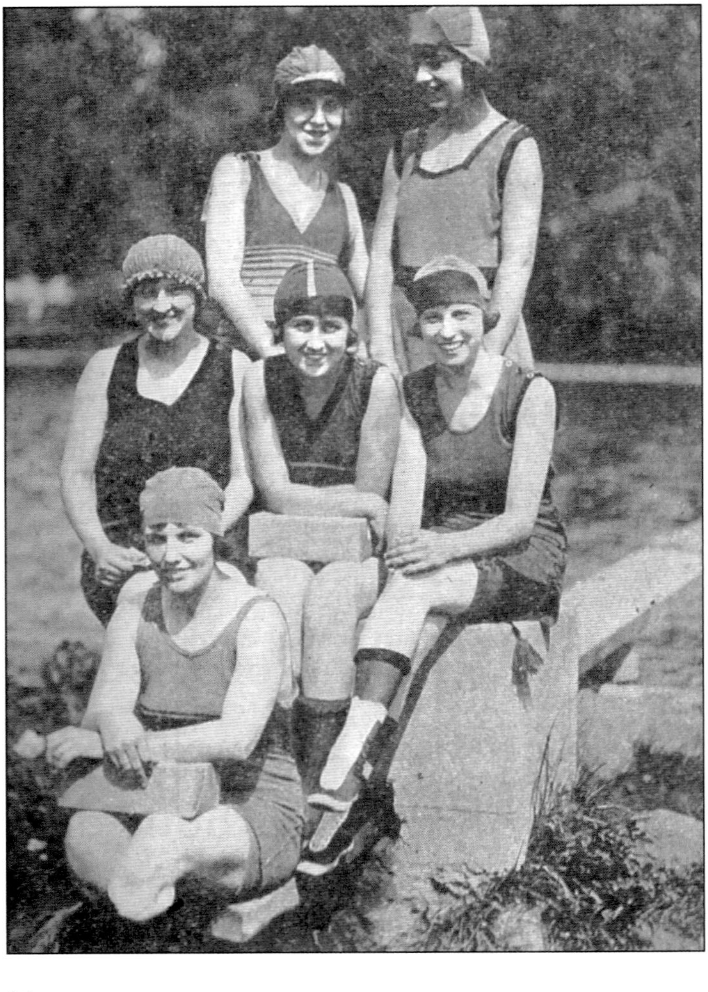

These bathing beauties were part of the Gerlach Barklow Calendar Company's 13th Annual Outing—an employee's picnic—at Electric Park. They were the entrants in the Bathing Girls Parade at the park on July 24, 1920. The calendar company mentioned in its newsletter that everyone at the picnic was on hand for the parade to pass judgment. First and second prizes were awarded for the bathing parade. During the evening of the picnic, girls and boys enjoyed dancing until the last trolley car left at 11:00 p.m. The Gerlach Barklow Calendar Company was a large employer in Joliet that had its picnic at Electric Park each year.

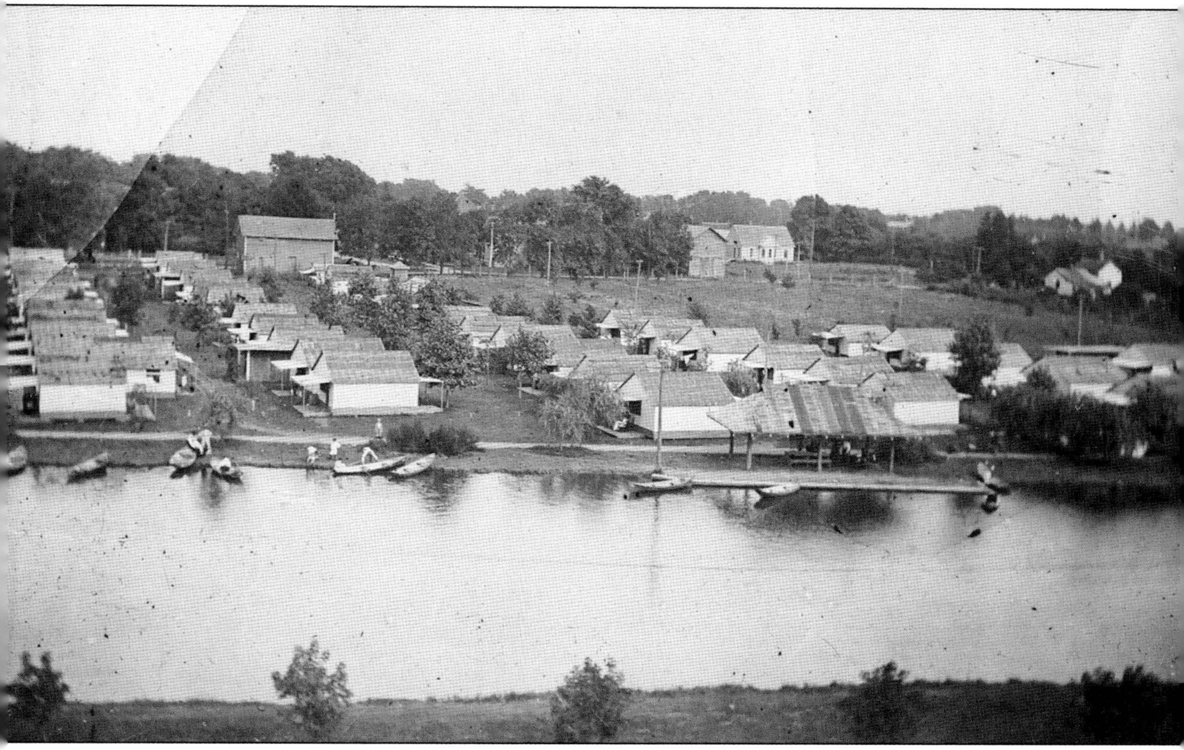

This glass negative is cracked in the upper left of this great bird's-eye view photograph of the cottages looking east across the DuPage River. The Electric Park program's description of summer life at the park states, "This novel summer habitation is purely an Electric Park creation. You will not find it at any other resort and you will agree, after living in one for a season, that it is the most convenient, healthful and thoroughly satisfactory abode in which you have ever spent a summer's vacation. The canvas cottage secures to you all of the open air advantages of the tent, with all the comforts of a modern home. The canvas cottage withstands the severest of storms and brings the occupants through safe and dry." Included in the rental of a cottage were a kitchen table, a two-burner gas stove, a Welsbach light, and the cost of gas to operate for cooking as well as lighting.

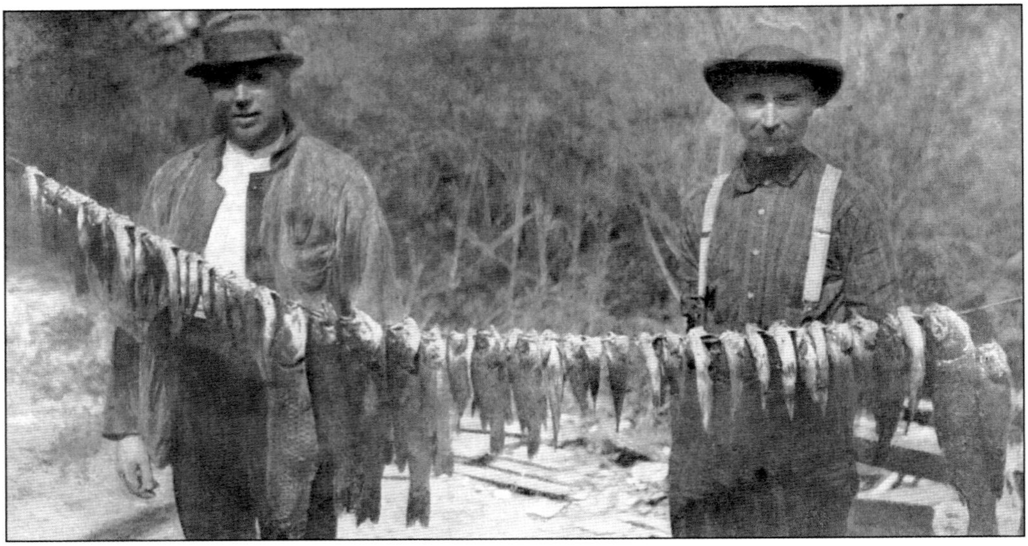

The DuPage River was noted for excellent fishing during the era of Electric Park. Rock bass, pickerel, perch, and channel cat were bountiful in the river. The park's program advertises, "The DuPage River is noted for its clear spring water and abundance of game fish. In the first place, a stream or body of water affording good boating, bathing and fishing is absolutely essential." The above c. 1906 photograph indicate how good the fishing was at Electric Park; this is not too bad for an afternoon's catch. In the photograph below, the family is enjoying the day fishing near the dam. The man is wearing a suit, and the woman is wearing a long, white dress and a flowered hat as the children watch him fish.

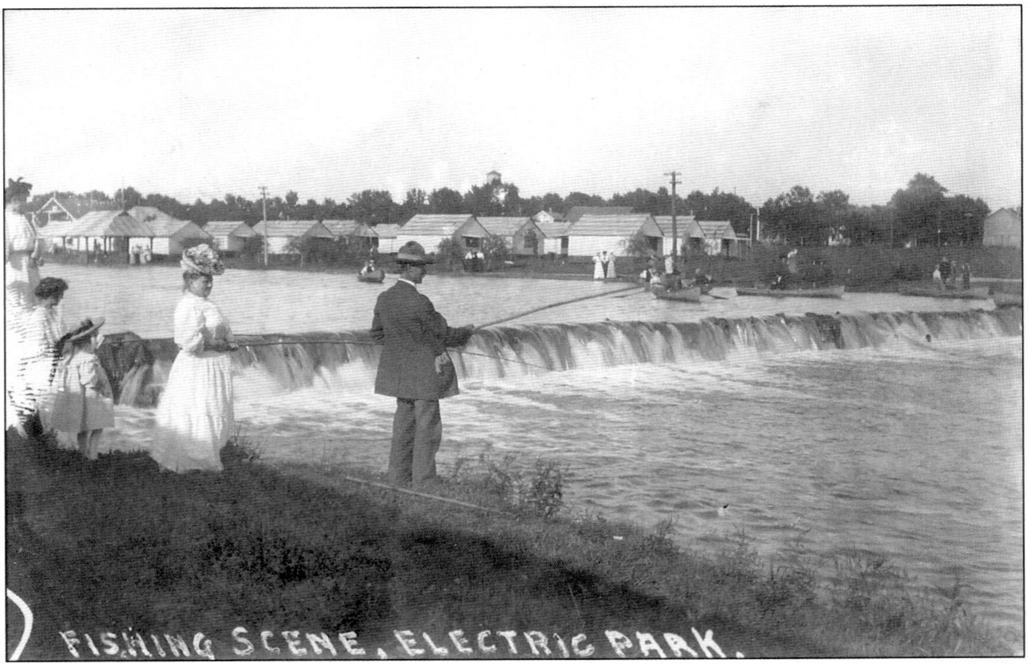

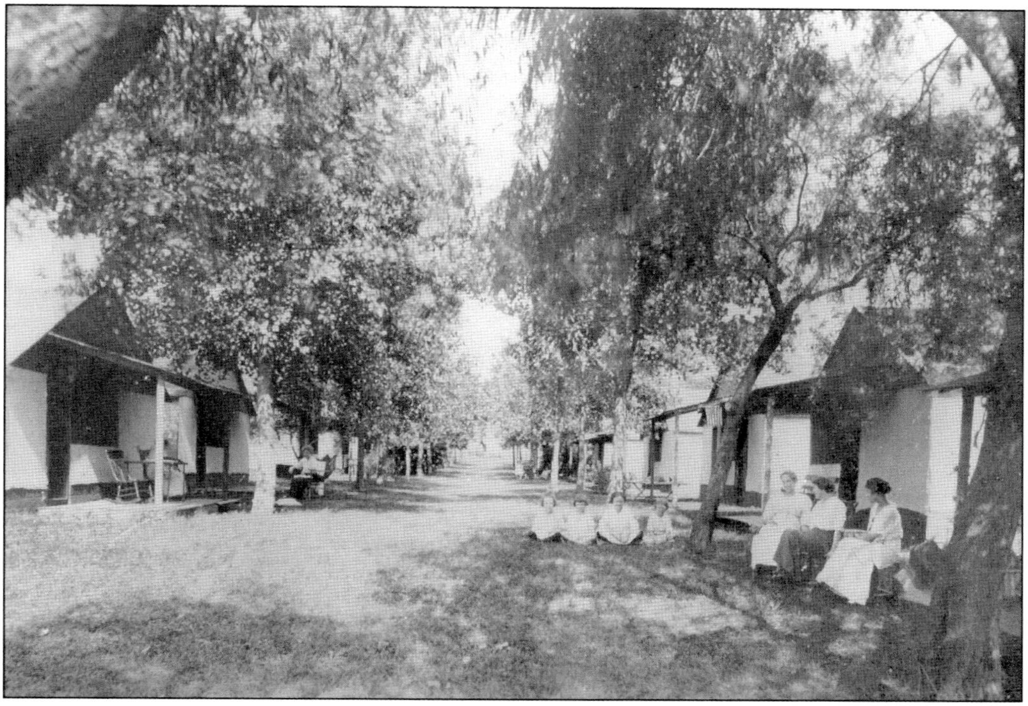

The cottages came in three sizes, usually divided into two, four, and six rooms. In a six-room cottage, there was a hall running through the middle, and the rear portion of the cottage was a dining room. There were 6-by-12-foot canvas awnings over both the front and rear doors, with a wooden platform under them. Each cottage was provided with burlap curtains that served as room dividers, as desired by the occupants.

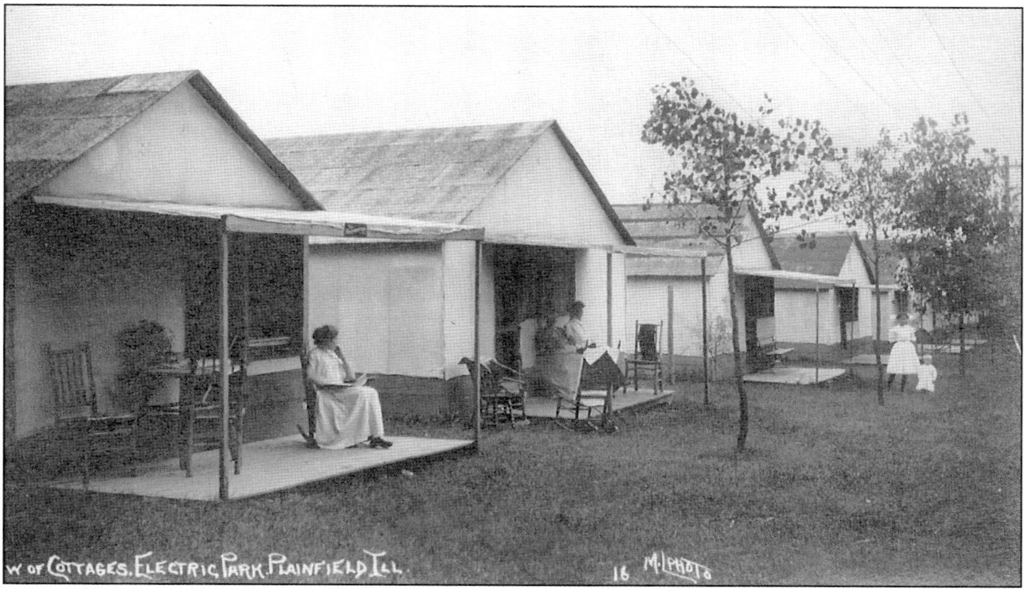

The cottages did not have running water. Near the rear door of each cottage was a hydrant of artesian water. The internal sink was described at the time as a slop sink and was connected to a sewer system. The sanitary toilet rooms for both ladies and gentlemen were distributed around the park grounds to make them convenient for all the cottages.

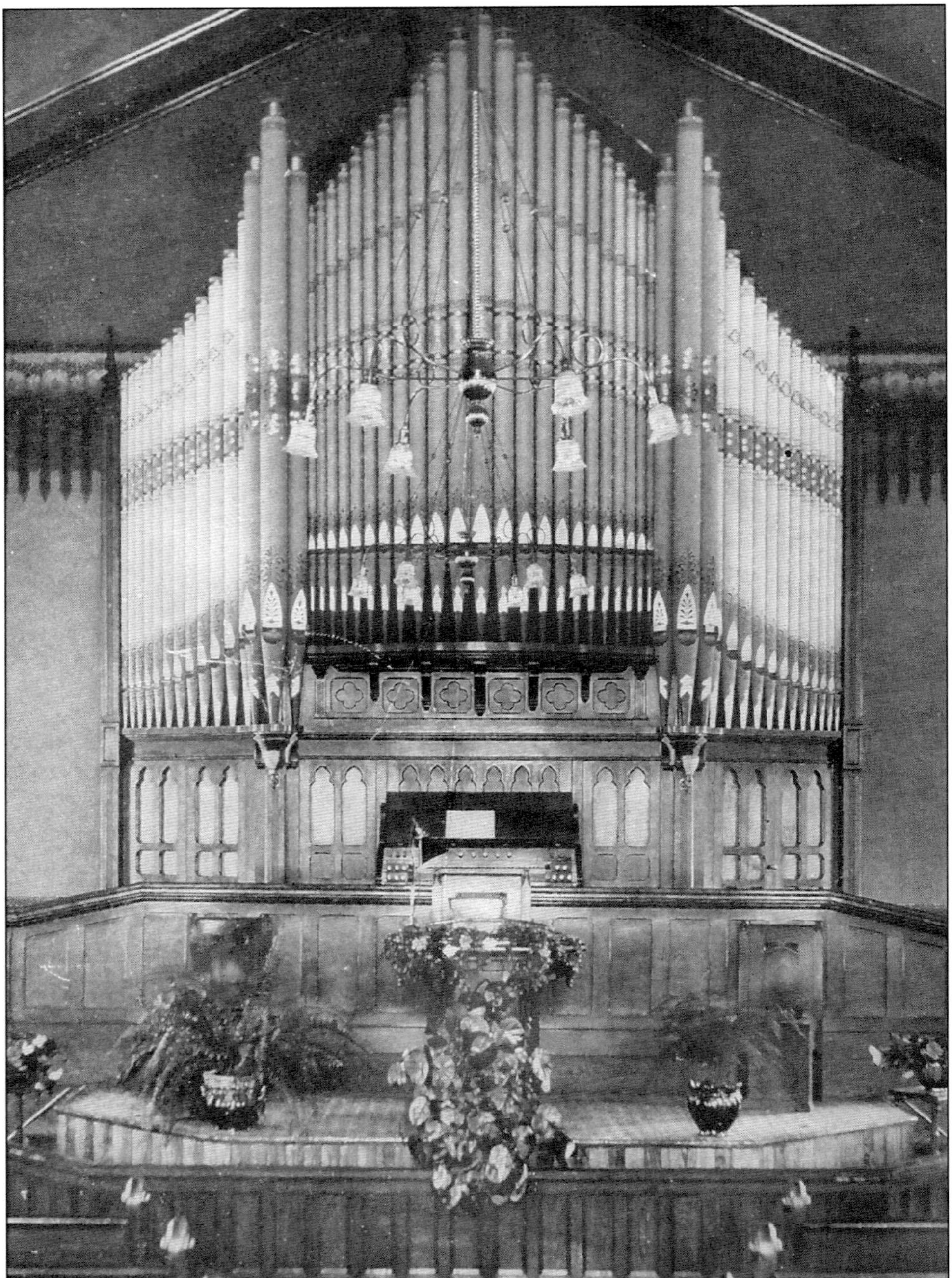

The grand pipe organ inside the auditorium was built at a cost of $2,500. It was manufactured by the Hinners Organ Company of Pekin, Illinois. The auditorium could seat up to 3,500 and had a stage for entertainment. The structure was made of steel and was 135 feet in diameter. This made an ideal setting for a Chautauqua to come to the park. The 1909 Chautauqua ran for nine days at Electric Park, with the cost of adult season tickets at $1.50 for all nine days. Adult admission for a day was 25¢. One could also buy one single-day ticket for $2.75, which allowed 18 admissions on that one ticket. Children's season tickets were 75¢, and a single-day admission for a child was 15¢.

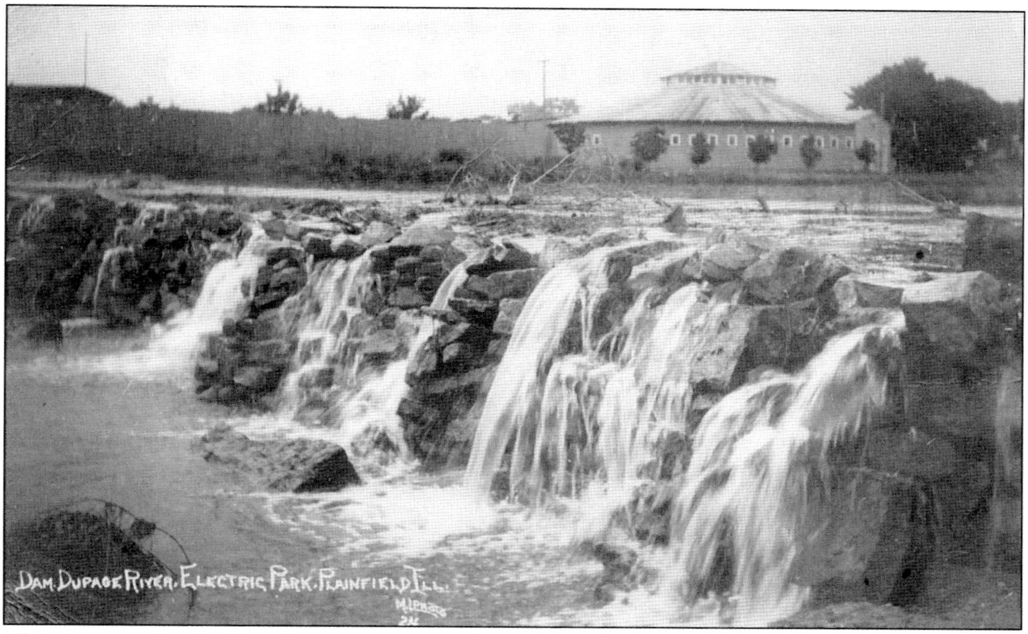

This dam on the DuPage River was across from the auditorium at Electric Park. It was located south of Lockport Street. The dam kept a consistent water level of around five feet, affording park visitors use of the river for such activities as swimming, boating, and fishing.

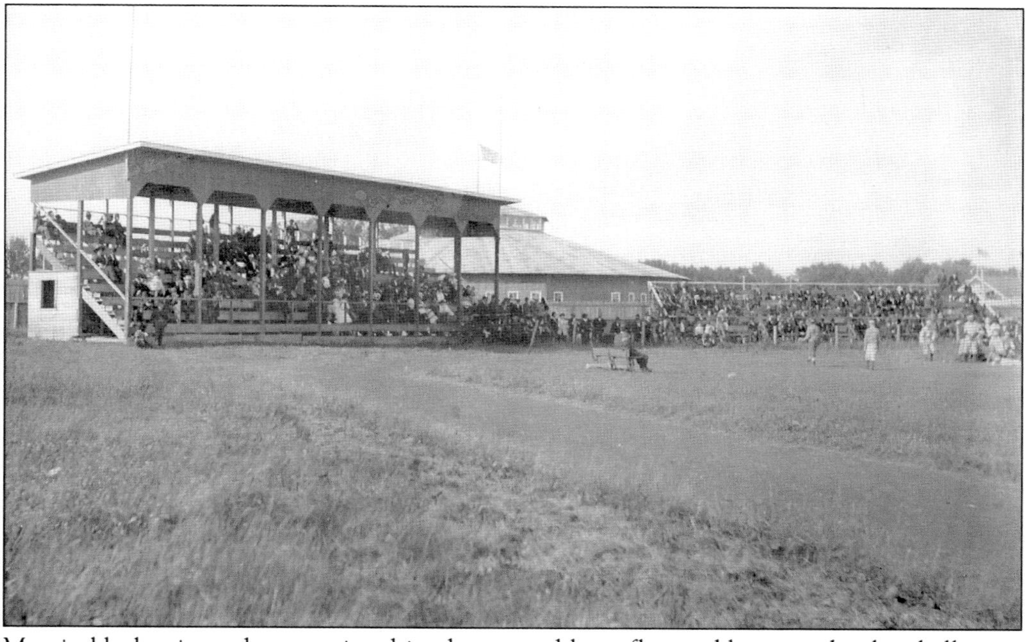

Men in black suits and women in white dresses and large flowered hats watch a baseball game at Electric Park. The grandstands are full, as the US flag flies high at the top of the auditorium behind the baseball field. Chicago Cubs pitcher George Pierce lived in Plainfield and pitched ball at Electric Park after leaving the major leagues. He pitched for the Cubs from 1912–1915. Pierce was sold to the Cardinals in 1916.

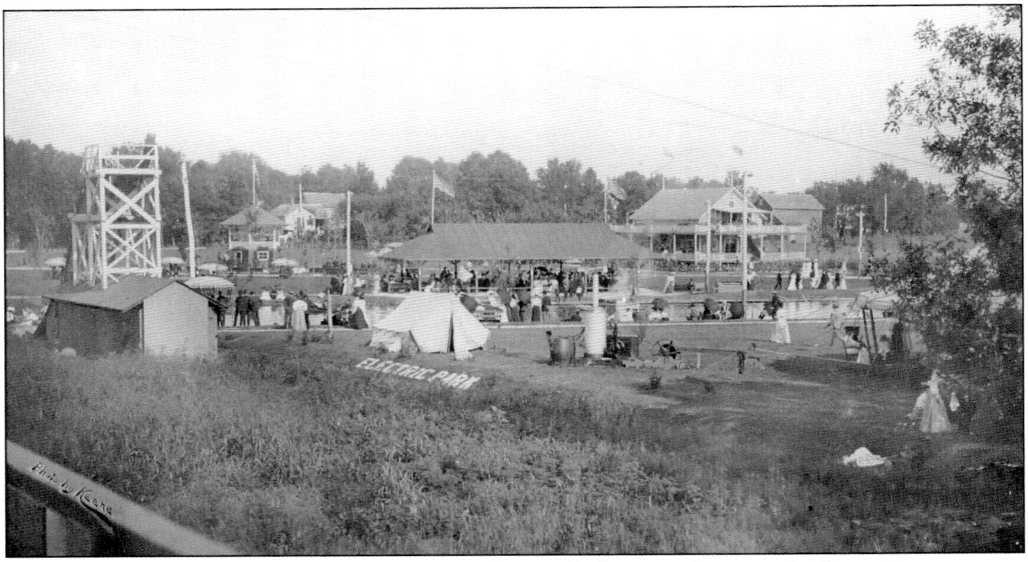

In the above photograph, the name Electric Park is spelled out on the ground. The trolley company advertised the park as "just such a spot, as you wished for nearby, where the wife and babies can conveniently hike, escape the sweltering rays of the midsummer sky, and welcome tired father as he comes home every night." Often, the husband would take the trolley to work each day while the family stayed at the park. The trolley company boasted, "It is a short ride from the smoky atmosphere of the great city of Chicago in just ninety minutes to a trip back in nature in one of the prettiest rural spots to be found in this western county. You will be along the grassy banks of the spring fed waters of the historic DuPage River, inviting you to a refreshing plunge beneath its gently rippling surface."

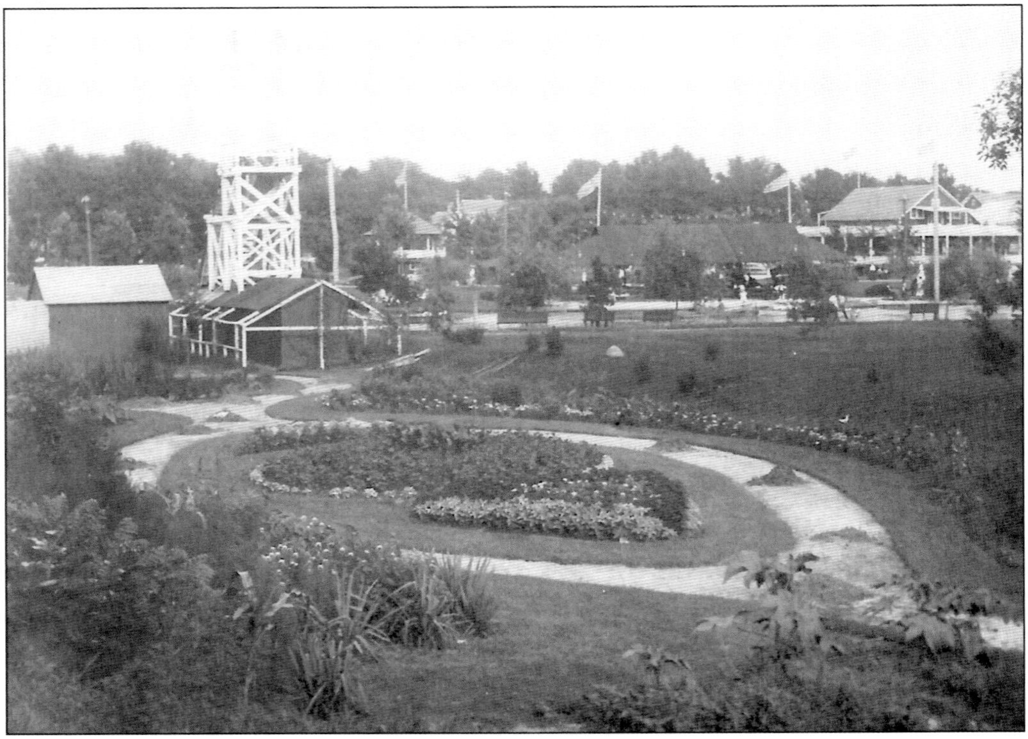

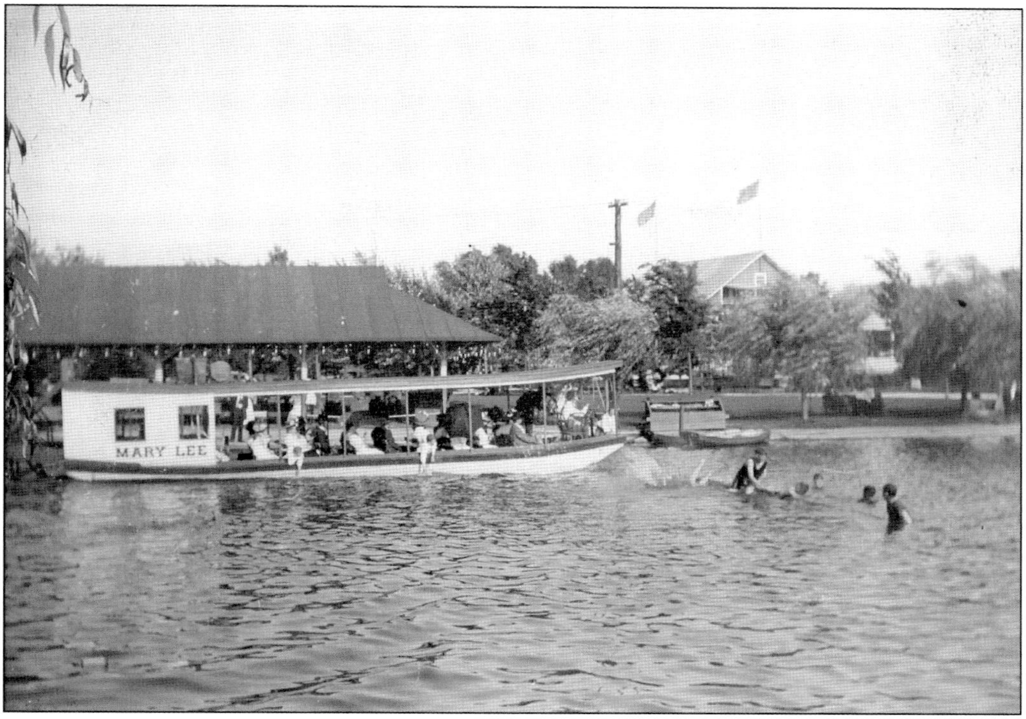

The *Mary Lee* paddleboat would take park visitors up and down the DuPage River while they relaxed after a busy day at the park. Bathers would often be next to the paddleboat as it passed by. The park program states, "The children could frolic in the water practically unattended, hours at a time, and nearly all learned to swim in the first season at the park. Parents soon discover there is no occasion for anxiety on account of the water, and this fact contributes materially to the perfect enjoyment of Electric Park."

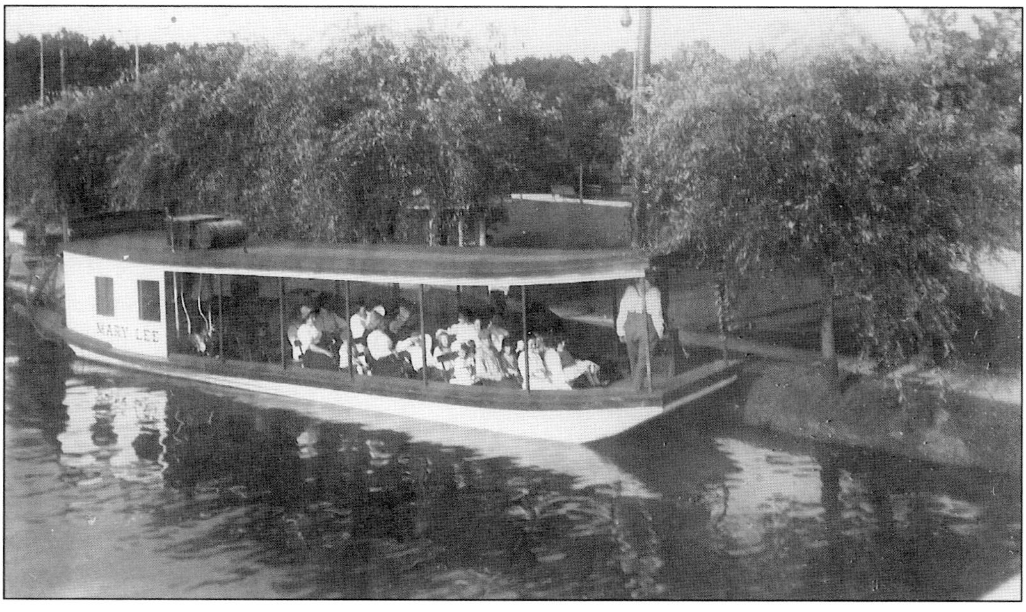

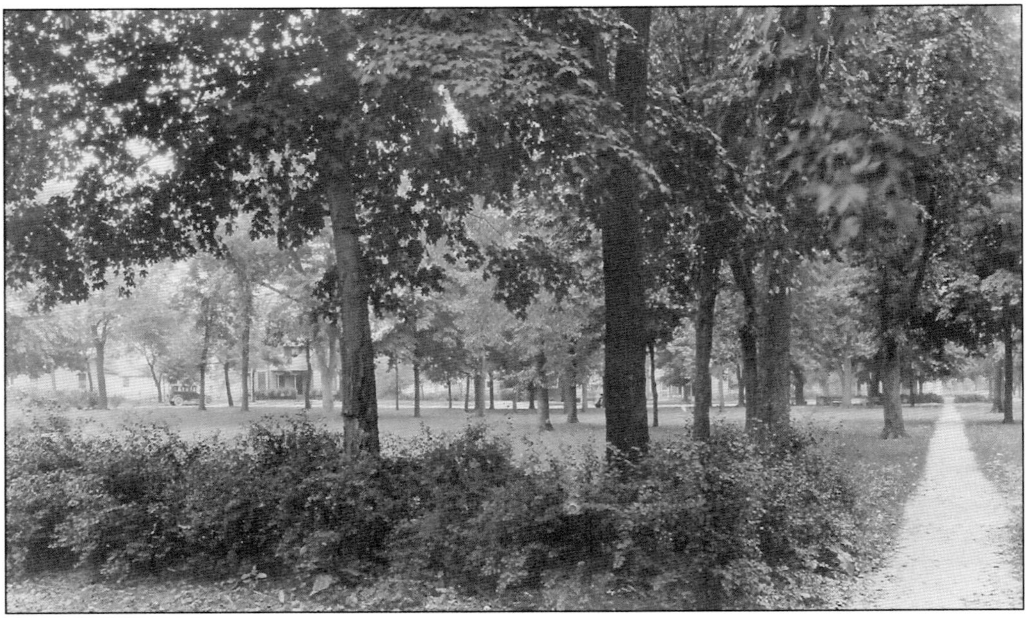

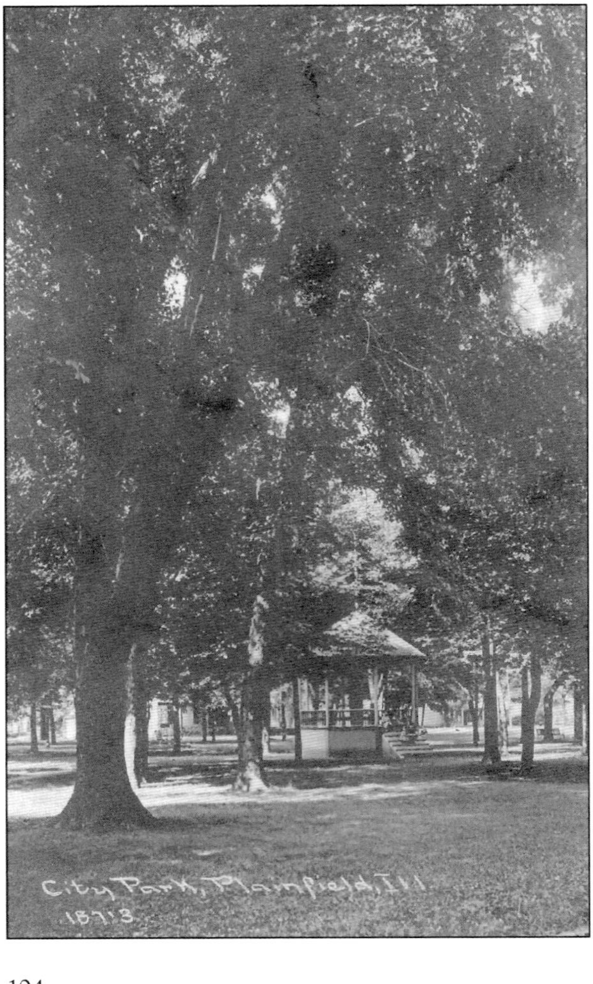

The Village Green Park is located one block south of Lockport Street in the middle of downtown. Chester Ingersoll platted the south side of town in 1834. He donated the land that the park is on with the stipulation that no buildings could be placed on it. On the back of the real-photo postcard at left, the sender writes, "I am now at Plainfield. Will stay two weeks, then it will be back to the grind. Frankie is wild out here. It is pretty here, but so lonesome. This park is across the street from grandpa's house."

Four

Schools and Churches

Plainfield has always had the good fortune to be well supplied with churches. The Methodists erected a church in 1836 and later built a fine, large stone structure in 1868. The Baptist Society and Congregational Society were both organized in 1834, while the Evangelist Church was erected in 1855. The Universalists soon followed, building their church in 1868. This structure was purchased by St Mary's Catholic Church of Joliet in 1908. A new Catholic church was built on Route 59 in 1971 and would be rebuilt after the 1990 tornado. In the early days, Plainfield was often designated as the "Village of Churches."

Plainfield has also been known since the 1830s for its good schools. The first school was held in a log cabin along Division Street. The village and township had many schools in the early days, consolidating into Plainfield District No. 202 in 1920. In 1876, the township and village schools recorded 340 students, with 445 being documented in 1906. In 1990, District 202 reported about 3,500 students. In 2011–2012, the district reported that it served 28,910 students from a 64-square-mile area, making it the fourth-largest school district in Illinois. Plainfield District 202 has 30 schools, including 17 elementary schools, seven middle schools, four traditional high schools, an alternative school, and an early learning center.

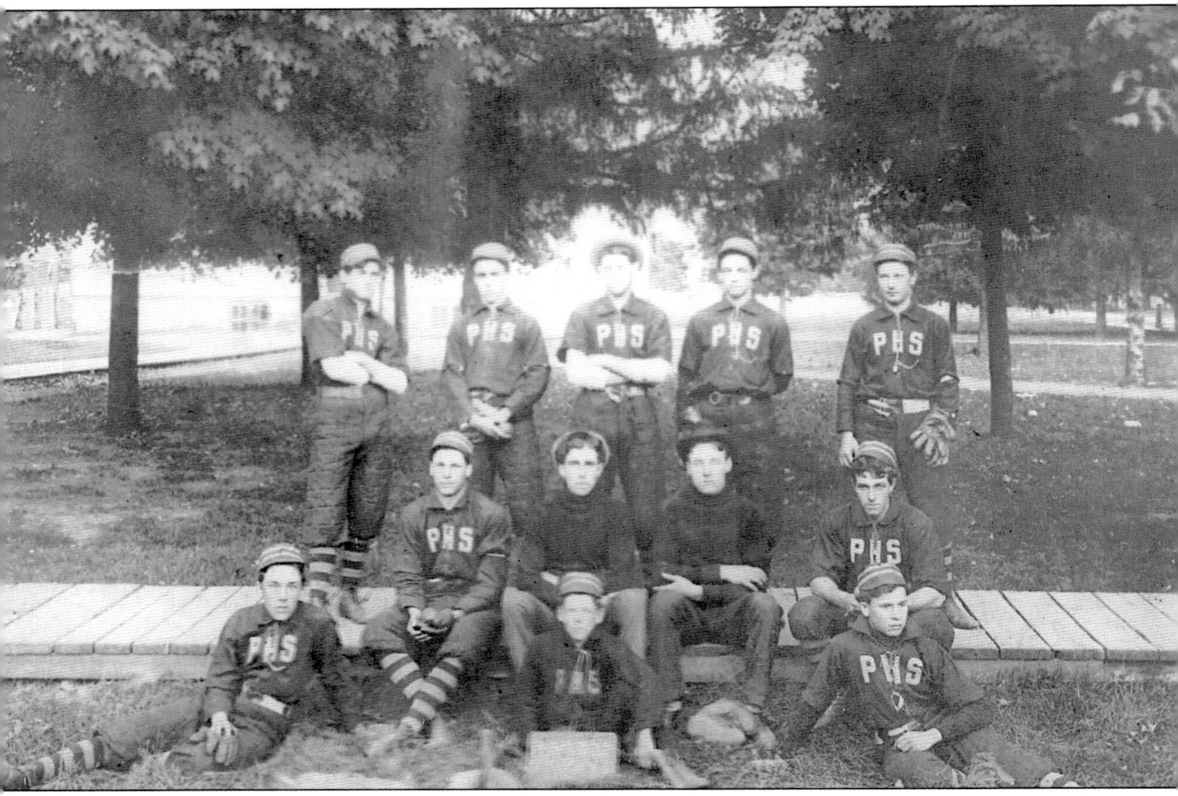

Pictured is an early Plainfield High School baseball team, with players sporting "PHS" across their shirts as well as some very fashionable striped stockings. Pictured are, in no particular order, (on the ground) Warren Klett, mascot Guy Overman, and Fred Pratt; (on the sidewalk) ? Schwartz, Clayton Smith, Clyde Essington, and Harry Spangler; (standing) Frank Boughton, Floyd Worst, Ed Spangler, John Pennington, and George Parker. The school is in the background behind the players. The White School, as it was called, was located at Lockport and Division Streets. It opened in 1882 and housed both grade school and high school students. In 1915, a brick high school was built next door to the White School on the same property.

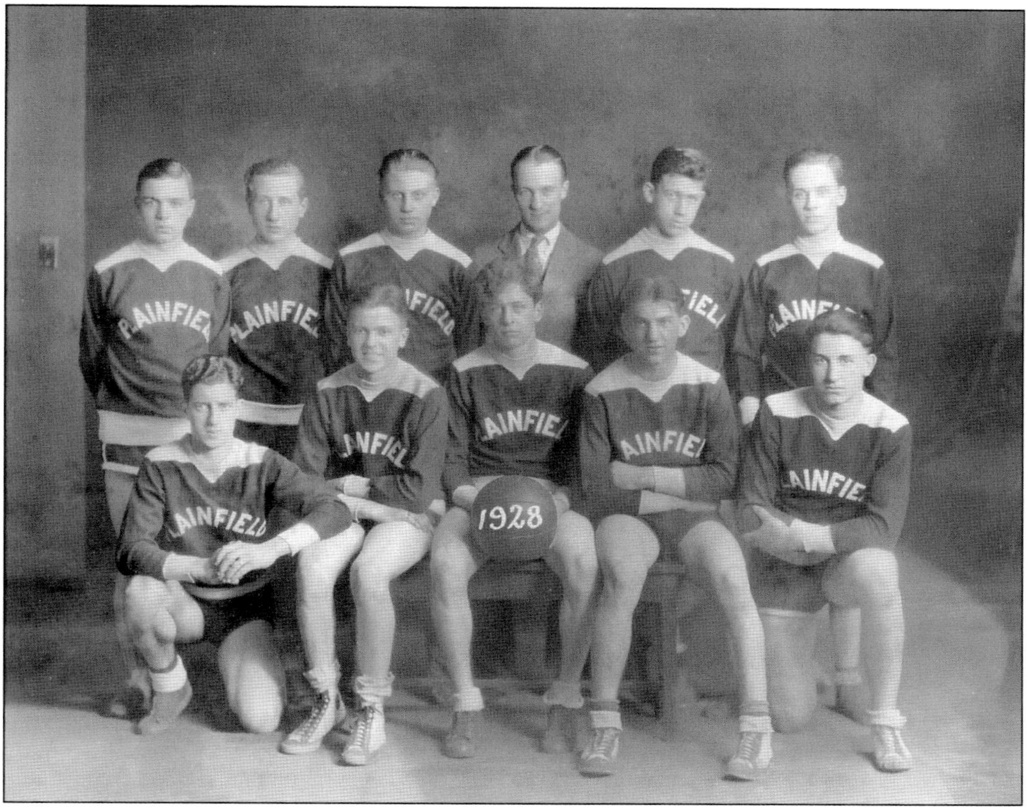

Ready for action, the 1928 Plainfield High School basketball team is pictured here. In 1914, the first Plainfield High School boys' basketball team was organized and coached by a Mr. Bassler, the superintendent from 1913–1919. In 1921, a football team was organized. On October 29, 1921, the football team won a game by a score of 68-0 over Aurora East High School. The first boys' wrestling program was not introduced until 1963. Below is an early Plainfield High School Wildcat patch. The wildcat is still the mascot of Plainfield Central High School.

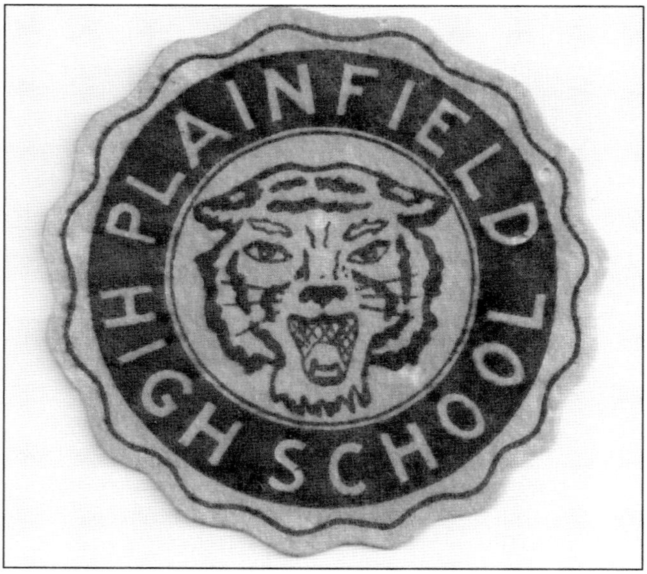

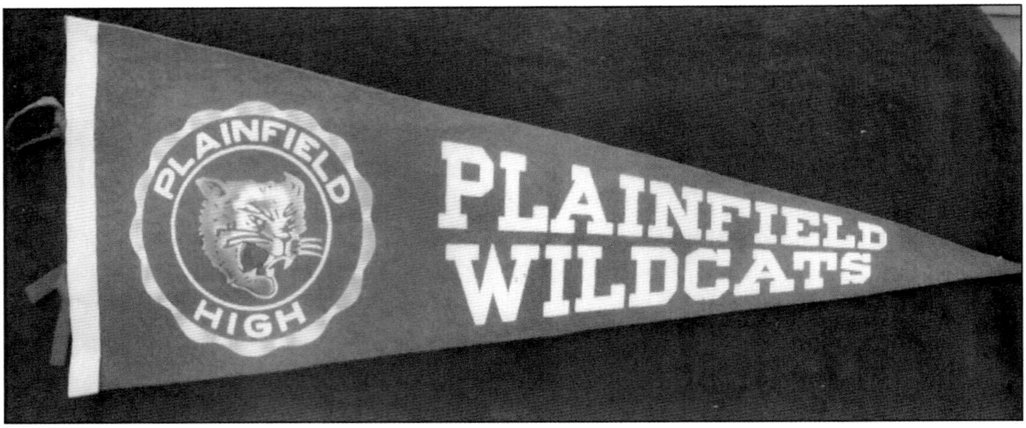

Pictured are early Plainfield High School Wildcat pennants. The first Plainfield High School homecoming was held in October 1952, with the theme "School Days." The first homecoming queen was Anne Dodge. She was joined in the homecoming parade by May Sennitt, class of 1891, and Carrie Munroe, class of 1892. The first Plainfield homecoming king was William Pommerening, in 1969. Plainfield schools have celebrated with a very well-attended homecoming parade every year since 1952. The parade route cuts through downtown Plainfield and runs down Lockport Street.

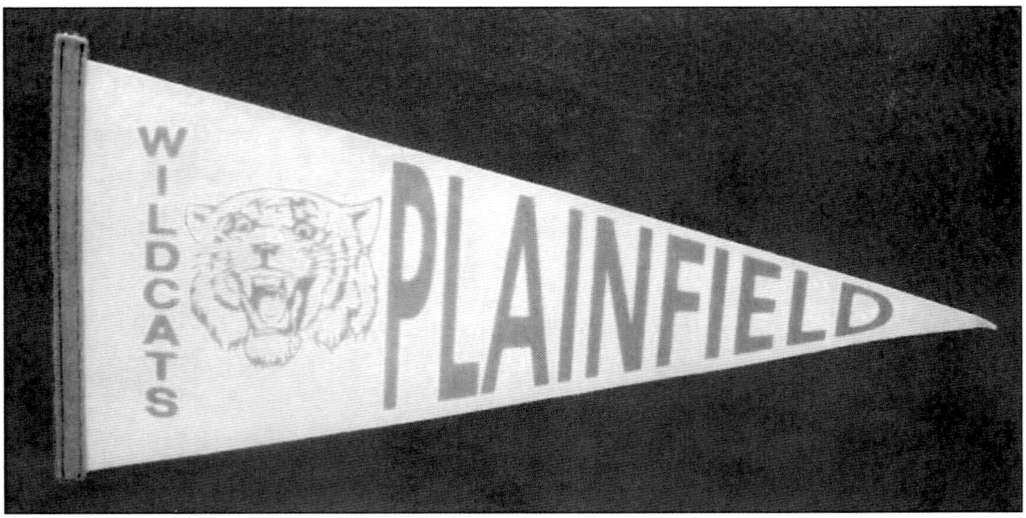

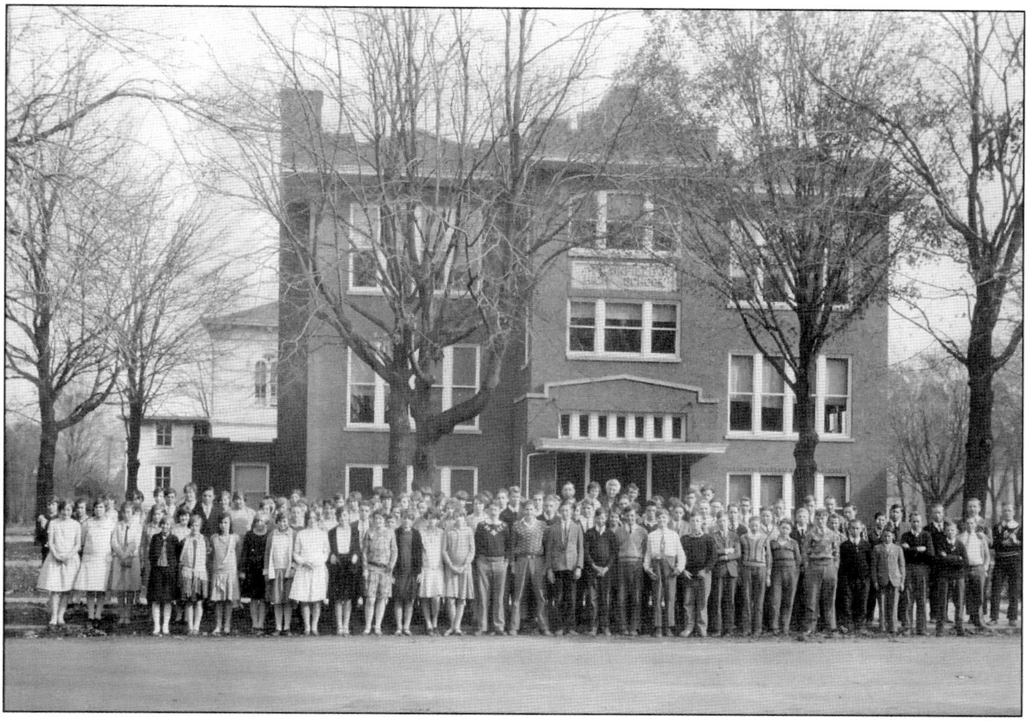

Plainfield High School and its students are pictured in this early photograph. They are facing Division Street, which is now known as Route 59. This school was built in 1915 on the corner of Division and Lockport Streets at a cost of $25,000. It had six classrooms. One room housed seventh and eighth grades. The rest of the building was used as a high school. In addition, there was a study hall, two lavatories, and a gymnasium. This school became Plainfield Junior High School in the fall of 1957. A new high school was built at 612 Commercial Street and also opened the fall of 1957. Pictured below is the high school with the White School, as it was called, next to it.

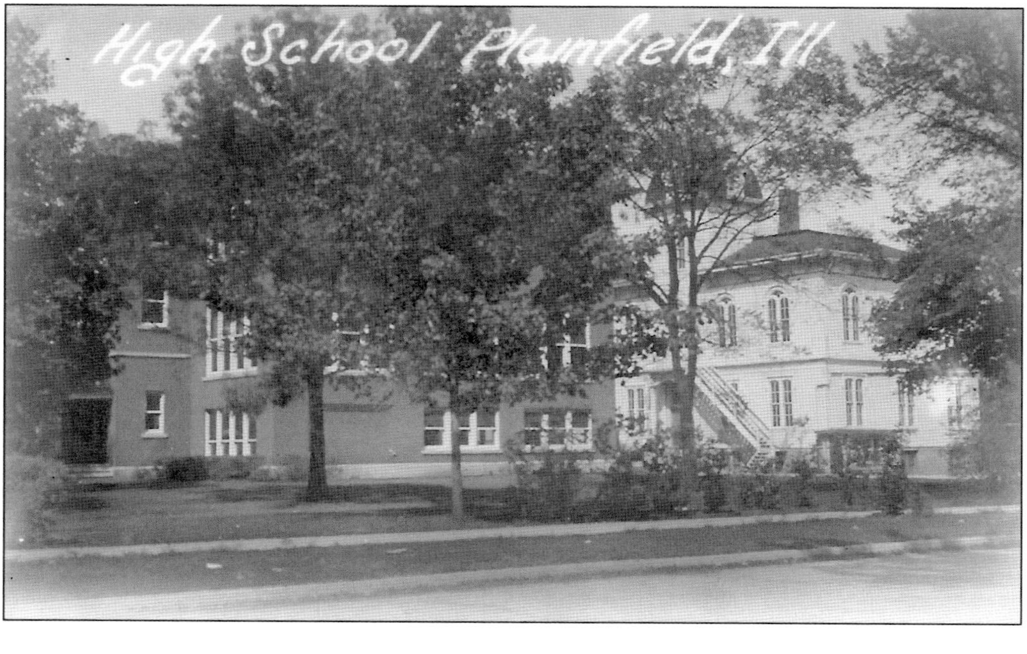

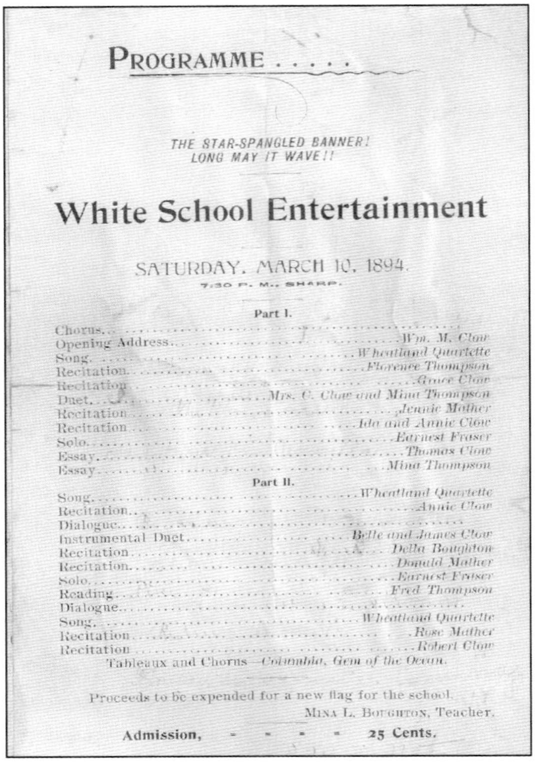

PROGRAMME . . . . .

THE STAR-SPANGLED BANNER!
LONG MAY IT WAVE!!

White School Entertainment

SATURDAY, MARCH 10, 1894.
7:30 P. M., SHARP.

Part I.

Chorus. . . . .
Opening Address. . . . . *Wm. M. Clow*
Song. . . . . *Wheatland Quartette*
Recitation. . . . . *Florence Thompson*
Recitation . . . . *Grace Clow*
Duet. . . . . *Mrs. C. Clow and Mina Thompson*
Recitation . . . . *Jennie Mather*
Recitation . . . . *Ida and Annie Clow*
Solo. . . . . *Earnest Fraser*
Essay. . . . . *Thomas Clow*
Essay . . . . *Mina Thompson*

Part II.

Song. . . . . *Wheatland Quartette*
Recitation. . . . . *Annie Clow*
Dialogue. . . . .
Instrumental Duet. . . . . *Belle and James Clow*
Recitation . . . . *Della Boughton*
Recitation. . . . . *Donald Mather*
Solo. . . . . *Earnest Fraser*
Reading. . . . . *Fred Thompson*
Dialogue. . . . .
Song. . . . . *Wheatland Quartette*
Recitation . . . . *Rose Mather*
Recitation . . . . *Robert Clow*
Tableaux and Chorus—*Columbia, Gem of the Ocean.*

Proceeds to be expended for a new flag for the school.
MINA L. BOUGHTON, Teacher.

Admission, - - - - 25 Cents.

The White School on Lockport Street was completed in 1882 at a cost of approximately $10,000. This 1894 White School entertainment program has several names from the Wheatland area. They include William Clow, Grace Clow, Ida Clow, Thomas Clow, Annie Clow, and Della Boughton. Admission was 25¢. The proceeds were to be expended for a new flag for the school. Below is a real-photo postcard showing the White School. The former school at this location was known as Plainfield College and later as the Plainfield Academy. The Plainfield Academy burned in 1873, and the White School was built on its foundations.

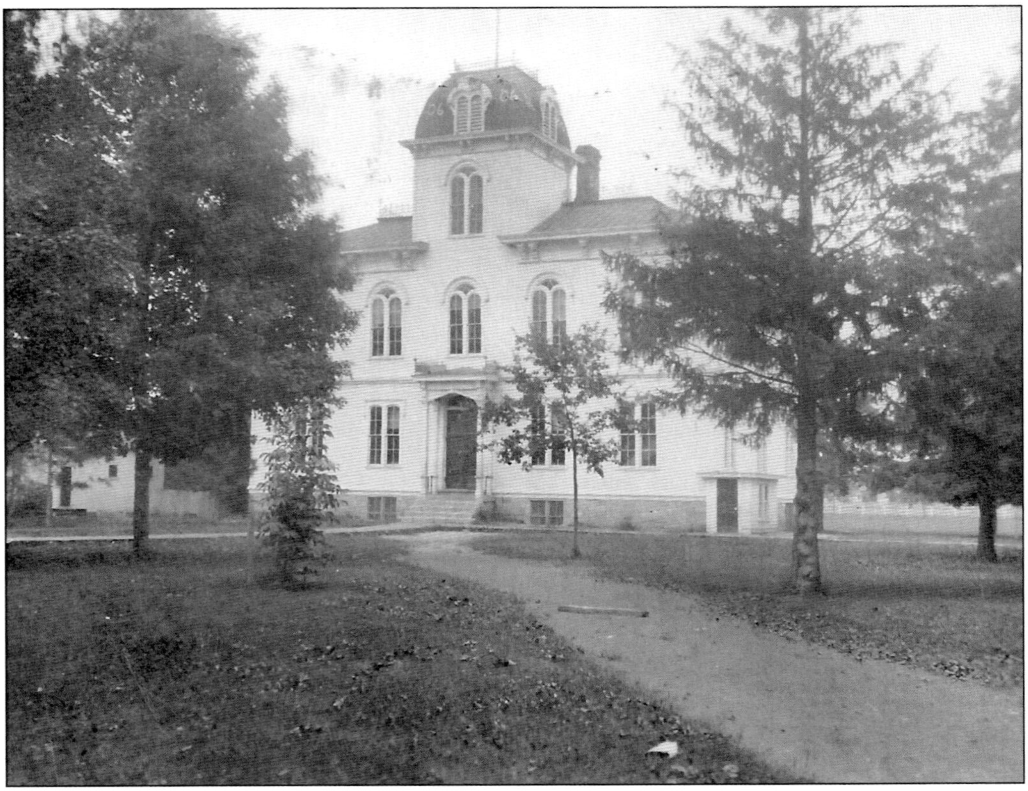

The 1896 Plainfield High School Class Day and Commencement programs held on June 22 and 23 detail the activities for both days. Both are held at the Methodist Episcopal church in Plainfield. The first high school was organized in 1888, with the first three-year class graduating in 1891. The class of 1891 consisted of three girls and one boy. Listed in the program as speakers are some well-known early Plainfield names, such as McAllister and Sennitt. The 1896 class motto, *Esse non videri*, is a Latin phrase for "To be, rather than to seem." The first four-year Plainfield High School graduating class, consisting of seven students, was in 1904.

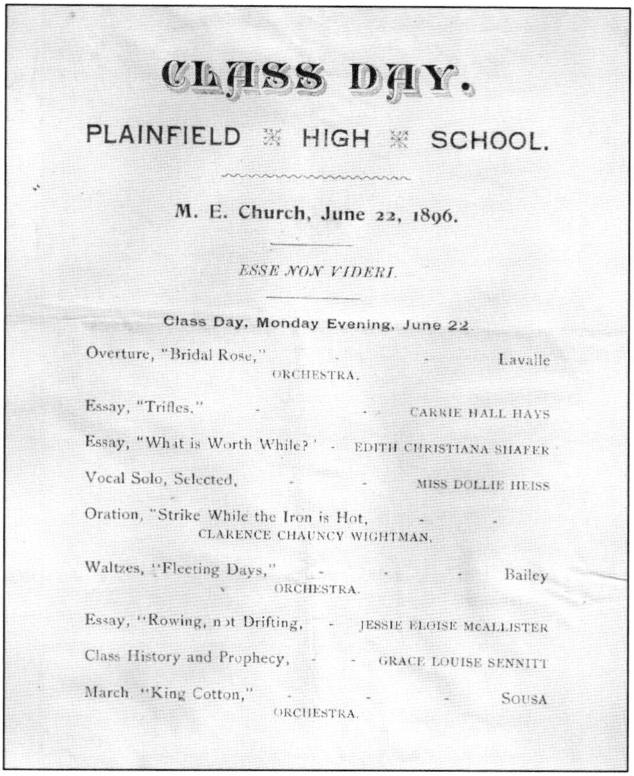

CLASS DAY.

PLAINFIELD HIGH SCHOOL.

M. E. Church, June 22, 1896.

ESSE NON VIDERI.

Class Day, Monday Evening, June 22.

Overture, "Bridal Rose," - - Lavalle
ORCHESTRA.

Essay, "Trifles." - - CARRIE HALL HAYS

Essay, "What is Worth While?" - EDITH CHRISTIANA SHAFER

Vocal Solo, Selected, - - MISS DOLLIE HEISS

Oration, "Strike While the Iron is Hot, - -
CLARENCE CHAUNCY WIGHTMAN.

Waltzes, "Fleeting Days," - - - Bailey
ORCHESTRA.

Essay, "Rowing, not Drifting, - JESSIE ELOISE McALLISTER

Class History and Prophecy, - - GRACE LOUISE SENNITT

March "King Cotton," - - - SOUSA
ORCHESTRA.

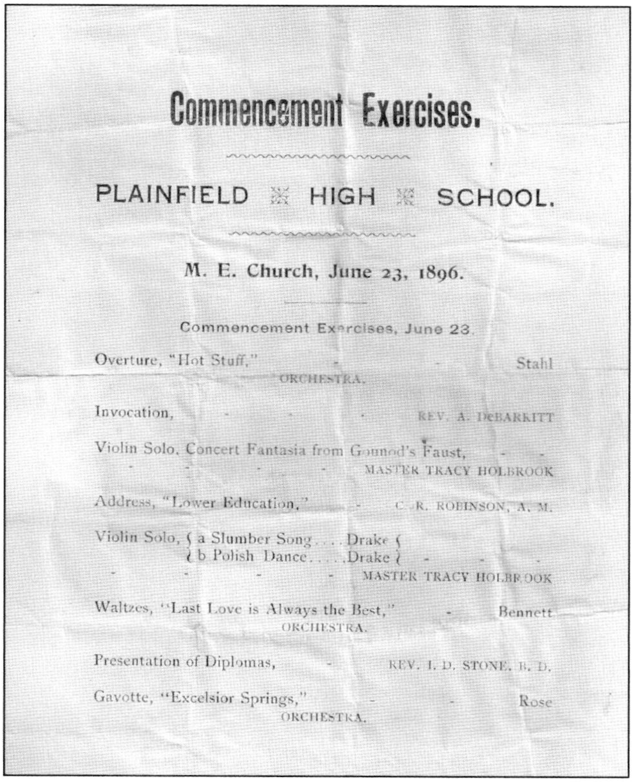

Commencement Exercises.

PLAINFIELD HIGH SCHOOL.

M. E. Church, June 23, 1896.

Commencement Exercises, June 23.

Overture, "Hot Stuff," - - Stahl
ORCHESTRA.

Invocation, - - - REV. A. DeBARRITT

Violin Solo, Concert Fantasia from Gounod's Faust, - -
- - - MASTER TRACY HOLBROOK

Address, "Lower Education," - C. R. ROBINSON, A. M.

Violin Solo, { a Slumber Song....Drake }
{ b Polish Dance....Drake } - - -
- - - - MASTER TRACY HOLBROOK

Waltzes, "Last Love is Always the Best," - Bennett
ORCHESTRA.

Presentation of Diplomas, - REV. I. D. STONE, B. D.

Gavotte, "Excelsior Springs," - - Rose
ORCHESTRA.

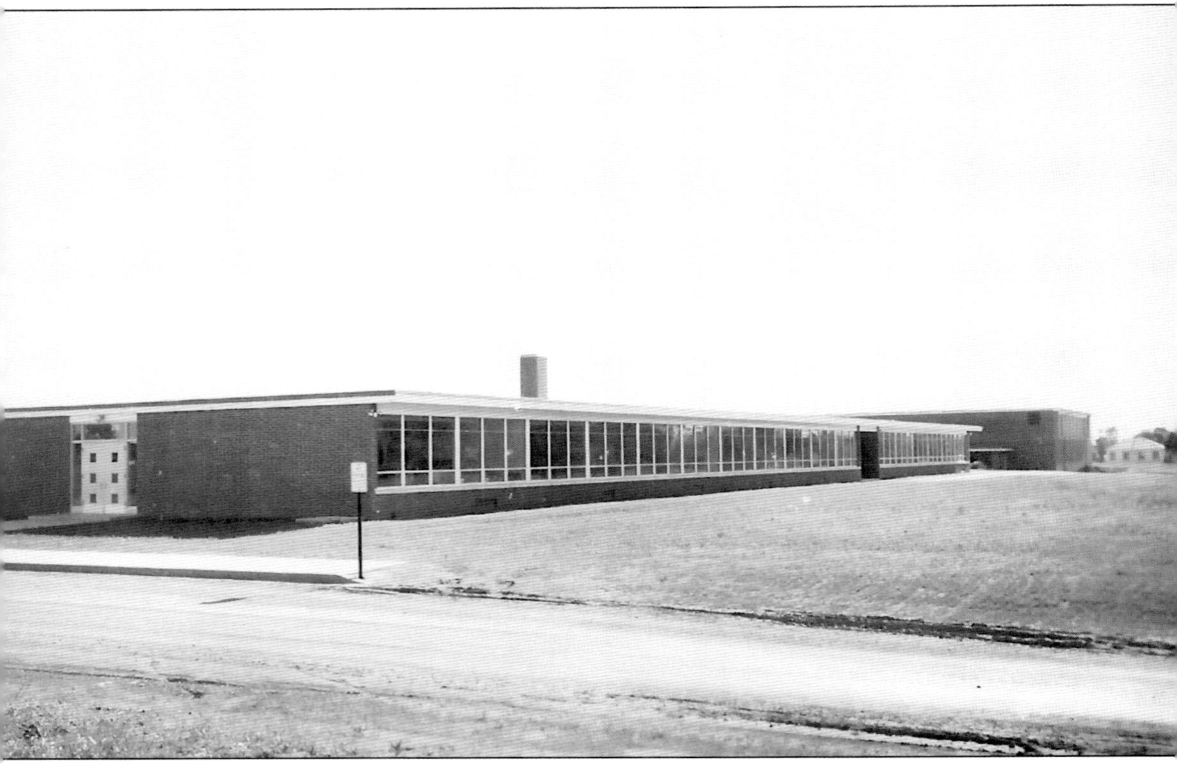

The doors of the high school on Commercial Street opened in September 1957. The 1959 *Green and White Plainfield High School Handbook* includes a "code of dress" for the students. The girls were not allowed to wear blue jeans or slacks to school; they were to wear skirts and dresses that were appropriate, have well groomed hair, and were instructed, "Do not over use cosmetics." The boys' dress code states, "Do not wear black leather jackets or articles that will lower your standard of decency." The school offered the Future Nurses, Future Homemakers of America, and Future Farmers of America clubs. Students who brought a lunch to school were asked to use the basement as a lunchroom. Ping-pong, dancing, and conversations could be conducted in the basement, according to the handbook. This school was destroyed in the 1990 Plainfield tornado.

The Plainfield Riding Club Horse Show was held at the high school athletic field on Eastern Avenue in Plainfield. The Plainfield Riding Club's goal was to stimulate and maintain interest in saddle and harness horses. Competition included the open barrel race, polo bending, flag race, western pleasure competition, along with several other contests. In 1959, the show was sponsored by the Plainfield Riding Club and the band boosters. Also included was a contest to choose the "Queen of the Horse Show." Each ticket purchased gave the purchaser votes toward the girl of his or her choice for queen.

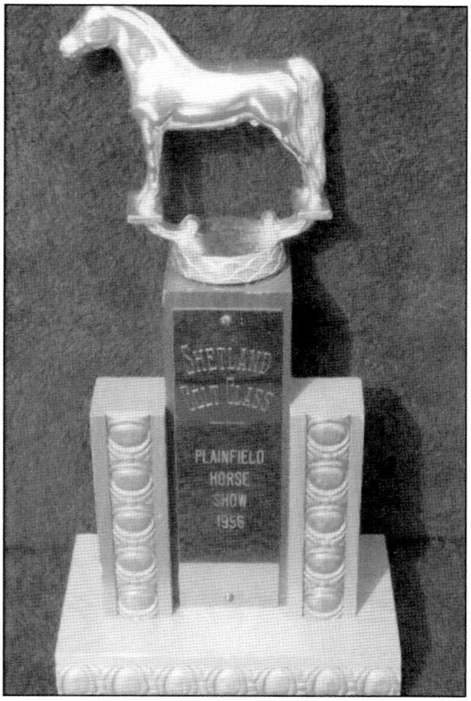

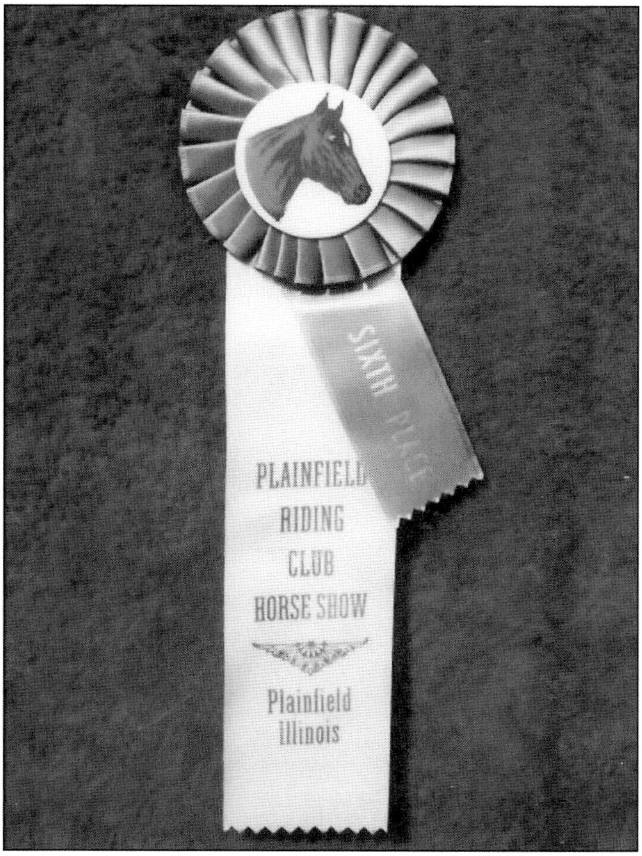

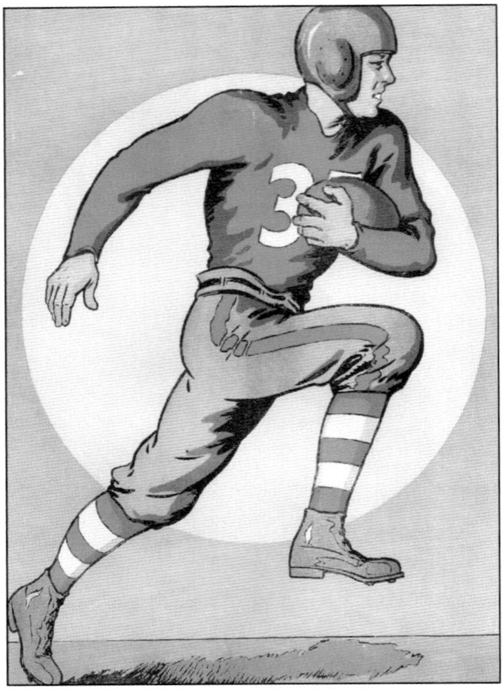

This 1956–1957 high school football program lists the Plainfield High School football team members. It also lists the team coaches as Albert Trumpy and Paul Crafts, the team physician as Dr. Frank Bender, and superintendent of Plainfield schools as W.G. Niehus. In this game, the Wildcats were playing the Marseilles (Illinois) High School team. The homecoming was held on October 5–6, 1956, with the homecoming theme being "Circus." The 1956 homecoming queen was Lenore Paluck. The 1953 Plainfield football team, also coached by Albert Trumpy, had been one of 16 undefeated teams in the state that year.

1956-57 Football team

PLAINFIELD WILDCATS

21	LARRY HOULE	L.E.
27	ALVIN RIESER	L.T.
40	JERRY LEAMAN	L.G.
33	ROGER BRONK	C
44	EUGENE BOESE	R.G.
43	DICK DAY	R.T.
30	JIM MAUER	R.E.
35	FRED HADFIELD	Q.B.
31	PAUL MONTGOMERY	H.B.
32	HARVEY JOHNSON	H.B
37	BRUCE FLEMING	F.B.
20	JIM FERGUSON	
22	FLORIAN CHWASZ	
25	BOB PALUCK	
26	JOHN BERST	
28	LEONARD HUMO	
24	TOM FINDLAY	
34	BILL ALSTOT	
36	CHUCK WOOD	
39	WAYNE SCHIEBER	
41	DICK TAYLOR	
42	DICK RUSSELL	

PLAINFIELD COACHES:
ALBERT TRUMPY
PAUL CRAFTS

TEAM PHYSICIAN:
DR. FRANK BENDER

SUPT.: W. G. NIEHUS

Rev. Bertram Dickens was the pastor of the Methodist Episcopal church in Plainfield in 1907 when new bells were installed. The bells were purchased with donations made by James W. Beggs and John D. Shreffler a few years earlier. The first to ring the chimes were Reinette Dickens and John Morgan. Reinette was the reverend's daughter. Trays, such as the one shown at right, were sold to raise money for the church, which is still located on Illinois Street in downtown Plainfield. Below, the church is shown in this photograph made from an early glass negative.

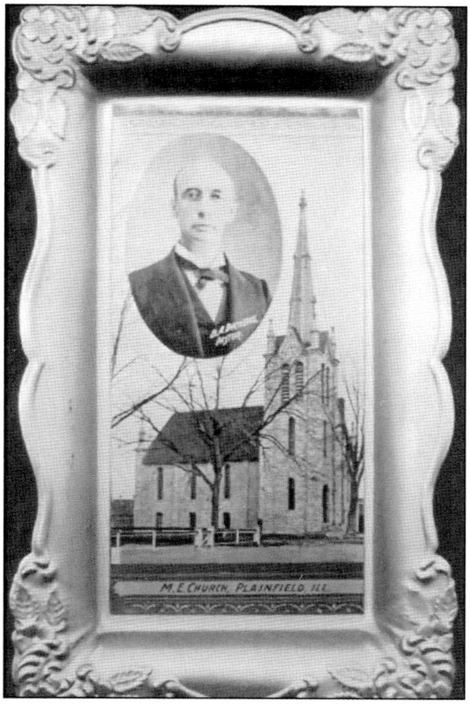

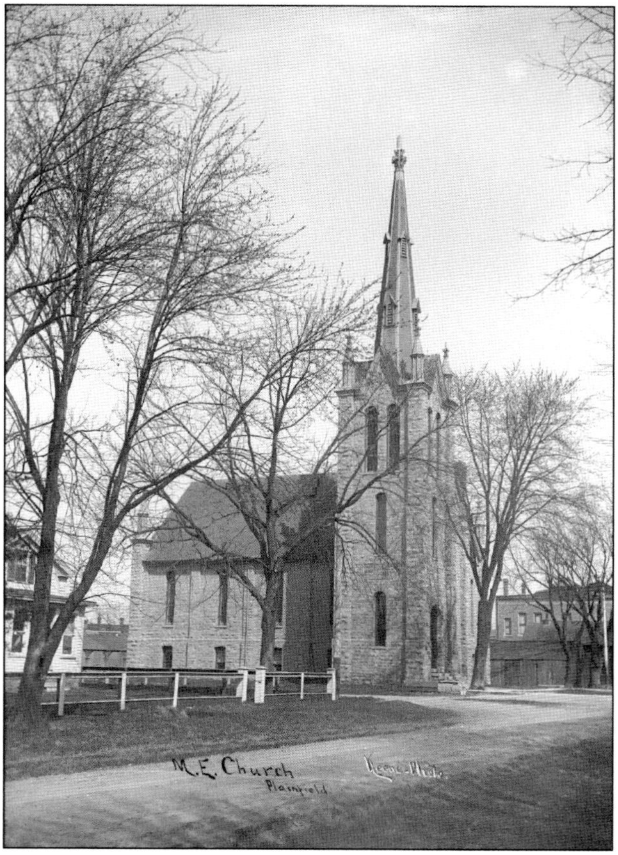

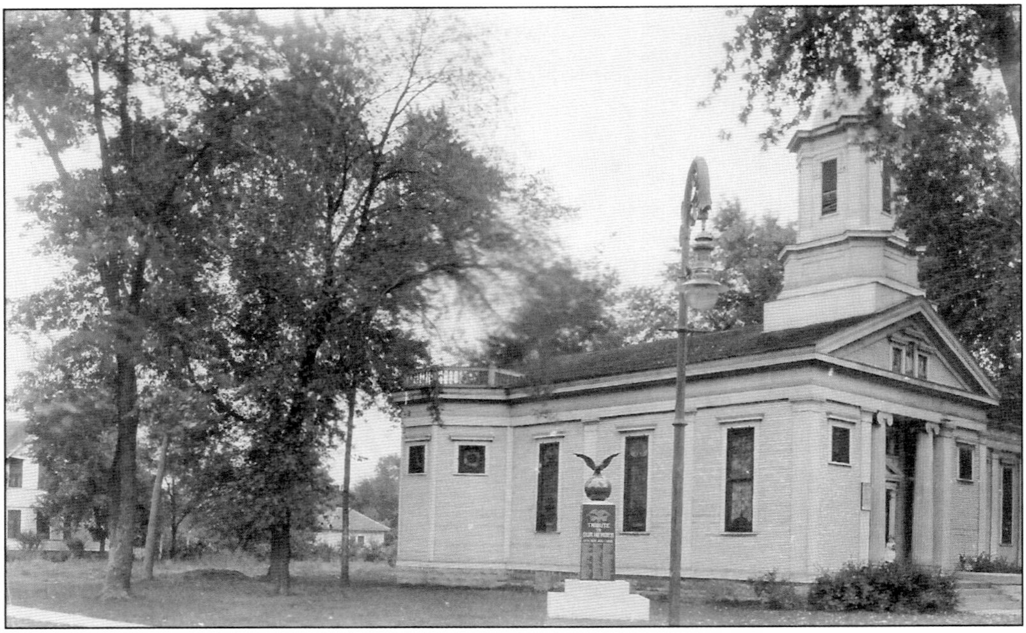

The Congregational Church was built in 1850 at the corner of what is now Lockport and Illinois Streets at a cost of about $2,200. The church was dedicated in June 1851. One of the first resolutions recorded was requiring church members to "abstain from drinking ardent spirits, manufacturing, trafficking in it or otherwise using it, except for medicine." As of 1878, the church had about 80 members. In 1907, an east wing was added to the church. Note the Soldiers' Memorial next to the church in both photographs. It is now located at Settlers Park in Plainfield. The photograph below was taken in the 1950s and shows an Illinois Route 30 sign along the highway.

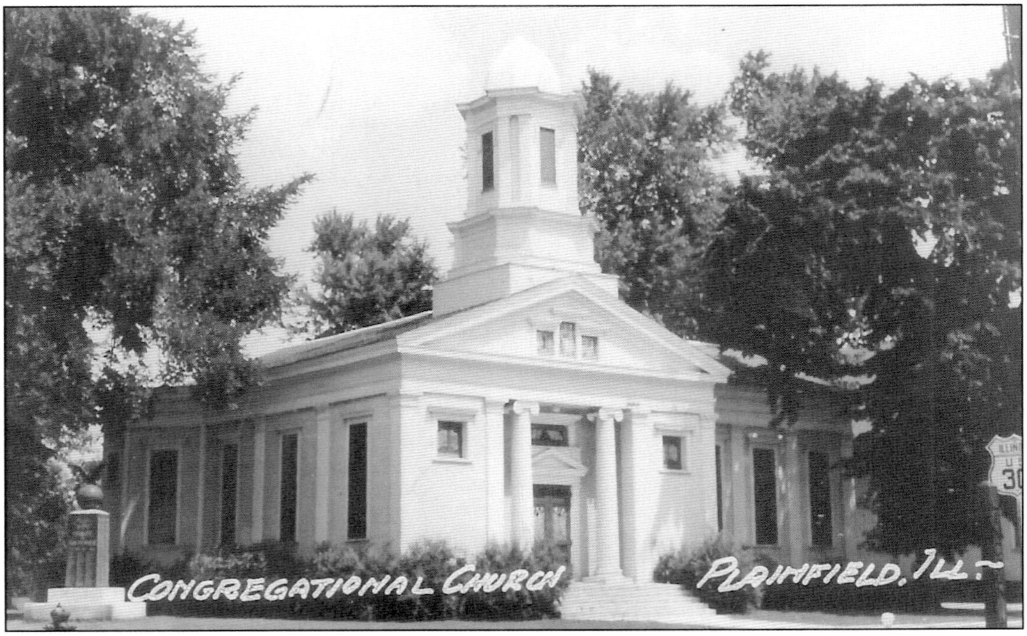

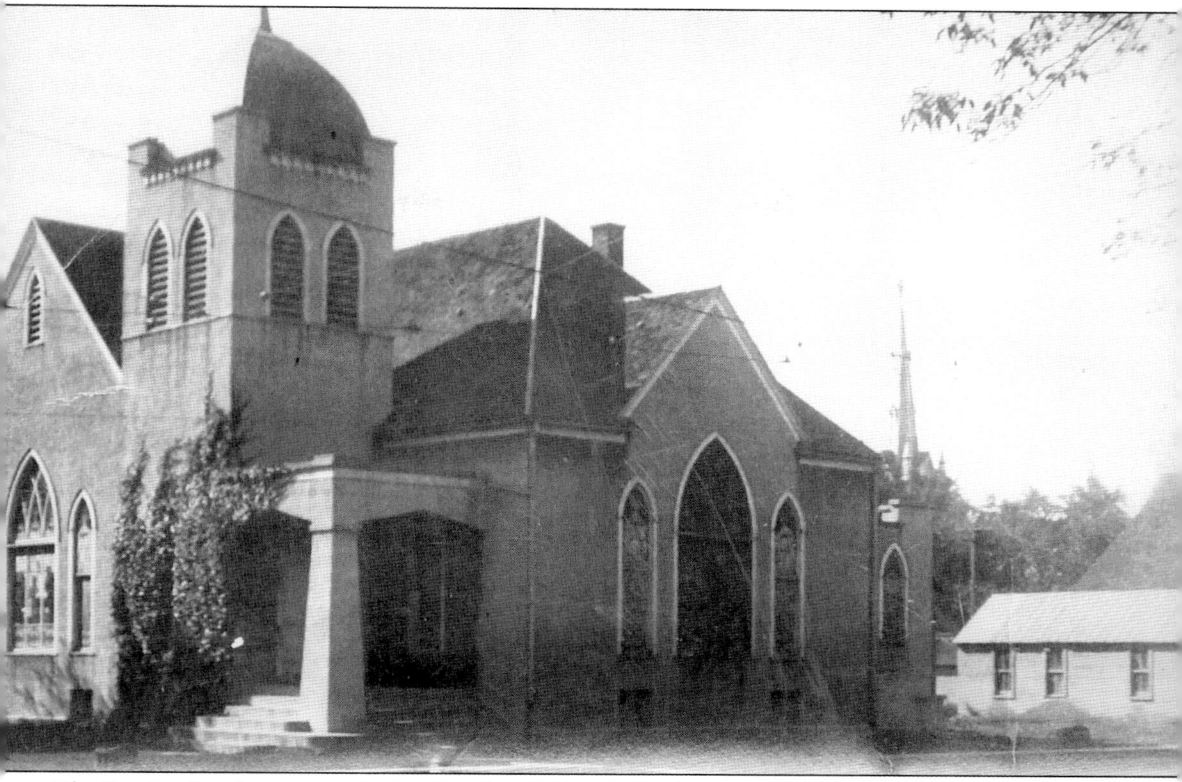

The Baptist church was organized in October 1834 with J.E. Ambrose as the first pastor. It originally had six members. It was part of four churches that joined the Northern Baptist Association. In 1836, the first church building was constructed at a cost of $2,500. It was about 26 by 36 feet and was later used as a blacksmith shop after a new church was built in 1857. This newer church was built at a cost between $4,500 and $5,000. In 1878, it was reported that the church membership was at 131, with an attendance at Sunday school of 70 children. In 1914, the church that was built in 1857 burned, and the church shown in these photographs was erected on the same site at Division and Lockport Streets. An addition was built on to the church in 1959.

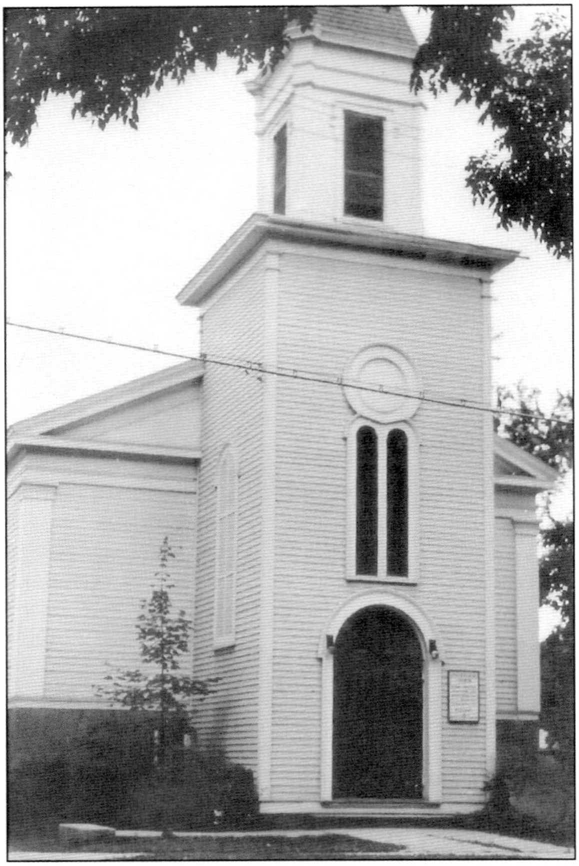

The Evangelical church was built in 1855 at a cost of $3,000. It was dedicated by Rev. Tobias, the presiding elder of the church. The first pastor was Rev. John Kamer. The Sunday school was organized at the same time. The first superintendent of the Sunday school was David Shreffler. In the late 1870s, the church had a membership of 113 and an average Sunday school attendance of 70. The early church services were given in both English and German. In 1907, gaslights were installed in the church, and in 1921, electric lights replaced them. This church still stands at the corner of Lockport and Dillman Streets.

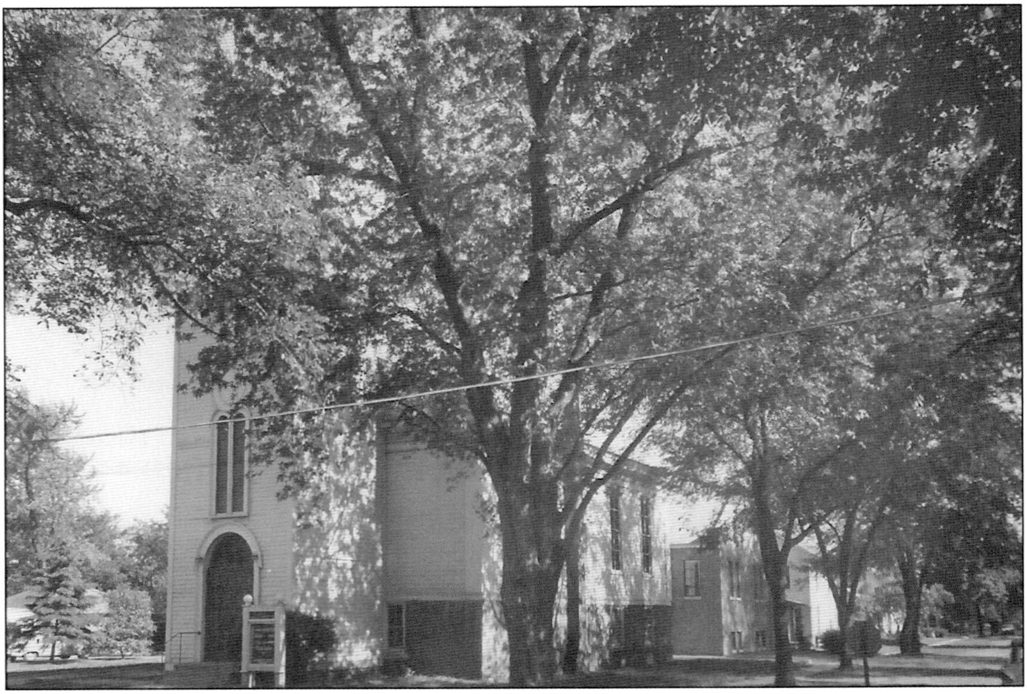

This church was originally the Universalist Church. It was built in 1868 at a cost of about $6,000. The church initially did not have a steeple, but one was added later. St. Mary's Catholic Church in Joliet purchased the church in 1908. Prior to this, local families traveled to Joliet or Lockport to attend mass. This travel was done by horse and buggy or sleigh. The church was operated as a mission for two years before a resident pastor was appointed.

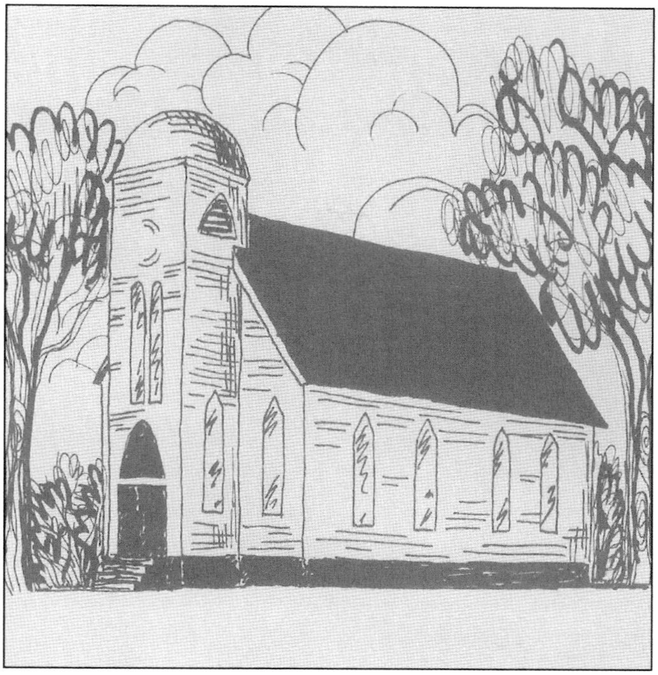

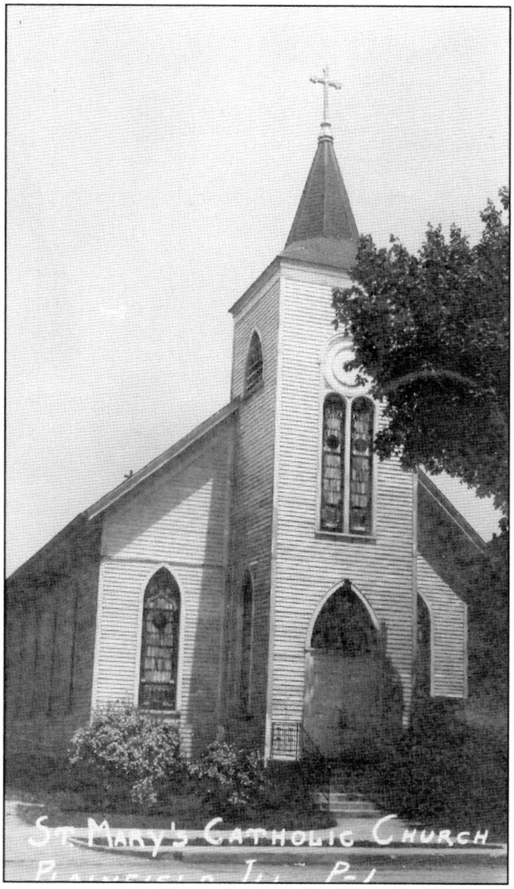

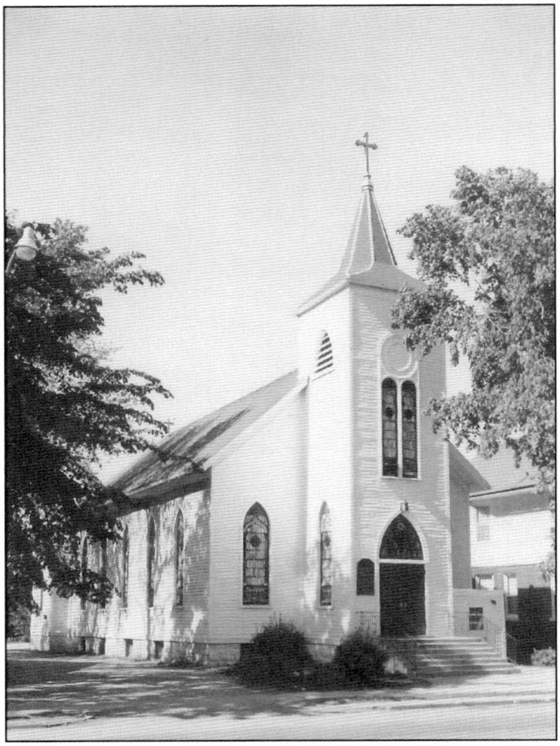

In 1938, the roof of St. Mary's Church caught fire during a storm. The steeple of the church was destroyed, but the church structure was saved when the steeple was blown off. It was believed that the fire started from a short circuit. During the roof and steeple repairs, an accident took place when the scaffolding collapsed and fell. This accident caused the death of William C. Miller and injury to Edward Glasgow and Maurice Smiley.

This church was built and dedicated in 1971, when St. Mary's Church was deemed too small. The parish had grown from around 40 families to over 600 by 1971. Six families of the original parish were sons or daughters of Elizabeth Drauden. This church was located on Route 59 on the south end of town. This church building was destroyed in the 1990 tornado.

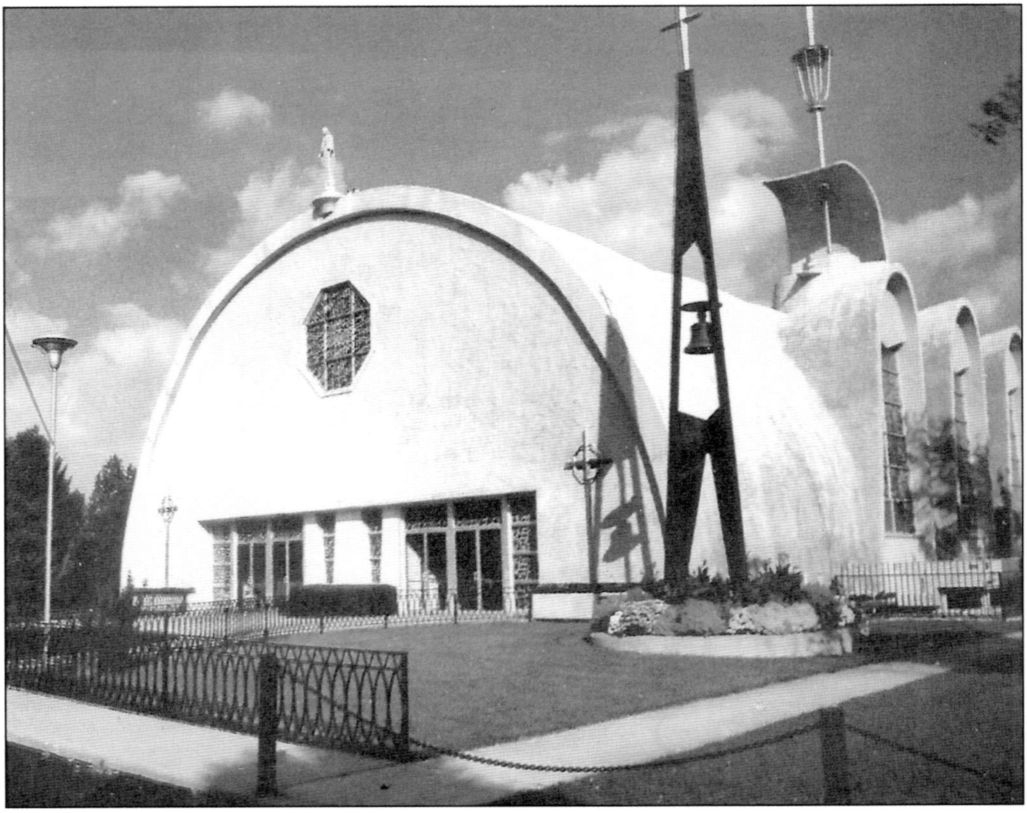

Five

The Plainfield Tornado

August 28, 1990, was a horrific day in the history of Plainfield. It is a memory etched in the minds of those who survived the devastating F5 tornado that carved a path through Plainfield around 3:30 p.m. That afternoon, the heat index reached an unbearable 98 degrees. Around 1:30 p.m., a thunderstorm system developed near Janesville, Wisconsin, moving in a southeasterly direction and spawning several tornadoes. One of these tornadoes struck without warning in northwestern Will County, leaving a path of destruction for 16.4 miles. Much of the destruction was in Plainfield.

Wheatland Plains subdivision was the first to be hit, with the tornado damaging nearly 50 homes, destroying 12, and injuring several people. As the tornado plowed its way through Plainfield, nearly everything in its path was destroyed, including Plainfield High School. The school year was set to begin the next day. Some teachers were present as well as about 100 athletes from the football and volleyball teams. Due to the quick thinking of the coaches, they and the athletes survived. People were hurried from the gym into the hallway as the roof of the gym collapsed and the walls came down around them. Three people died at the high school.

The tornado raced its way across Route 59, setting out to destroy St. Mary Immaculate School and Church. Three more people lost their lives at St. Mary's. From there, the tornado went on to Peerless Estates and Lily Cache Acres subdivisions, where one person perished, and much of what lay in the storm's path was badly damaged or destroyed. As the tornado continued on through Crystal Lawns subdivision, two more people lost their lives. Grand Prairie School was badly damaged, but the lives of those present at the school were spared. The tornado moved on to Joliet and Crest Hill, leaving more death and devastation in its wake.

In a matter of just a few minutes, 29 people had lost their lives, over 350 people were injured, and hundreds of homes were damaged or destroyed. August 28, 1990, is a day that many of in Plainfield will never forget, as their lives were forever changed.

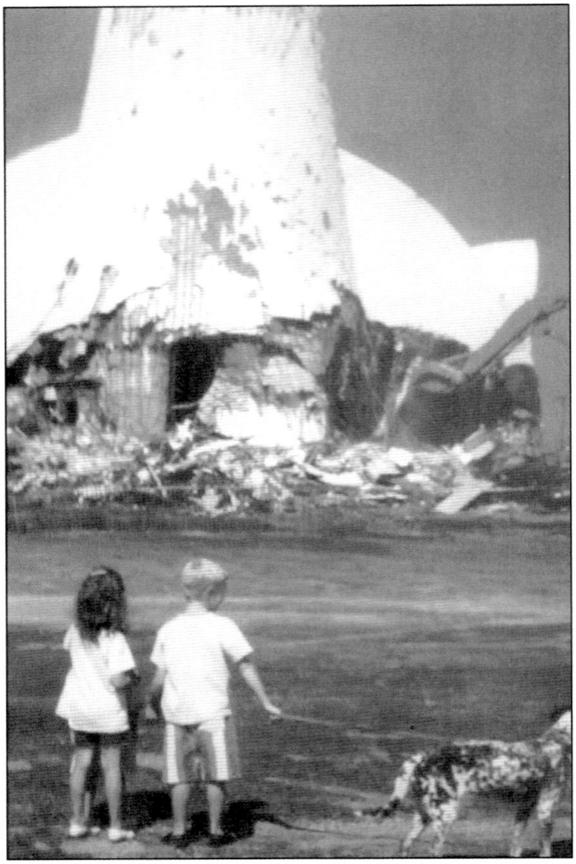

Amanda Cecil and Tim Child are pictured at left with Amanda's dog, Pokey. They are looking at St. Mary Immaculate Catholic Church, which stood along Route 59 with the school. Both were destroyed by the August 28, 1990, tornado. This church had been dedicated in 1971 and built at a cost of $750,000. Both families of the two children in this photograph lived near the church and had homes destroyed in the tornado. What remained of the church was torn down. A new church was built, and a dedication was held for the new church almost four years later to the day, on August 27, 1994. (Left, courtesy of Amanda Cecil; below, courtesy of John and Patti Child.)

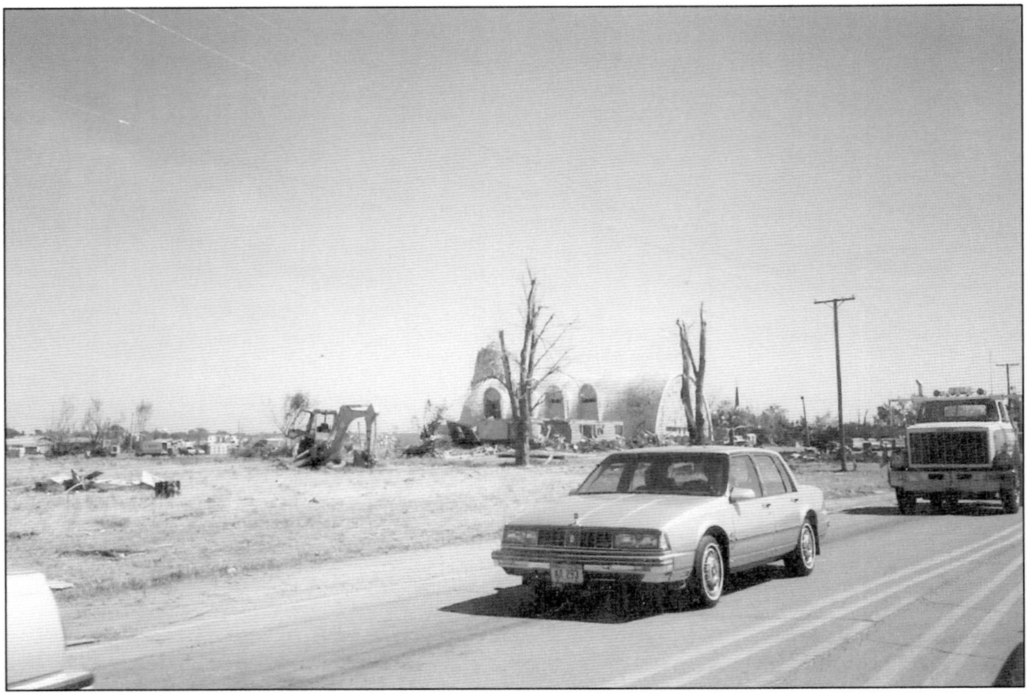

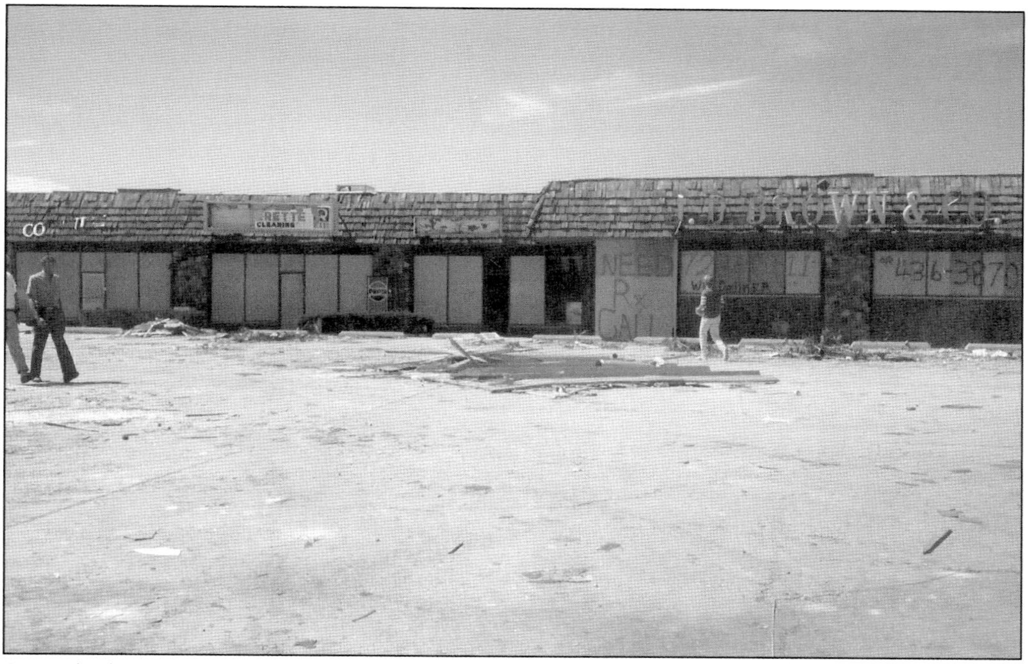

Several schools and business were destroyed in the tornado. This shopping center along Route 59 took on the brunt of the storm and suffered very heavy damage. The storm was, without a doubt, the worst tornado in Will County, Illinois, history. The tornado touched down around 3:30 p.m. at the Kendall County–Will County line, in the Wheatland Plains subdivision about two miles northwest of Plainfield. Its path of damage stretched over 16 miles, traveling through Plainfield into Joliet and Crest Hill. This was a very large and intense F5 storm, with winds approaching 300 miles per hour. (Both, courtesy of John and Patti Child.)

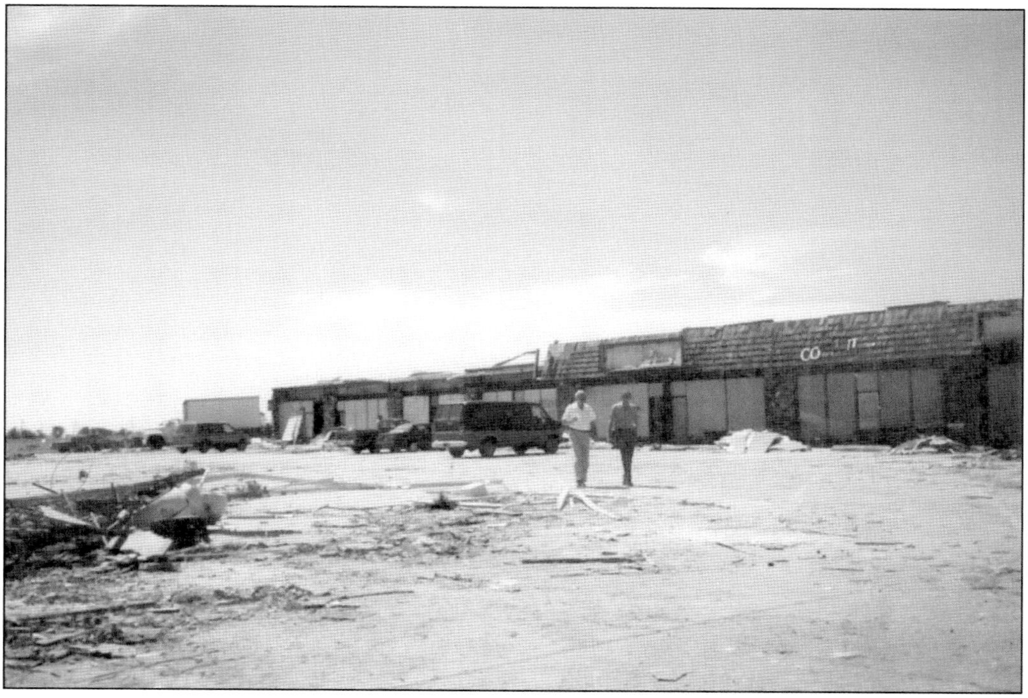

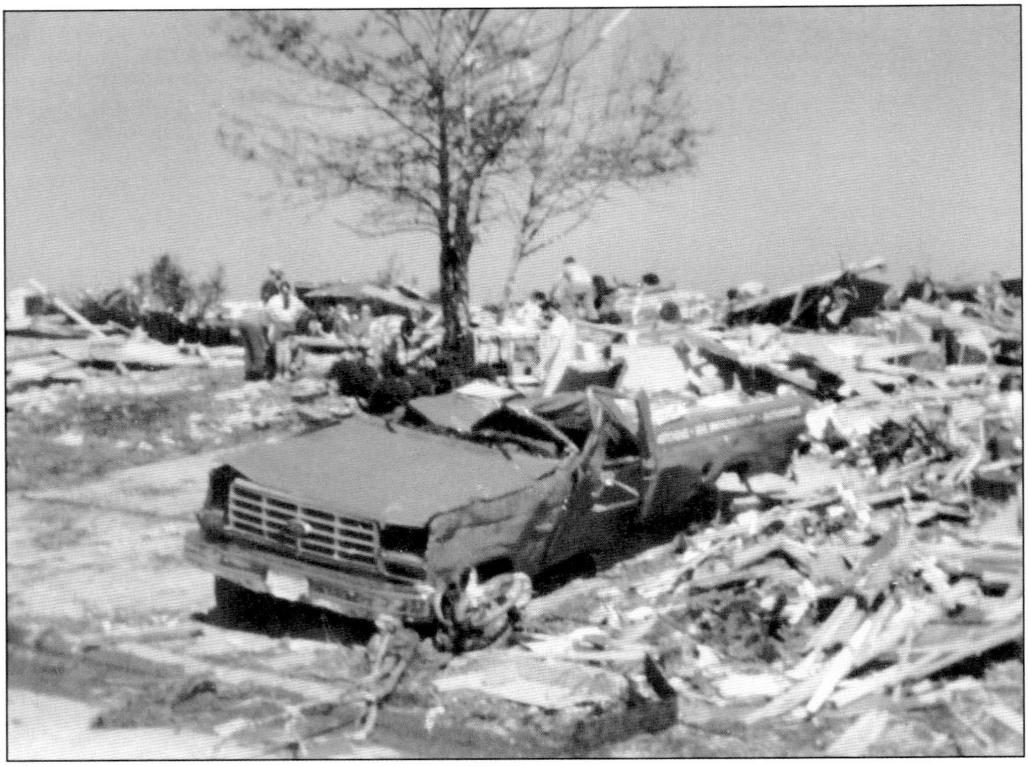

The Plainfield tornado caused over $140 million worth of damage. In the months following the disaster, the National Weather Service was criticized for providing Plainfield residents no warning of the approaching tornado or that a tornado was on the ground. Even today, many meteorologists refer to "Plainfield Syndrome" as the idea that it is better to issue too many warnings and be wrong than miss one critical warning, as was the case with the Plainfield tornado.

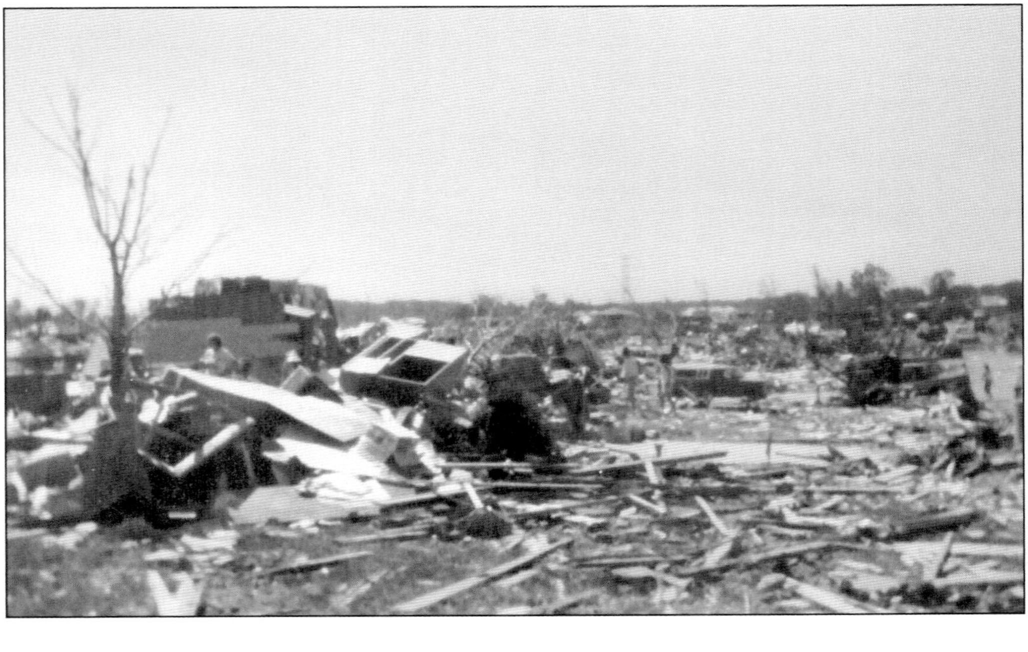

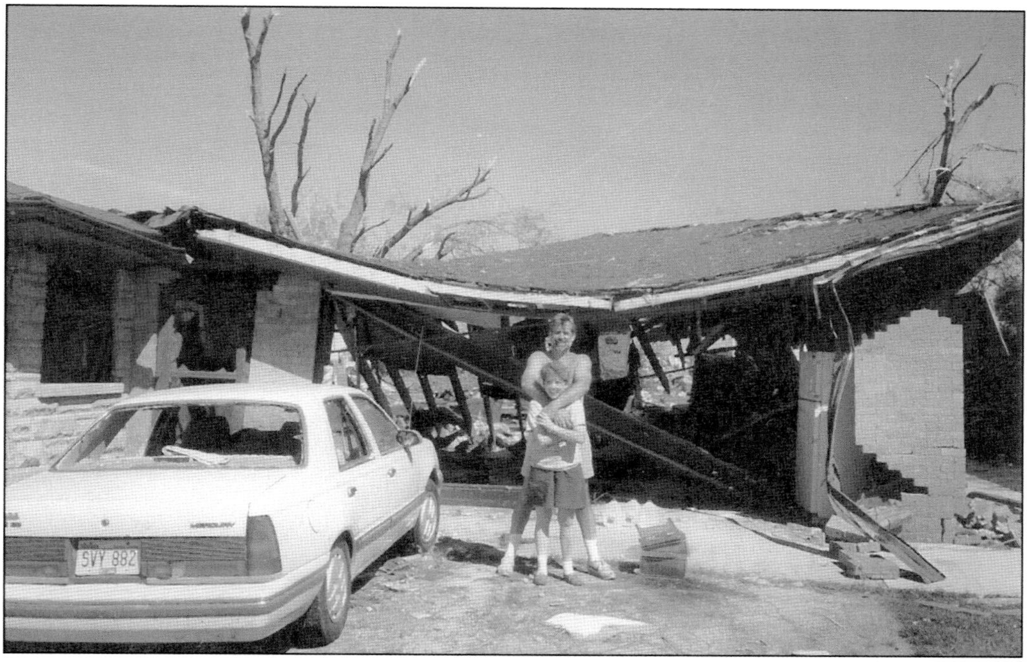

Many Plainfield homes sustained damage or were destroyed by the wind, and the cleanup of debris was a huge undertaking. Countless volunteers supported the cleanup effort within days. The development of NEXRAD (Next Generation Radar) has contributed greatly to the ability to recognize tornado activity. The ability to see rotation inside a storm has allowed forecasters to issue tornado warnings in a more timely fashion with higher probability of detection. The Plainfield tornado in 1990 was the only F5 tornado ever recorded to strike in the Chicago area. (Both, courtesy of John and Patti Child.)

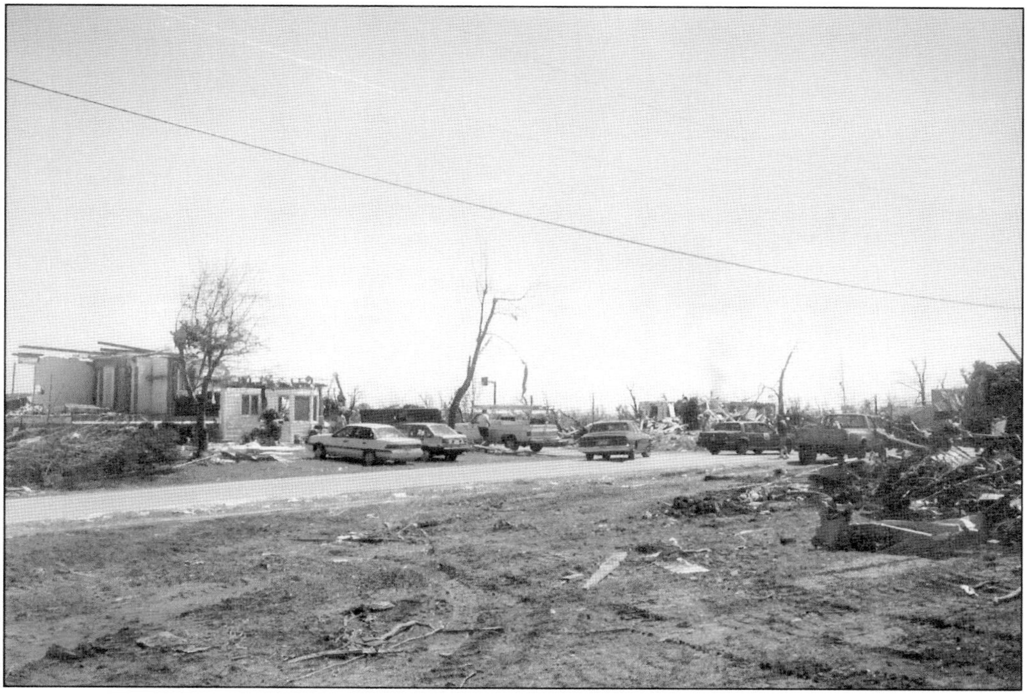

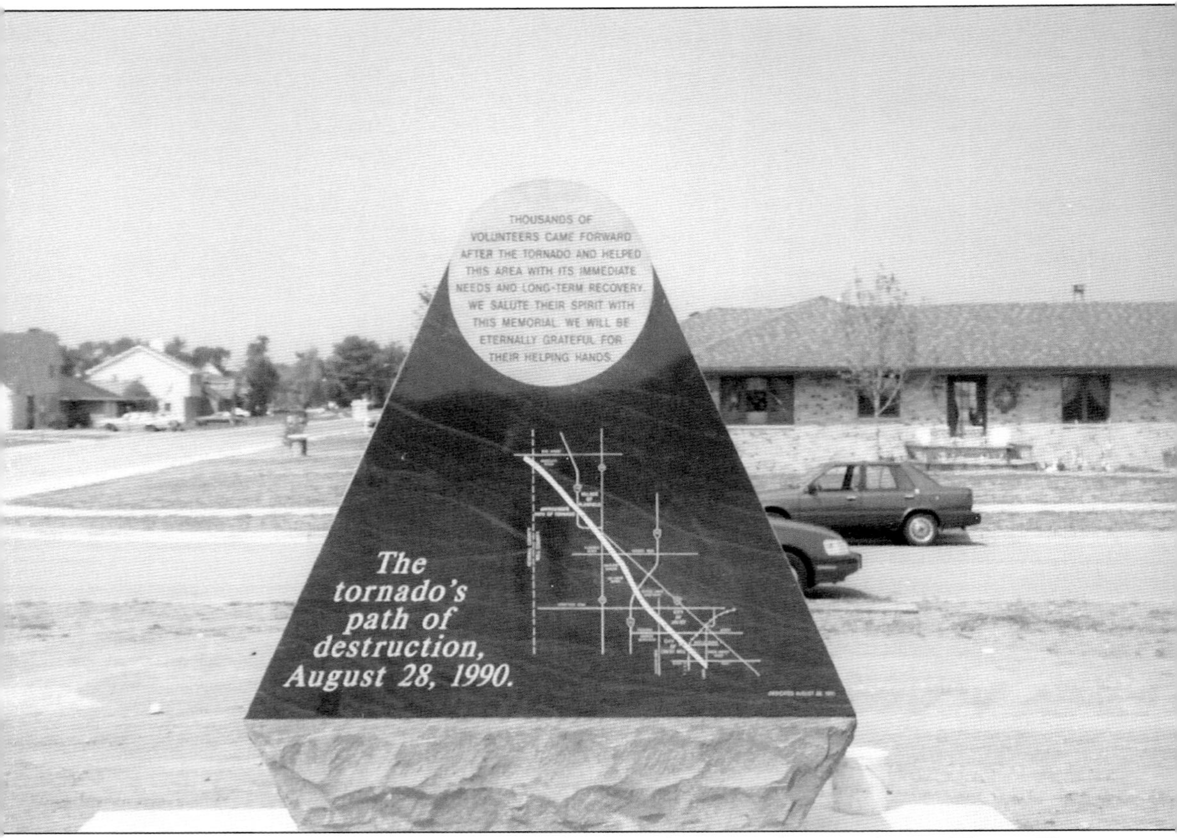

The people who lost their lives in the tornado were Alice Jean Johnson, Thomas Thayer, Phoumy Senephimmachac, Henry T. Berquist, Stephen P. Hunt, Pat Skoien, Howard Hawes Jr., Sr. Mary Keenan, Gloria Sanchez, Vicki J. Egizio, Thomas Egizio, Leslie Egizio, Virginia Lydon, Charles Likes, Sarah Brower, Ryan R. Glaser, Janis Granat, James Pullen, Patricia Sue Combs, Frank Riffel, Alida Riffel, Leticia Herrod, Tatiana Brown, Eddie Lee Jr., Brian Paul Strohm, Eric Wilson, James L. Niccum, and James E. Kachel. This memorial is located near Plainfield Central High School on West Fort Beggs Drive in Plainfield.

Bibliography

Crook, Richard J. *Jesse Walker, Pioneer Preacher.* Plainfield, IL: Plainfield Enterprise, 1976.
Electric Park, Plainfield Ill.: The Ideal Summer Resort Right Here at Home. Joliet, IL: Joliet Republican Printing Company, 1908.
Genealogical and Biographical Record of Will County, Illinois. Chicago: Biographical Publishing Company, 1900.
Hartong, Miles. Research files. Plainfield, IL: Plainfield Historical Society.
History of Will County Illinois. Chicago: Wm. Le Baron Jr. & Company, 1878.
Maue, August. *History of Will County Illinois.* Topeka: Historical Publishing Company, 1928.
Plainfield Bicentennial Commission. *A History of Plainfield Then and Now.* Plainfield, IL: Plainfield Enterprise, 1976.
Portrait Biographical Album of Will County Illinois. Chicago: Chapman Bros., 1890.
Prairie Farmer's Reliable Directory of Farmers and Breeders: Will and Southern Cook Counties. Chicago: Prairie Farmer, 1918.
Schofield, William W. *The Trail of the Potawatomi.* Joliet, IL: Will County Historical Society, 1967.
Stevens, William Wallace. *Past and Present of Will County, Illinois.* Chicago: S.J Clarke Publishing Company, 1907.
Wiggins Joliet and Will County Directory. Chicago: Joliet Directory Company, 1895–1896.
Will County Atlas. Elgin, IL: Thompson Brothers and Burr, 1873.
Will County Chautauqua Electric Park. Will County Chautauqua Association, 1909.

Discover Thousands of Local History Books Featuring Millions of Vintage Images

Arcadia Publishing, the leading local history publisher in the United States, is committed to making history accessible and meaningful through publishing books that celebrate and preserve the heritage of America's people and places.

Find more books like this at
www.arcadiapublishing.com

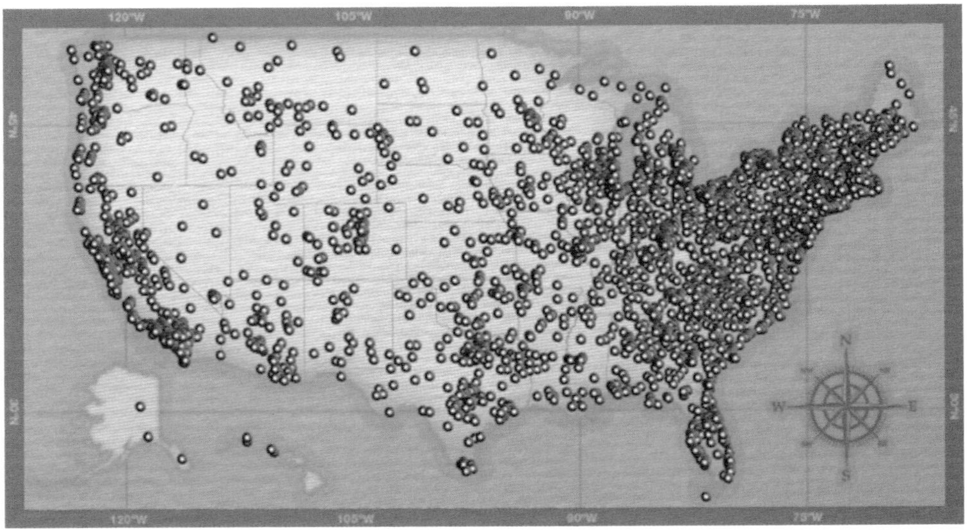

Search for your hometown history, your old stomping grounds, and even your favorite sports team.

Consistent with our mission to preserve history on a local level, this book was printed in South Carolina on American-made paper and manufactured entirely in the United States. Products carrying the accredited Forest Stewardship Council (FSC) label are printed on 100 percent FSC-certified paper.

MADE IN THE USA